The cover of the *Philadelphia Stories* 15th Anniversary Anthology
is comprised of the magazine's cover art from the past five years.
Featured from the top left to the bottom right are our covers from
fall 2019 through winter 2015. This artwork by twenty individual
artists embodies the spirit of *Philadelphia Stories* as we strive to share
the finest, most unique, boldest and most beautiful "voices" from
the Delaware Valley. These cover images have often set the tone
for each issue's visual direction and selections. The visual voices
found on and throughout each issue are selected for their overall
aesthetic harmony as a collection while also offering a variety of
artistic approach and intention. Thanks to our twenty featured
artists for their continued support of *Philadelphia Stories* and for once
again sharing their work.

– Pam McLean-Parker

Art Editor *Philadelphia Stories*

Masthead

Publisher/Editorial Director
Carla Spataro

Publisher/Executive Director
Christine Weiser

Managing Editor
Yalonda Rice

Fiction Editor(s)
Trish Rodriguez (Fall 2019-Present)
Mitchell Sommers (Winter 2015-Summer 2019)

Poetry Editor
Courtney Bambrick

Nonfiction Editor(s)
Adriana Lecuona (Winter 2018-present)
Susette Brooks (Spring 2017-Fall 2017)
Julia MacDonnell Chang (Spring 2009-Spring 2017)

Art Editor(s)
Pam McLean-Parker (Fall 2015-Present)
Melissa Tevere (Winter 2015-Summer 2015)

Contest Coordinator
Nicole Marie Pasquarello

Art Director
Derek Carnegie

Marketing Assistant
Dom Saunders

Event Director
Lena Van

15th Anniversary Book Design
Roma Narkhede

Board of Directors
Concha Alborg
Jacqueline Hopkins
Alex Husted
Daniel Johns
Madeleine Keogh
Patricia Thorell

Editorial Boards
Fiction
Elizabeth Greene
Aimee LaBrie
Nathan Long
Walt Maguire
Lena Van

Nonfiction
Brittany Leonard
Deborah Off
Elaine Paliatsas-Haughey
Rachel Mamola
Jacqueline Massaro
Andrea Vinci

Poetry
Hayley Allison
Peter Baroth
Deb Burnham

Liz Chang
Blythe Davenport
Liz Dolan
Margot Douaihy
Stephanie Durann
Monique Gordon
Colette Grecco
Pat Green
Vernita Hall
Angel Hogan
Kathryn Ionata
Donna Keegan
David Kozinski
Ed Krizek
Nicole Mancuso
Shira Moolten
Kristina Moriconi
Charlie O'Hay
Aimee Penna
Jennifer Rohrbach
Thomas Jay Rush
John Shea
Luke Stromberg
Maria Thiaw
Eli Tomaszewski
Valeria Tsygankova
Kira Wells
Notus Williams
Basia Wilson
Donna Wolf-Palacio

Assistant Editor(s)
Shelley Schenk (Fiction)
Nicole Pasquarello (Poetry)
Amy Luginbuhl (Fiction)

Published by PS Books, a division of Philadelphia Stories, Inc.

Philadelphia, PA 19148

©2019 by Philadelphia Stories

Printed in the United States of America

Cover Image: Collage of Philadelphia Stories Covers from 2014-2019, various artists

ISBN: 978-1945101007

Table of Contents

2018

2019

*Sandy Crimmins Poetry Prize Winner
**Sandy Crimmins Poetry Prize Runner-Up
+Marguerite McGlinn Fiction Prize Winner
++Marguerite McGlinn Fiction Prize Runner UP

Introduction

When you're young, 15 years seems like a long time into the future. Now that we're here, I can't quite believe how quickly the time has flown. That's how things go, when you're lucky enough to live a life doing what you love. Time flies by in a blur and yet at the same time, can feel elongated, as if it might stretch out forever.

Back in 2003, when Christine Weiser and I first decided to launch a regional literary magazine, we really had no idea what we were getting ourselves into, but we made a plan and took a chance. What's that saying, "a goal without a plan is just a wish…" Well, we planned and raised money, and then launched our little dream in September of 2004 at the now long defunct Brasserie Perrier restaurant in Center City Philadelphia. There were hundreds of people there, most of whom we did not know, but many who have become fast friends and ardent supporters. There were also some people there that we lost too soon— passionate supporters like Sandy Crimmins and Marguerite McGlinn. Every year, through the generous support of their families, we honor the memories of Sandy and Marguerite with our contests. Many of the winners of those contests are featured in these pages. I'm confident that Sandy and Marguerite, both of whom were brilliant and talented and opiniated, would be pleased that we're able to celebrate poets and short story writers, not only with money, but with recognition, something that only the very highest echelon of our profession usually receive.

Every issue of *Philadelphia Stories* is a labor of love. The journal is free, and 5,000 copies are distributed to individual donors and through county libraries, coffee shops, and bookstores all across the Delaware Valley. Our mission is to cultivate a community of writers, artists, and readers in the Greater Philadelphia Area through publications, professional development, and promotion of area writers. Community is a word that gets bandied about quite a lot these days, but it really means something to us. Christine and I didn't really know how big the writing community was until we launched *Philadelphia Stories*. We were honored to join the great literary tradition here in the city and are thrilled to see so many other journals and outlets for writers flourish.

These stories were chosen by the current editors of the magazine, but if you don't see your favorite, you can always visit our website and see nearly every piece of writing we've ever published. The proceeds from this anthology will go to support our mission, as does everything we do. The board of directors, editorial board, and host of dedicated volunteers would like to thank you for being part of our community.

Carla Spataro
Editorial Director

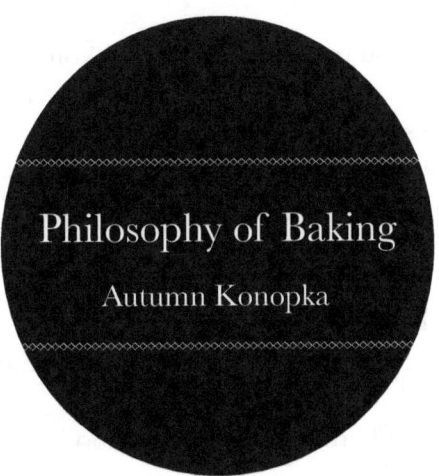

Philosophy of Baking

Autumn Konopka

In the oven there are secrets:
drippings,
crusts burned and flaked,
black bubbles that still smoke every time she fires up.

She says:

> *Give me bitter lemons; I will sweeten them.*
> *Give me brown bananas, sour milk.*
> *Give me the chocolate so dark it chokes you.*

You train yourself to listen.
Give the oven what she wants,
and she gives you
coconut custard, marble pound,
red velvet cupcakes, cranberry scones.
You tune out the cacophony:
"Mommy! Mommy! Mommy!"
the doorbell bringing women who want
to know if you're saved,
men who want
to know if you're saving enough on your gas bill.

Sometimes the oven says
eggs, bacon, gruyere, chives.
And you obey
without hesitation.

Other voices hurl pages
of unwritten poems, echos of your husband's lover
singing "Oh yes! Oh yes! Oh god, yes!"
And him: "There has never been another woman
so beautiful."

You don't listen to them.
You lean in closer to the oven.
Closer still.
Deep inside where it's quietest.
Maybe today will be your day
to change, to puff and flake,
turn golden and rise
without sinking in the center.

Without His Fingers

Ona Russell

The day was hot and humid, typical of a Philly summer. Bernie and John couldn't wait for their ocean swim. They always took a dip before a concert, no matter what the weather. It was their ritual, a way to release tension and diffuse the jitters that accompanied a performance. But with sweat already clinging to their shirts, they were even more eager than usual.

The concert would be held at the Metropolitan Opera House or perhaps the Academy of Music on Broad and Locust at 8 p.m. that evening. So it must have been around noon, after a morning practice, when they felt as ready as they'd ever be, that they hopped a bus for Atlantic City, arriving an hour or two later.

I can see them during the ride, jibing each other, laughing, joking. And I hear Bernie asking John to pinch him, still in disbelief that he was a violinist in The Philadelphia Orchestra. Perhaps that night, Leopold Stokowski was conducting, the innovator who encouraged "free bowing" and was helping to create a unique, Philadelphia sound. The New York Times had just praised the Orchestra as possessing "uncommon excellence," and Stokowski had no small part in its evolution. Would the program include Mendelssohn's Violin Concerto in E Minor? I like to think so, like to believe that Bernie was anticipating playing one of his favorite pieces, the last great work of the Romantic composer, with its immediate entrance of the soloist, who, if Bernie worked hard enough, he would surely one day be.

In Atlantic City, the sand must have felt good under their feet. Soon, hard shoes and stiff tuxes would bind them, but now they were as free as their bows, imbibing the sea air, running toward the waves, admiring the female bathers. It was 1923, early in the decade, and they, too, were in their early twenties, embodiments of the period's youthful exuberance. They dove into the surf, perhaps hearing in the rush of water the concerto's frenetic, final coda.

After an hour or so, Bernie swam back to shore. Time to go. Their towels were where they left them, in a heap. In the water, he and John had drifted apart, one doing a fast crawl, the other lazily floating. Bernie must have been drying himself off, looking casually to the placid blue surface for his friend. There had been a light current, a bit of an undertow, but nothing out of the ordinary. He spotted a curly blond head that he at first thought was John, but no. He glanced toward the dressing stalls, their established meeting place, but John wasn't there either. Bernie returned to the water's edge, getting his feet and then legs wet again. With his hand blocking the sun, he gazed more carefully now, out, far out, and up and down the coast. And then, the first inkling that something was wrong. His stomach must have tightened, his breathing grown rapid. Time passed, and then the real panic set in. Rushing to a lifeguard. Shouting down the beach, questioning everyone he saw. Thirty minutes, sixty. Longer.

That night, the string section was surely a little off. Someone had to fill in for the missing player, and if Bernie played at all, it must have been out of key. The search continued for weeks, but John was never found, drowning listed as the official cause of death. Soon thereafter, one of Bernie's fingers began to ache.

Bernie, Bernard Greenberg, was my great uncle, and before I tell the rest of that story, here are a few things you might want to know: Bernie grew up lower-middle class in the Logan area of Philadelphia, the second child of four in a secular Jewish family. His parents owned two delicatessens in Strawberry Mansion. He was a happy, loving kid, known for being a prankster, often dangerously so. Once, pretending he was Zorro, he carved a Z into my aunt's arm with a pocketknife, and that was tame in comparison to some of his other antics. My grandmother Rosella, married to Oscar Kahn, brother of noted architect Louis, was his sister. The family was close and Bernie, despite his mischievous nature, was a favored member. He was handsome and athletic, known for his nasty English, both on a ball and in speech. And then, of course, there was the music, the combination of passion and talent, charged with that ineffable something that separated him from the crowd. His pranks were infamous, but everyone knew that his violin would make him famous.

His left ring finger was the first to suffer. Why that one, I don't know, maybe because Bernie never had the chance to marry, even though, before he got sick, he had a girl in mind. Soon all of his fingers turned cold, went white, then blue. For a while he could play through the soreness, but soon the pain became unbearable. One, then another and another, until he was forced to quit the orchestra and seek medical help.

The family thought his symptoms were related to the shock of losing his friend. And maybe in part they were. But on what I can only envision as a gray winter's day, with snow beginning to fall, Bernie was diagnosed with Beurger's disease, a circulatory disorder where the body essentially attacks its own blood vessels. All organs can be involved but the limbs and digits are especially affected. Pathologist and namesake, Leo Beurger, first identified the disease in 1908, and Bernie was one of the first patients to undergo Beurger's trial and error treatments at Mt. Sinai hospital in New York.

I could describe in graphic detail his twenty-two years in and out of hospitals, the freezing and boiling baths, the nerve surgeries, the eventual amputations. I could tell you of the constant agony, of pain so excruciating that my uncle became addicted to morphine. And I could, and should, tell you that cigarette smoking was related to the disease, and that, despite being told that he would lose his toes as well as his fingers if he didn't quit, Bernie continued to smoke. That was before the tobacco industry even knew enough to lie about how addictive their products were. I could tell you about this nightmare. Yes, I could tell about when the music stopped. But I'd rather tell you about when it began again, when spring finally returned.

By the time I came into consciousness, the disease had burned itself out. I wasn't there when Bernie swore there were bats flying in his hospital room or when he stood over my parent's bed, begging my father, a physician, for a fix. By my time, Bernie was in his forties, living with my great-grandmother in L.A. He had gone cold turkey off all drugs and was a frequent visitor in our home. The only remnants of his illness were his constantly perspiring forehead, and of course, the mangled stubs where his shapely, violinist fingers used to be. I grew up with those stubs and thought nothing of them. It took others' reactions to make me understand that they could be disturbing. Nor did it strike me odd at all when, after taking a year of piano lessons with a mediocre instructor, Bernie became my teacher.

I don't recall how the deal was struck, but I'll never forget those sessions. I was young, only nine when they started and seventeen at the end. Bernie was patient, but also demanding. He wouldn't tolerate a sluggish trill, too heavy of a pedal. Every note was to be defined, every passage a delicate balance of restraint and force. Often, it was too much for me. Sometimes I'd run out the room, screaming and crying. I'd tell him I hated him. But there were other times, when we were in a groove, when his stubs would sway over me like a conductor's baton, and the music came to life. All those scales, those repetitions until I thought I'd go mad, suddenly paid off, and my hands flew over the keyboard, smooth and clear. At those moments, I cared for nothing else. My mother might call us to dinner, and I'd shoo her away. We were in a world of our own, one that, without his fingers, my uncle had made possible.

Soon, word spread. "Ona's pretty good at the piano. Who's her teacher?" "Bernie, her Uncle Bernie."

"But he doesn't have…"

That must have often been the reaction. But it didn't prevent anyone from pursuing him as a teacher. First to sign up was a friend of mine down the street, and then another around the corner. As his fingers had once fallen, one by one, his list of students, for violin as well as piano, grew, until he had more than he could handle. It was the autumn of his life, but he was in high demand.

Now he was Bernard Green, music teacher. He'd dropped the "berg" to make his Jewish identity less certain, although the Yiddish obscenities that peppered his talk were a bit of a giveaway. He lived, as did we, in an area where vague and sometimes overt anti-Semitic sentiment was common. The change was purely a business decision, and it may have contributed to him getting his foot (minus his toes) in the door. He frightened some initially, more with his expectations than his deformity, but everyone recognized his gift. He breathed music, and the air entered our lungs, traveled to our brains, and sent a special message to our fingers.

A few other things about Bernie:
He had a cockatoo that stood on his head and ordered him, by name, to wake up.

He was an animal whisperer before the term was known.

His room was crowded with National Geographics and smelled like Old Spice.

He repeatedly dropped cigarette ashes into our Steinway.

He feared my Beatlemania.

He pretended to hate my mother's meatloaf.

He drank up my father's scotch.

He could have done stand-up comedy.

It is lately, as I approach the age when he died, that I think not only about what Bernie might have been, but what he was. To say that he overcame adversity is an understatement. Like many artists, he created beauty out of anguish. But also, in his quiet way, he transformed lives. When children asked him in horror what had happened to him, he would say that he didn't listen to his mother when she told him not to play in the street. When adults stared, he smiled back. Without his fingers, he touched everyone he met. Still, I like to think of him that summer day back in '23, before the drowning, with John alive, and all possibility before him, running toward the waves, with his hands outstretched, reaching for the horizon.

Cul de Sac

Oindria Mukherjee

The first night her parents arrive from India is the one that means the most, because there is so much to look forward to, even now, even after everything that's happened.

As the car turns into Swapna's street, evening is creeping in on the neighborhood. The house that will soon belong exclusively to her is white with gold squares of light at the windows and stands at the end of the cul de sac. Even as families gather for dinner in the other homes, this one waits in silence. Swapna's parents notice as soon as they climb out of the car.

"It's so quiet," says her mother, putting a hand to her chest. The crickets chirp in unison, emphasizing the silence when they pause.

"This is a residential neighborhood," Swapna shrugs. "That's why we – I – chose it."

She opens the door with some hesitation. What she has grown accustomed to is likely to appear unnerving to her parents. They have always found America lonely. But tonight, the quiet desolation of the living room, which Linda cleaned only yesterday with such meticulous care, slams them in the face. Swapna catches a glimpse of their surprised and tired faces and wishes again that she hadn't yielded to their requests to come and "help."

Her father is too exhausted to reflect but her mother, never quite able to switch off her intuition or her concern for her daughter, looks around and sniffs. Swapna wonders with sudden panic if she is searching for Tom's smell. Linda and she have sprayed bottles of bleach, window cleaner, floor polish, fabric softener, carpet stain remover, and other liquids in the last six months, in a maniacal bid to sanitize, but one never knows. Swapna hopes her mother cannot smell the debris of her marriage on her first night here.

The longer the interval between their meetings, the more significant the reunions become. She knows her parents feel it too, because even though they are so tired they feel like they are walking inside a cloud, they insist on staying up with her for a while. Eventually, when her father goes to bed, Swapna and her mother sit on the cream leather sofa. They barely talk, and every few minutes her mother lets out a yawn so wide and mournful that it makes Swapna want to curl up right there and doze off. Finally, her mother's eyes start to close and Swapna nudges her towards her room gently.

"Tomorrow," Ma says, as she stands up. "Tomorrow, we will talk about everything."

Swapna goes to her own room and slips under the covers from where she can stare out at the large ghostly moon in the blue-black sky. Tonight she feels like a child again. She feels safe and warm and knows that unlike the last five months, tonight she will sleep through the night.

The next morning, as soon as she wakes up, Swapna remembers that some remnants of Tom linger around the house. The mug with the picture of the Eiffel Tower that he brought back from a European History conference stands among the other mugs on the top kitchen shelf. His toolbox lies in the garage for a time when Swapna might need to fix something even though she, like most other Indian women, has never learned to fix anything in her life. His faded brown corduroy jacket, which he wore on his walks every evening through the mild Atlanta winter, hangs in the closet. His books are in the library they built together over the years. Most of them are biographies. Of American presidents, European royalty, country musicians, baseball players. All of them have his name on the first page, scrawled in ink, alongside the dates and locations where he purchased them. Vienna, New Orleans, Toronto, New York, Jaipur. Somewhere there is a box full of Italian ties in various shades of red, the one vanity he permitted himself despite the jeers from his scholarly colleagues. When Swapna opens the top drawer of her dresser each morning, a blue Tiffany's box stares at her. She never glances inside. She doesn't need to. She knows what lies there, how it sparkles in the sun, and how it feels against her skin, hard and cold.

The way she speaks of Tom, anyone would think he were dead.

She wonders if her parents will discover any of these objects. It makes her almost smile to think how things remain the same over the years. The first time her parents visited her in the apartment she then shared with two roommates up north, back when Swapna was just a graduate student, she had removed things before they arrived. The bottle of whiskey from her bookshelf, the tube of KY Jelly from her bathroom closet, the packet of condoms from her nightstand, the subscription to the adult channels, and all pictures of Tom. This time, she did not bother to hide anything. That is the strange thing about marriage, even a failed one. It gives you a kind of legitimacy that no relationship can, at least not if you are Indian.

She finds her father in the living room, studying the switch for the air conditioning.

"Why do you have it on all the time?" he asks. "How much is your electricity bill?"

The question irritates Swapna. The temperature is in the eighties outside, and soon the house will warm up. It's summer in the deep south, she wants to tell him. Everyone uses air-conditioning. It's not India. But she says nothing and goes into the kitchen where her mother is making tea.

"What will you eat for breakfast?" her mother asks.

"Ma," Swapna protests. "It's the first day. Don't do chores."

It's no use of course. By the end of the day the kitchen looks different. Drops of water cover the sink and the counters, and even splash on the tile floor. The trashcan goes from empty to full. Swapna finds crumbs everywhere. She wonders why she bothered to get the house cleaned. When her parents go outside to admire the backyard, Swapna grabs a paper towel to and wipe the counters dry and mop up the floor. It is not India, she wants to say to her mother. Don't make everything wet.

But when her father goes to bed right after dinner, her mother fights her jetlag and sits on the couch with her again. Swapna opens her Facebook page. They scroll down the newsfeed while she points out all her friends. Her colleagues, her grad school cohorts from Philly, and some of her old friends from Calcutta. Her mother looks intently and listens to every word, asking questions about the people she used to know. Where is she now? How old are her children? Are his parents alright? Then, suddenly, comes the question that catches Swapna off guard.

"Is Tom on Facebook?" her mother asks casually, without looking at her.

"No," Swapna says.

There is no need to go into detail. Her mother does not need to know that she unfriended him the day they had the talk, back in the winter when the trees were bare and reached into the sky with skeletal arms.

That night, still shaking from the confrontation, she hadn't been sure if the unfriending was irreversible. But the gesture, ripe with symbolism, was not to be undone. Her mother does not need to know that she still goes to his profile sometimes, even though she can't see his posts. Swapna looks at his profile picture, an old one, where he wears a red T-shirt and baseball cap and a two-day stubble, still looking like the Tom she knew. If she stares at the thumbnail photograph long enough, he morphs into a stranger. Her mother doesn't have to know that Swapna needed to unfriend him, not out of anger or pride, but because she could not bear to see the girl's casual posts on his wall. The photographs of helpless animals in shelters, the blogs about photography, the updates about running. And then his comments on those posts, so courteous, so decent.

"That," her mother says, pointing. "Who is that?"

They both look at the picture of the Indian man with a receding hairline and a soft, round belly. He is not on Swapna's friend list, but Facebook recommends that she add him.

"Joydeep," her mother says peering.

And so it is. Despite the softening of his body and the roundness of his face, despite the thinning of hair, he still looks boyish and sweet. He is wearing a dress shirt tucked into black trousers, looking a lot more dapper than before. A pair of sunglasses hangs down the front of his shirt.

"Do you talk to him?" she asks, with the innocence of one who does not really understand the complicated mechanics of Facebook.

Even before she finishes the question, Swapna sends him a friend request. It has been so long. Surely, he has forgiven her by now. They are both middle-aged. They have found other people to direct all their strong emotions at in the past two decades.

It is after midnight when her mother finally goes to bed. Swapna keeps checking her Facebook page until Joydeep accepts her friend request. She lies in bed and looks at his photographs, trying to piece together a lifetime, when he sends her a one-line message saying, *Good to hear from you, you look happy.*

She takes her parents to see the Coca Cola museum, where they gaze at vintage ads. Her father and she stand in the tasting room side by side, sipping miniature plastic cups filled with different flavors of soda from around the world. Green tea from Japan, raspberry from New Zealand, candy pine nut from South Africa. He tastes each one with a serious look on his face and makes a brief comment as if the company's future depends on him. Swapna watches him drink the fizzy liquids with the sincerity of a professional taster. His forehead is lined with creases and he looks frailer than she remembers from two years ago. He always looks less authoritative in America than in India. He speaks more softly and does not laugh as much. She wonders if it is the old uncertainty he feels in this foreign land, or if he is particularly debilitated because of her situation. He will turn seventy-seven in a few months. She should not have gone four years without seeing her parents.

He turns to her and says, "Try this one Buri. It's very refreshing."

He offers his cup. The soda is golden, like ginger ale. So many beverages on tap here in America, on every office floor, in public Laundromats, rest areas on the highway, the lobby of every apartment complex, and all over on university campuses. How Swapna had marveled at this when she first came here as a graduate student in the nineties. How jaded she has become since then. But when her father calls her by her pet name, Buri, for a moment she feels innocent again.

The last time Swapna was at the Coke museum was with a tourist friend from Germany, and Tom. Afterwards the three of them had gone to eat tapas. They drank two pitchers of sangria between them. Tom was a far better host than her, ensuring that their guest was constantly entertained. Swapna allows herself a little fantasy. If he were here now, he would walk ahead with her father, pointing out things to him, citing scientific facts about soda. Baba would keep up an endless stream of questioning, making Tom swell with the sense of his own importance. Meanwhile, her mother and she could have talked too.

There is so much Swapna wants to talk to her about, but where does one begin? On the night when she came home slightly drunk from the office Christmas party and extended an arm to Tom, only to be pushed away? Or on the afternoon at the gallery when she caught a glimpse of his former student, twenty-something and thin as a reed, laughing like she was high at something Tom said? Or maybe one begins much earlier, on the day when they bought this house when her bank balance was a third of his, and yet they decided to split the mortgage in equal halves because she fancied herself a feminist.

No, none of them is the beginning of course. Swapna knows that. She knows there was a morning back in Calcutta eighteen years ago, when her mother woke her up at first light of dawn for the turmeric bath. Bulu pishi led the other aunts on her father's side to begin the ulu-uli, until the sound of their high-pitched voices rang out through all the rooms like a siren. The guests stared at the Americans. How the cousins nudged one another and giggled when Tom startled himself and everyone else by pricking his forefinger on a fishbone during lunch. Swapna apologized later for not having warned him but he simply laughed.

She had tried to see the wedding circus through Tom's eyes. The heavy crimson sari and layers of gold jewelry that wore her down until she could barely move, the mournful notes of the shehnai that played all evening until the last guest was gone, the giant paan leaf she used to shield her face from the groom, the exchange of marigold garlands. Through it all, Swapna pretended she was an onlooker, white, foreign, fascinated, watching everything for the very first time. And despite her abhorrence of ritual, the sight of Tom, wrapped in a white and gold dhoti and silk kurta, made it quite charming.

Swapna finds herself thinking of that day for the first time in years, and wonders what she would do if she had a time machine. If she could go back to that day with the hindsight she now has, would she still go through with it? Her parents walk ahead, not speaking. Her father is almost a foot taller than her mother. The back of his head is bald and hers grey. Swapna watches them walk side-by-side, in sync. They have been married forty-eight years and they met only once before their wedding. It seems improbable but there it is. Yet another cliché from the country she has left behind, but all the sneering in the world cannot make her marriage more successful than theirs.

At night, a message from Joydeep pops up on her iPhone screen. He asks how she's been. It's a strange question, given how much time has passed since they last spoke. She considers the question, wondering how she has been since that night twenty years ago, when she hung up the phone after breaking up with him.

"Fine," she tells him. "You?"

He tells her the basics. He moved to Bombay some years ago, to work for Microsoft, which she finds ironic because that's what Indian men are supposed to do in America. He lives alone in a western suburb and has a small house in Goa where he spends many of his weekends.

"That sounds wonderful," she says.

Swapna recalls the flat he shared with his parents when they were in college. It was right next to the busy market where hawkers set up their fly-by-night stands and sold oily fried snacks, cheap plastic jewelry, and produce. Sometimes, on their way back from college, Swapna and Joydeep would climb off the bus and stop at the market to buy guavas and oranges. During the frequent power cuts, the shopkeepers would light their kerosene lamps and lay them on the ground. The streets and houses stood in darkness, but the bazaar flickered with the yellow lights from the lamps.

Now he drives a Honda City to his weekend house on the beach.

"So," she types. "You finally became a capitalist."

He adds a laughing emoticon. "If you can't beat em, you know." He sounds almost American. "Living in India is expensive now, especially Bombay. One has to survive."

Swapna wonders when survival in the motherland became synonymous with vacation homes and Japanese sedans. But, immediately, she feels guilty. It is the guilt of the Non Resident Indian, the latent double standard of one who casually pulls out cans of soda from vending machines placed strategically for maximum consumption. Besides, something in Joydeep's voice suggests a lack of contentment. Or maybe, in her misery, she is simply seeking company.

One morning, she wakes up to find her mother muttering as she opens shelves in the kitchen. She randomly takes out unopened cans and jars and reads labels. She starts to throw away things from the fridge.

"Buri," she says decisively when she sees Swapna. "I need to cook. You cannot live like this. You are not a student any more. You are." She does not complete the sentence, which makes Swapna wonder what she thinks she is. Scientist? Middle-aged? Divorced?

There is no stopping her mother now. She makes a list. They go to the grocery store. Her father comes along because he is fascinated by American grocery stores. He insists on calling them supermarkets. Swapna hopes they do not run into any black people because her father also refers to them by the wrong word. His idea of America has changed little from when she was a little girl. Now, he pushes the cart while Swapna leads the way and her mother makes the selections. The women pour over things and consult while her father stares at the rows of cereals. A customer barks at him to get out of the way because he's blocking the aisle.

"Sorry, sorry, sorry," he says instantly, ashamed and concerned about the breaching of grocery aisle propriety in America.

To compensate for his apologies, Swapna glares at the woman's back as she walks away. How uncharacteristically rude she has just been for this gracious city.

Her mother leans toward her and whispers, "Racist?"

"Maybe she's tired or frustrated about something or unhappy. Maybe," she pauses. "Her husband left her for another woman." She grins.

Her mother looks at her without smiling.

"I don't think you should joke about serious things. This is your problem, this is why you annoy people," she says, with her lips pursed.

Swapna avoids speaking to either of them for the remainder of the trip. The thought of carrying the tilapia filets, ground beef, spinach, carrots, and beets back home, makes her weary. She already bought all the things she thought her parents would enjoy, stocking up the fridge in the days before their arrival. Liver pate, prosciutto, various cheeses, portabella, asparagus. What was all that for?

"This is for you," her mother says. "You need to eat the things you miss. Especially now that you don't come to India."

She wants to tell her mother she misses nothing, at least nothing edible. What she misses is not from India, and her mother can't cook it up for her. But since she is trying not to have conversation, she says nothing. While they wait at the checkout counter, Swapna glances at her phone to see when Joydeep was last online.

That night, when she gets under the covers she feels an old familiar stirring. It is almost like excitement. As the computer lights up, she finds herself shivering a little.

"How can you chat at work?' she asks.

"Don't worry, I'm the boss." He adds a smiley, fat, yellow, infinitely cheerful. "No one's in my office. I can do whatever I want."

"Why did you never marry?" It is only a faint curiosity.

"Never found the right person after you. I was too cynical and angry, then time passed, I got busy with work, and it seemed too much of an effort."

"Do you have a girlfriend?" She wonders if he will protest this intrusion, or say she has no right to ask him things like this.

"Yes. In Goa. I see her when I go."

"Ah."

"It's fine. Life is fine. Just enjoy the moment."

"Yes, I suppose."

She thinks he must be a good lover. In college, Joydeep, Swapna and their friends often skipped classes and hung out at each other's homes in the afternoons. The fun part about going to Swapna's parents' flat was the food her mother would make for them. Cheese pakoras, home made pizza, fish fry, potato tikkis. They would sit on the balcony and eat, drink numerous cups of tea, and talk. Sometimes, her mother would join them briefly. Her friends tried to include her in the conversations. *Mashi, join us*, they would say, making room. *The food is delicious as always*. Only Joydeep would look uncomfortable. He would stare at his scrawny hands or long feet, and not say a word while her mother was there. Later, he admitted that he was intimidated. It was the little things, he would say. The thin gold necklace her mother always wore. The piano in the living room, which he knew she played. The pipe her father smoked. Whenever her mother was around, he seemed to freeze. Swapna wanted so much for him to be lively, to tell his jokes and impress her with his knowledge of Marx and Jung and Derrida.

The Joydeep that Swapna knew privately was a boy of simple but acute pleasures. In India they did not have enough privacy for sex. Instead, they went to the movies. Mostly afternoon shows, when the sun beat down on the streets with unrelenting force. To escape the heat and humidity, they bought plastic packets of salted popcorn and hot chips, and sat in the cool darkness of Lighthouse or Globe or New Empire, the three theatres around New Market that played Hollywood movies a few months after their global release. In the darkness, Swapna glanced at Joydeep's profile many times. His cheekbones were so sharp and his face so thin, they made him look ghostly in the blue light of the screen. His goatee made him look slightly older than his years. They sat with their elbows touching on the same armrest. He always watched the movie so intently, observing every detail of filmmaking, while she let her mind wonder. The seats around them at that time of day were nearly all empty. If he had wanted to, he could have kissed her. Many of their friends went to the movies for that. She waited for him to turn to her with blazing eyes, but at the movies he never did.

Some winter days, when the nip in the air chapped their lips and the sunshine actually felt good, they took a bus to the zoo. Swapna still remembers thinking that the animals looked uniformly depressed. And there is this one memory, an image, of monkey pairs searching one another for head lice. Joydeep and she spent hours outside the monkey arena, watching them do this. How carefully, how patiently, they would look for the lice. *That is love,* Joydeep once said to her. It was unlike him to speak overtly about emotions. *When I grow up, he said, I want to be a monkey.*

The cooking begins on Sunday. Her silent, cold kitchen is transformed into a cauldron of scents and sounds. The pressure cooker hisses and whistles. The microwave beeps. Oil sizzles in the pan. A cloud of steam rises from the pot. The kitchen smells of turmeric and cumin. Swapna chops vegetables on the counter facing the backyard. She can see the back of her father's bald head as he sits out on the porch, reading the newspaper. The grass is lush after a night of rain. She watches her mother cook, hoping to acquire some magical culinary talent from the act of observing. Her mother in the kitchen is brisk and confident. Her fingers move swiftly. She asks Swapna for the garam masala. But Swapna has no idea where it is. It's been so long since she made Indian food. Tom did most of the cooking until six months ago. Even the last night, before he left, he cooked spaghetti and meatballs. They drank a glass of wine. Swapna drank two. No, three. She drank a lot that night. She broke a glass. He stayed calm. He calmly cleared up the table, loaded the dishwasher, wiped the counters. He wanted to make sure, he said, that the house was tidy before he left. Because he knew how much she sucked at housework. He said it without malice.

Swapna is impressed with her mother's efficiency in her foreign kitchen. It is not just about making food for her family, though that is her mother's calling. It is the shrewd wisdom with which she senses things, what to buy, how much to pay, when to cook, when to eat, what medications to track, whether or not to nap. While she is here, Swapna is tempted to abandon all responsibility and let her make the decisions. She wants to simply crumple up like a used paper towel and yield. She is so tired of being self-sufficient.

"How is he doing?" her mother asks as the turmeric-coated tilapia fries in the hot oil.

"Who?"

She glances sideways at her daughter.

"Tom? He's fine I think. We don't communicate. His lawyer talks to my lawyer."

"Surely he will pay you something? After what he did?"

"We'll see. It's hard to prove."

"But he was? Wasn't he?"

Why won't her mother utter the words? Why won't she say adultery or cheating or any of those words that would instantly condemn him to some Hindu hell? Swapna doesn't respond at first because she doesn't really know. What she wants more than anything else is to know. But she cannot bear the thought that his denials were true, that the marriage in fact disintegrated for other reasons.

"What do you think Ma?" She finally asks. "Do you think he was having an affair with that girl? They were always texting. They went to art events together. They had so much in common."

"They were both American," her mother says.

That's all. That's all she has to say. As if that is enough.

The kitchen smells of fried fish, warm and fragrant now, but tomorrow, and over the next few days, it will turn into a stink that will refuse to go despite copious quantities of air freshener. If Tom were here, he would have thrown a fit. *Broil the fish, don't fry it*, he would yell. *The house will stink for days.* Perhaps her mother is right. Perhaps his American self couldn't bear the burden of her any longer.

But now that they have broached the subject, her mother looks deflated. Her movements are suddenly slower. Swapna feels so sorry to have done this to her aging parents.

"It's ok Ma. Lots of people get divorced nowadays. You should understand. You're not like other people of your generation." She wants to point out how her parents eat beef, how they read poetry, how they watch documentaries on the Middle East. How her mother has even exchanged her Bengali sari for the salwaar kameez. They should be fine with divorce.

"You don't understand," her mother says, laying down the wooden spatula with some force. "We will not live for long. Baba is nearly 77. I am 70. How long do we have? Then, what will you do?"

"I have friends."

"Who? Where are these friends? No one visits you. You are always alone."

"Not always," Swapna protests. "They are busy with work and families. And besides, it's the summer. You know that during the summer I don't see people much."

"You will have no one when we are gone." She turns to the skillet, and carefully picks up each piece of fish and places it on a paper towel.

Swapna leaves the kitchen to demonstrate her anger, and joins Baba on the porch. They talk about the world news. He says nothing about Tom or her marriage or her lonely future. The grass is moist, and Swapna can see her mother cooking tilapia in yoghurt and a light meat stew with vegetables through the kitchen window, as she sits with her father and discusses current affairs. She could be sixteen, in a condo in south Calcutta, with a future as open as the sea.

In the middle of the night, with all the lights off except the blue from the computer, Facebook offers a virtual party, with videos, photographs, news reports, jokes, confessions, and recipes streaming constantly on her news feed. How can anyone ever feel alone again, she wonders, with all this stimuli from all these people playing endlessly in one's bedroom? The inevitable thought occurs to her. If such a platform had existed when she first left India as a nervous young grad student, would she have kept going with Joydeep? If they could have talked on Skype on weekends and kept abreast of one another's activities every second of the day, would they have stayed together?

The evening before she left India, twenty years ago, a college friend had invited them all over for a proper farewell. In the middle of the party, the group of friends ceremoniously handed her a goodbye gift. It was a brown and tan upright suitcase. Joydeep gave her nothing. When the others were preoccupied with their drinking, he pulled her into the bathroom and kissed her. They ran the tap so it would drown any sounds. He was a scrawny boy whose bristly goatee tickled her chin. She had stifled a laugh. The next day, after the airplane took off, leaving a trail of lights below, she thought of how the kiss felt and wept quietly in her seat.

They wrote letters for a while and gradually she wrote less and less. His became more and more desperate. His accounts of the unshaven, scruffy Bengali boys sitting on the steps of their fathers' houses and smoking, talking about Communism and Kafka, began to fill her with disgust. No one went anywhere or did anything interesting in Calcutta. One day, she met Tom at a seminar on the French Revolution. He was nearly a foot taller than her, and so confident, and so curious about everything Indian. The first time she visited his parents in suburban Ohio, everything was so clean. The wine glasses shimmered on the table, the fireplace flickered all evening, and snow fell softly outside. Everything in her old life seemed to fade away in a few brief months.

But now Joydeep and Swapna chat like old friends, and she wonders if she erred in picking a midwestern white man over someone who grew up listening to the same music, speaking the same language, and smelling the same odors. How had she lost herself so, in just two years in the West?

The elections have just ended in India. Swapna's newsfeed is crammed with reactions, celebratory and otherwise. Joydeep falls in the latter camp.

"Bloody rightwing Hindus," he types. "They will fuck us and squeeze every shred of independent thinking from their followers and dignity from the rest of us."

A wave of relief washes over Swapna. She can imagine the look of disgust on his face and the snarl in his voice. Here is the same old Joydeep, fiery and passionate about politics and human rights. She remembers how he marched across campus with the red Communist Party flag. She remembers his torn jeans and khadi tunic, and the canvas tote bags he swung across his shoulder. She is tempted to provoke him further, to drive him to a point of frenzy.

"But the economy? Your jobs? Aren't those important? The new government is supposed to lure in foreign investors again. Doesn't the prime minister have an impressive record in his home state?"

"Impressive record???!!!!"

Swapna pulls the comforter over her even though it is a warm and humid night. "You mean the murders and riots??? The rest is his crony media campaign. The poor haven't benefitted. Muslims haven't benefitted. What fucking record are you talking about?"

She smiles in the semi darkness. "You haven't changed that much after all."

"But you have."

It catches her by surprise. "Really?"

"Yes, you're calmer, and not in a good way. Like something's left you. Spirit or romance or that innocent faith in the world."

"I'm a realist now," Swapna says.

"It's not enough," says Joydeep. "I will retire in a few years and move to Goa, where I can climb coconut trees and sip feni, watch the waves lap the shore, and write a book."

Tears spring to her eyes at the vision. It is like the cover of a romance novel. So foolish, so embarrassing.

"You should come visit me in Goa. Or better still, come live with me. Rekindle."

"What?" Her heart may have stopped as she waits for his response. It has been a long time since anyone has flirted with her.

"Your romantic side," he says. "Innocence."

"What about your girlfriend?"

A chubby yellow smiley appears on the screen, before the chat abruptly ceases and the green light next to his name goes out.

The night before her parents leave, she finds it impossible to sleep. She gets out of bed in the middle of the night and wanders to the living room. It is raining softly and the large bay windows are fogged up. Swapna makes her way to the couch and finds her mother sitting there, staring out of the same window. She sits next to her and they gaze outside as if the window is a TV.

"What will happen to you when we leave?" her mother asks.

"The same things that happened before you arrived Ma," she says. But the truth is she is a little afraid too. This departure feels different, more significant somehow.

"How will you live alone?"

"Please Ma, I am not a child. I came here alone, when I knew no one and had nothing. Now look." She waves her hand around the house. She is a senior researcher for the US government, she has colleagues and friends and even in laws though soon they will not be hers. Still, she has built a community in this country, and lives on her own terms. All this she wants to tell her mother but instead she simply waves her hand as if that gesture might encompass an entire existence.

"Perhaps it is our fault," her mother says.

Swapna looks at her, surprised. She expected blame, not guilt.

"How can it be your fault?"

"We should not have allowed you to come here. You could have lived in India, married Joydeep or some other Bengali boy, and we would all have been nearby. We should have put our foot down when you wanted to marry an American."

"Ma," Swapna begins, startled by the anger rising in her breast. "Allowed? You would not have allowed me?" she pauses to collect herself. "What would I have done in India? Got a nine to five job and popped out a couple of babies? Or stayed at home and not even worked like so many of my old friends? I love my job, Ma. And you know, I did love Tom too. He was so interesting." She yells out the last word and realizes only then that it is true.

Her mother starts to weep. Swapna shakes her head in frustration. Behind them a light comes on in the hallway. It is her father.

"What are you both doing? It is the last night."

He stands in the arched doorway, silhouetted against the light.

"Stop crying. Stop," he says abruptly to his wife. "This is not the time to cry."

"Isn't it our fault?" her mother asks him. "Your sisters had warned us before the wedding. Maybe we should have tried to stop her."

He comes towards them in the dim light and Swapna sees that he is shaking his head. "Stop her from what Malati? It was twenty years ago. How could we know? No one knew what the future held, not even Tom. He was so sincere. Don't you remember? He took the bus everywhere in Calcutta, and ate with his hands. Don't you remember how he cooked with you in the kitchen and how he tried to learn Bengali? It must have been so hard for him, and yet I never heard him complain."

Swapna feels her father's hand on her head. It is surprisingly steady. She wills it to stay there awhile and tries to memorize its shape on her head. Her father strokes her hair and beside them her mother's tears slowly subside into an occasional sniff. They stay like that for a while, and watch the sky. Tomorrow her parents will disappear into it. A day later, they will look at it from different hemispheres. But now, in this moment, they are united.

Swapna wonders what Joydeep would say if he knew that she has begun to think of him during the day. Or that she checks her phone for messages every few hours. There is a level of comfort in their online conversations that reminds her of a less complicated time. Despite the superficial changes, Joydeep and she belong to the same community, and share the same sensibility. This is what she had thought of Tom once.

He begins tonight's chat with the most intimate of questions. "Where's Tom now?"

"He lives with Julia," she says. "She's very young. And not even very pretty."

"Who's paying whom?

"She's a student, works as a bartender to pay her bills. So he must take care of her."

"No I mean you and he. Who's paying? Settlement? Is the house yours?"

"Oh that. Our lawyers are working on that. I've been asked to stay single for a few months." Swapna adds a smiley.
"You should squeeze him. Don't let him get away. When in the States…"

"I don't know if I care that much. I have a job. And in Georgia it's all about how much either of us needs. I do have the house because it was half mine anyway." Swapna looks around her room at the floral wallpaper, the shag carpet, and the furniture they had bought slowly, over months, with their first paychecks. The large window reveals the dark night sky over the backyard. The house has a sunroom, where Tom and she read on Sunday mornings after he brewed cappuccino for them both on his high-end espresso maker. The basement downstairs is full of their winter clothes which they haven't used since they moved down south. Tom's down coat and hers, their thick wool scarves and hats, and winter boots, lie entangled together in old boxes that haven't been opened in a few years. Yes, this house is hers, and she can live out her life in it, surrounded by their memories.

She glances back at the screen and sees Joydeep's words waiting for her. "Sorry, I didn't mean to make you uncomfortable. It's just that after all this time I still feel protective of you."

It has been a long time since Swapna has had a man feel protective of her. This was the patriarchal impulse she had once fought. In Tom she had found the liberal white man who treated her as his equal and expected her to solve her own problems. How refreshing it had seemed then. But now, this instant, faced with the prospect of her parents leaving the next day and a future spent in solitude, she finds herself longing for a pair of protective arms around her.

"My parents leave tomorrow," she says.

Joydeep sends her a little red heart. "It will be lonely. I wish I were there to keep you company."

"Their being here has been so comforting. I didn't realize just how much it would help."

"After they leave, we can chat every night before you sleep."

"You're sweet. Thank you." The thought of chatting with Joydeep relieves some of the weight that has lately settled in her chest. She wonders what might have happened if they had found each other online before Tom left. Then she thinks of destiny. Fate. Those Indian words she once sneered at. Is this how things were meant to be? With a return to her youth and to whatever she had left behind? In the next room, her parents sleep, her father's gentle snores drift through the walls. In the morning, her mother will make a last cup of tea for her. Swapna wishes this night could last eternally.

"I hope your parents are heavy sleepers," Joydeep types.

"Yes, unless Ma is up worrying about me."

"How long has it been?"

"Six months."

"You must miss things."

"It's only occasional now. The anger's faded. Some days I'm really happy to be free."

"But you must still miss some things."

Swapna looks at the screen, a little confused about what he means.

"What was it like being married to an American?"

"I don't know. How does one sum it up? Same as being married to anyone else I would think. Complicated."

"But Americans are less traditional. Especially a man like Tom who married an India. He must have been very liberal."

"Yes he was. That was one of the nice things about him."

"How nice?"

"What?"
"What kind of things did you do? Did you experiment much?"
"Wait, what are you talking about? You mean like drugs?"

"No, I mean, did he teach you stuff? You've been in the States 22 years, you must know all kinds of things."

The room suddenly feels cooler than before. Swapna tries to recall if she locked all the doors.

As if on cue, Joydeep types, "My door is locked. Tell me some of the things you did. While your parents are in the next room. More fun this way."

"Joydeep," Swapna begins. Her fingers hover over the keyboard, searching for words that might explain what she's feeling now, or any of the emotions she has undergone in the past six months.

"Do you remember us kissing in Janani's bathroom the night before you left for the States? How it turned us on but we couldn't do anything because of all the people right outside? I have never been more aroused in my life."

Her father's snores get louder. The clock ticks on the nightstand next to her. Its metronomic beat sounds like someone's heart.

When she doesn't respond for several minutes, Joydeep types, "Tomorrow, after your parents leave, ping me. It's ok if you wake me up."

She still says nothing. Posts keep streaming on her newsfeed. Baby pictures, someone's lunch menu, a conversation someone overheard in a coffee shop in Seattle. Minute-by-minute accounts of life around the globe pour in.

"I get lonely too Swapna. This corporate life, this traffic, the crowds, the noise. It's all deafening. All I crave is a human connection."

"This is your idea of a connection? Cyber sex?"

"Come on Swapna." Everyone in India is doing it. Young, old, single, married, everyone. And you? You're free, and in America. You of all people should not pretend to be a prude. We are both alone."

"You girlfriend in Goa?"

"She's sweet. Really shy and not very aggressive. Not a cosmopolitan, if you know what I mean."

"I should sleep," Swapna types. "I think you are not quite well. You sound a bit messed up."

"I am not well? And what about you?"

She knows she should let it go, end the chat, and turn off the laptop, but she feels compelled to type something definitive, as if putting the words down on the screen will make her life's decisions mean something.

"We have nothing in common Joydeep."

The words come faster at her now, and Swapna notices how he misspells them. "Oh yah? And what did you hsve in commmon with Tom? You on your high hoarse. You think I need help? What about you? What will you do for the rest of your life?"

Swapna closes the chat abruptly without saying goodbye. She lies in bed, trying to swallow the queasy feeling that's washing over her. Once or twice she gulps hard to push back the acid that's climbing up her throat. The room is plunged in cool darkness now, free of the harsh glare of the computer screen. She lies there and ponders Joydeep's final question to her. What will she do with the rest of her life, what will she do when her parents are dead and there is absolutely no one to call her own?

On the way to the airport, her parents argue about whether to leave the window up or down, whether her father has remembered the tickets, and whether they should grab a bite before boarding. Swapna drives absent-mindedly, listening to her mother scold her father for no reason.

"How can you fight constantly just when you're leaving?" she finally asks.

Her father turns to her. His tone is gentle when he speaks. "It is because we are leaving. She is upset."

This is how he sums up forty-eight years of marriage, Swapna thinks, with this primal understanding of the other person.

Swapna watches them leave at the airport, and bites her lower lip to concentrate on that pain. Their backs recede slowly out of sight. As always when her parents leave, she feels momentarily orphaned.

Instead of heading home, Swapna goes to the zoo for the first time in eleven years. She buys herself a ticket and walks slowly around the grounds. It is the peak of summer. Even the animals want to stay inside. Only a few other fools like her have ventured to the zoo today. Swapna makes her way to the primate section. They come in various sizes and shades. Drill, lemur, tamarin, macaque. Swapna stops suddenly in front of the orangutans. There are two of them. They are large, almost like adult humans, and they sit close together, their bodies touching. In fact, every time one of them moves slightly, so does the other, in tandem, as if tied with an invisible rope. They move slowly, inching their way across the large outdoor cage.

Swapna sits on a rock and watches them. A few other people walk by. A young mother pushing a stroller stops to look at the apes. Her baby stares at them from its seat and gurgles with what Swapna assumes must be pleasure, for instead of hurrying away, the mother lingers. If she had kids, Swapna might have been a regular at the zoo. The apes, dark brown and hairy, have long, mournful faces. One of them is slightly smaller than the other. The larger orangutan waits patiently for the smaller one to catch up. They touch each other constantly.

This southern summer is scorching and humid like the tropics. Sweat trickles down her back but she cannot turn away. The apes stop in the middle of the cage. The smaller one reaches up to the larger one and begins to search for lice. It works patiently, its fingers kneading through the other's hair. Every now and then the apes glance up and blink slowly at the sun, as if bewildered by the world outside.

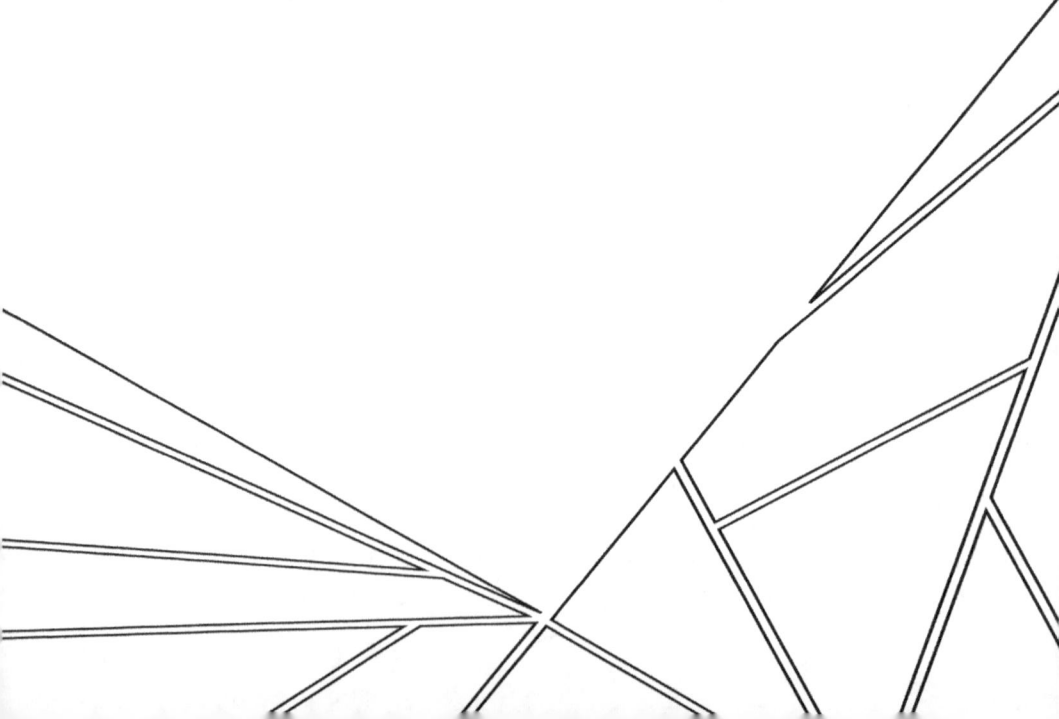

Self Portrait as Rapunzel

Emily Rose Cole

i.

My mother built her tower out of baby teeth
broken on stale communion wafers, out of dogs
choked by chicken bones, empty medicine cabinets,
every lullaby her mother never sang her.

When I was born, she mixed a mortar of bent
needles, busted harp strings, and porcupine
quills pulled from beneath her fingernails.

One day, she told me, *gold dust will pool in the hollow
of your tongue. Roses will track their roots in your spine.
Your body will chip like shale rock chiseled by rain.*

ii.

She shut me in. No door. One locked window.
A keyhole cut in the shape of my name.

I stayed inside for years, afraid of anything
that carried its shadow too close to itself.
My mother hoisted baskets of mint and dill.

She wrote notes that ended with *for your own good*
and planted morning glories that opened like eyes.

iii.

When a prince arrived, he used words like *trapped*
and *escape*. I offered a rope woven from daisy stems,
but he said my hair was stronger.

The shorn end of the braid thumped the grass
like a feathered body striking stones. Years later,
after he left me, I carved a hole in my tongue.

I came home. The tower had fallen. My mother's last gift:
a handful of pebbles shaping a word: *grow*.
I built my tower out of nettles and closed doors
and dropped seeds into my eyes.

iv.

Now, red petals curl behind my teeth.
Yellow pollen smears my lips and bees
drone at the corners of my mouth.

I swallow secrets that harden into keys.
All night, I listen to locks sliding shut.

Kielbasy Run

Rachel Garman

Tucked into Philadelphia's northeastern section, the small neighborhood of Port Richmond is still asleep. It's 5:30 on a cold December morning, and a fog has fallen over the narrow streets and row-homes. Abandoned factories and ornate churches, still illuminated by the moon, cast elongated shadows across the neighborhood. Most residents are still snug in the warmth of their beds, I am not one of them. For the past 17 years, my mom, Aunt Pat and I have embarked on the "Kielbasy Run." Set during the week before Christmas, we put on layer after layer of clothing and take the 20-minute drive on an empty I-95 to my family's old Polish neighborhood, Port Richmond. The ride is mostly silent; Aunt Pat tries to catch up on sleep after consecutive night shifts at Jefferson Hospital, and I stare out the window.

Our destination—Czerw's Deli—is located on Tilton Street, which closer resembles a back alleyway than a usable road. After parallel parking a few blocks away (the closest we can get to the store), we venture into the below-zero temperatures and wait in line outside. The store won't be open until 7 a.m., but the line already reaches the end of the block. We do all of this in search of one thing: authentic Polish food.

We wait in line with familiar faces from years past. There's the businessman taking a day off from work, the father with his young children who drove in from New Jersey and the old woman (hair still in curlers) who lives around the block.

Thirty minutes later, we pass the screen door leading to the back of the deli—a source of warmth and a sign we are nearing the main entrance. Through the screen, I can make out the faint figure of an old woman, hunched over with her cane faithfully by her side. Her hands move slowly and steadily as she packs beef into cabbage leaves. Her measurements are by memory, the movements of her fingers automatic. After wrapping up the finished product, she hobbles to the back hallway, calls out for one of her sons and hands off the package.

Just then, a large man—his white apron covered in reddish-brown stains—flings open the screen door and steps into the cold air to check the smoker. As he removes the lid, warm smoke and the woodsy smell of meat diffuses through the line. He grumbles to himself as he dips a finger in the juice pooling under the meat and raises it to his mouth.

"Needs more onions," he states with a smack of his lips. He disappears back into the kitchen.

After nearly an hour in the cold, we make it to the large, wooden door. Inside, the deli is long and narrow, with enough room for only 10 customers. The line stretches along the back wall next to shelves packed with everything from Jewish rye bread to kosher dill pickles. One shelf displays four kinds of babka—cheese, raspberry, poppy seed and sometimes chocolate. In the back corner of the deli is a freezer full of pierogis. A large barrel full of sauerkraut gives the store its distinctive sour delicious smell of onions and garlic.

When we finally reach the deli counter, one of the three blond brothers takes our order.

"What'll it be ladies?" the oldest brother asks in a gruff voice.

Mom recites our order like clockwork:

"Four pounds kabanosa, one pound fresh kielbasy, a pound of fresh bacon—sliced thick—one cheese babka, and four dozen onion & cheese pierogis."

The rounded glass case is filled with red meat ranging from slab bacon to smoked kielbasy. Yellowed newspaper clippings hang in frames behind the counter, and a photograph of Pope John Paul II dutifully overlooks the cash register. After making our purchases, our food is handed to us in a large brown paper bag—20 pounds of pure culinary heaven. Our parcels act as a source of heat as we make our way back outside. Customers in line outside eye the trophy in our arms as we walk past.

The rest of our day is spent driving to three or four Polish bakeries—most are easy to spot with the country's red and white colors proudly displayed. As we drive from bakery to bakery, my mom and aunt point out familiar landmarks:

"This is the cemetery where Babci [Grandma] is buried."

"There's the corner store our cousin used to own."

"Here is where I first learned to drive our orange station wagon."

Our foggy car windows display family history like a photo album. With each street comes another memory, and with each memory comes another anecdote.

By now it's nearly 1 p.m., and we make our way into the last bakery for our most valued item: paczkis. Paczkis (pronounced PUNCH-keys) are Polish doughnuts filled with fruit jelly or cream. Their airy dough makes them significantly better than traditional American doughnuts. We select a variety of paczkis in flavors such as plum, prune and apricot.

As I walk back to the car—paczki in hand—the chilling wind hardly bothers me. I remove my thick gloves and let the powdered sugar fall onto my skin. The purple jelly stains my lips and tongue. I gaze once more at the grandiose churches dotting the avenue. From where I stand I can see the churches where great-grandma Frances Rybicki, great-grandpa Mikolaj Czekaj and grandma Catherine Wojcik all lived out the major events of their lives. I smile as our car pulls away and these familiar landmarks disappear into the Philadelphia skyline.

Once back at Aunt Pat's house, the crinkling of the brown paper bag acts as the dinner bell. My five cousins—Brook, Matt, Monica, Chris and Erica—come running down three flights of stairs. We gather around my aunt's round table and immediately begin to unwrap food from its paper packaging. We laugh for hours as Mom and Aunt Pat continue to share stories while we feast. Once my belly is finally full and I can't bear to eat another paczki, there's one thought running through my mind: *I can't wait until next year*.

Brotherly Love

Warren Longmire

Philly all the emo with none of the moshpit.
Philly free jazz in a trashbag.

Philly's a synthetic weave tumbleweed down 69th street.
Philly's Schuylkill punch brown and meek mill's cadence for an anti-
     depressant.

Philly's a rust covered trolley rail used as a balance beam for cat sized rats.
Philly's a mouse that stands in the middle your living-room wondering
     what you staring at.

Philly's when the scent of urine feels comfortable.
Philly's a crackhouse where someone pulls out an ipod touch.

Philly's the seasoning left in potato chip bag, littered because fuck you.
Philly's bulletproof glass protecting blunt wrappers and raisinets.

Philly's a bed sheet ad for pet colonics.
Philly's four empty barber shops in a two block radius.

Philly is abandoned midnight unsafe even if desert.
Philly looks at anything but you as intensely as it can.

Philly is dubstep basement row-home hot pagan light-show for nobody
      Philly.
Philly's a cafe a bored new jersey dreamed into existence.

Philly bucktoothed street with caution tape floss.
Philly flosses through beirut in a hooptee.
Philly ain't no white car.
Philly For Sale sign.

Philly loose dutch tobacco on the 23. Philly loose money. Philly is cheap.
Philly chirps. Philly speaks it's first words. Philly lounges.

Philly is waiting.
Philly is waiting.
Philly is waiting and the teams choke.
The kids choke.

The fey smokers identical outside the whiskey bar chain smoke like it's new
      orleans downtown.
The buses weeze.

The roads are cracked and the sidewalk's grow flowerbeds beneath them.
Philly grows and shrinks. Screams "back door" but doesn't tell you to step
      down.

Doesn't speak. Gets cut. Names.
A paradox laughing at itself. The old friend with no money

    and a ugly mouth.

Bird Fever

Robert Johnson

When the baby's fever reached one hundred and five, they decided they could stand it no longer. A call to the pediatrician had reached an answering machine, and they'd waited an hour, but the child was hot as a charcoal briquette and had recently begun vomiting a white, mealy substance – a cross between grade school paste and cottage cheese – that was unlike any spit-up they'd seen. Finally they loaded the baby into the Volvo and drove to the emergency room. Thomas kept the accelerator to the floor, and Allison sat in back with their son. The boy cried hoarsely with each breath, and Allison asked if Thomas finally agreed the turkeys were to blame.

"Let's not go off the deep end," he said. "We're not the doctor."

"When this is over, you're speaking to Danny Baker," she said. "And don't talk to me like I'm crazy."

The emergency room doctor took the baby's temperature – now one hundred and six – and declared that the first order of business was to cool the child down. Seizures were a possibility if the fever remained that high. Thomas spent the next half hour lowering his screaming son again and again into cool water while a nurse tracked his temperature. The boy held tightly to him with arms and legs between soakings, and to get him free Thomas had to break the child's hold each time. He found himself panting and crying with his son, as Allison leaned against the wall in the mercilessly bright exam room, her face in her hands.

When the fever dropped to one hundred and two, the nurse wrapped the child in a towel and laid him in his mother's arms, where he cried and then fell into a jerky, croaking sleep. The doctor, a ruddy man with watchful blue eyes, sat with them and asked how long the boy had been ill.

"We think it's bird flu," Allison said.

Thomas sighed and laid a hand on her arm. "Of course we don't know what it is, Doctor. He's been listless for two days, no appetite, his diapers soft and yellow. The fever came on late this morning and has been building all day."

Allison swung toward him, the child against her breast like a shield. "I was on the patio with Declan four days ago," she said, "where we allow turkeys – wild turkeys – to come right up to the house. He was on a blanket and I was reading, and I thought I'd swept all the disgusting droppings into the grass, when I looked down and saw him playing with one of them – one of the bowel movements, I mean." She glared at Thomas. "It was at his mouth."

The doctor's eyes darted between them. This was good information, he said, though bird flu was doubtful. "Despite what you hear on the news, the transmission of avian influenza from bird to human is rare, and there are no reported cases in the United States. It's more likely your boy has a case of the everyday flu, though we'll need further – "

"Can we at least acknowledge," Allison cried, "that a five-month-old child handling bird shit is a bad idea? Can we at least acknowledge that?" She said "bird shit" so loudly that conversations outside the exam room went quiet.

The doctor blinked and lifted his palms. Yes, he said, handling bird feces was never a good thing. Several illnesses might result from such contact, and knowing that the child had done so would inform their testing. Allison's face crumpled, and she began to weep so convulsively that Thomas took the baby from her, and the nurse helped her to the examination table where she could lie down.

In the hallway the doctor put a hand on Thomas's shoulder. "This is hard on both of you. That's perfectly understandable."

Thomas sensed the man was prompting him to talk about Allison. He pressed his cheek against his son's hot forehead and whispered, "It's bad enough having Declan so miserable, but she always jumps to the worst – "

"She's right to be concerned," the doctor said, dropping his hand to cup the baby's skull. "This boy is very sick."

Allison had always been fearful, though there'd been a time Thomas found her timidity appealing. She was blonde and honey-skinned and an inch taller than he, and she walked with the loping, pigeon-toed stride of a model on the runway. Her father owned three restaurants in Chicago and had played outfield for the White Sox, and he'd made it clear in word and deed that his daughter deserved better than a high school math teacher. When Allison turned girlish and needy it salved a raw spot in Thomas's pride.

Once, soon after they were engaged, she made a roast beef dinner at her apartment, and when they sat down she asked if he would light the candles. When he looked at her curiously she told him she'd never struck a match in her life.

"Daddy always did it when we were little," she said. "And then later on it became like a family custom, and before you know it I'm in high school and college and – " She shrugged her shoulders and laughed. "I've still never done it."

Thomas lit the candles and savored knowing he'd taken the old lion's place. He bent to kiss Allison's lovely cheeks in the firelight and said if she needed someone to strike matches for the rest of her life, he would be that man.

And he meant it. But in the four years since, her qualms and boundaries had begun to eat at him. If he stood at an open refrigerator door more than ten seconds, she worried the pork chops would spoil and give them trichinosis. If they were sitting on the patio in the evening and a bat flew overhead, she bolted for the house for fear the creature would tangle itself in her hair, leaving Thomas to either sit alone or gather the wine glasses and follow her inside.

But whenever he'd explained the flaws in her thinking – the few times he'd tried to help her face her fears logically – there'd been hell to pay.

Shortly after he'd begun his first teaching job, they spent a weekend in the city with another couple and visited the Sears Tower, where the observation deck promised a view of four states from its thirteen-hundred-foot perch. Better yet, you reached it by one of the world's fastest elevators.

Allison stood at the ticket booth reading the description and biting her lip, but when their friends suggested going for it she shook her head. Thomas had drunk a second beer at lunch, and he laughed more loudly than he'd intended and said, "Of course not. We could *all die*."

Allison scowled at him and walked away in the Wacker Drive lobby with her arms folded across her chest. He followed her – loaded with righteousness more than regret – and their argument in front of a Baskin Robbins had clerks staring and mothers gathering their toddlers close.

"You didn't have to embarrass me," she said when he caught up and took her elbow. She shook him off and stared at the travertine floor.

"Do just one thing for me," he said. "Admit that this is ludicrous. On an *intellectual* level at least, admit there's nothing to be afraid of."

"You treat me like a child."

Thomas's voice took on a tone he used in the classroom. "A child gives in to irrational fears, but an adult knows better. An adult knows there's near zero chance the elevator will malfunction. An adult knows – "

Her chin snapped up. "I know if you don't leave me alone I'll claw your eyes out. That's what I know."

He shook his head. "Have you ever once considered facing your demons and telling them to fuck off?"

She startled him by smiling. "Fuck off," she said.

In the end she waited in a tea shop while Thomas and the other couple rode in silence to the top of the world. There, he put his forehead against the glass and looked over the seamless reaches of Lake Michigan and asked himself how Allison could name him as a tormentor, when no one cared for her like he did.

The boy's temperature had begun to climb again, and the doctor suggested admitting him for a day or two. A regimen of anti-viral meds, fever reducers and a cool-mist vaporizer should do the trick. Allison insisted on staying, and Thomas said he would drive to the house and pack an overnight bag for both of them. She shook her head. "I want you to sleep at the house and talk to Danny Baker first thing," she said. "I don't want to see you again until you've talked to him."

"I don't think there's any reason to – " Thomas began, but she turned away, the child a sodden, reproachful weight on her shoulder.

Their neighbor Danny Baker was the town marshal. When he and his twelve-year-old son Mitch weren't hunting or fishing, they stacked bales of straw at the wooded end of their back yard and shot steel-tipped arrows into them. They cleaned blue gills and smallmouth bass on their deck and threw the guts into the weeds, where raccoons feasted in plain sight. Lately Allison had seen Mitch spreading ears of field corn in the grass, so wild turkeys and quail would come out of the pines to feed.

But though the quail scurried for cover the moment Thomas or Allison opened the sliding door to the patio, the turkeys had grown bolder by the day. One early June evening Thomas and Danny Baker stood at the hydrangea bed that connected their back yards, and the man told him that springtime was the birds' mating season, and the young males – "jakes," he called them – were loaded with spunk.

"We're either wives or rivals to them," Danny Baker said. "They want to fuck us or fight us." As if on cue, a male turkey stepped from the pines and strutted toward them, its head high and thrusting and its eyes fixed on their faces.

"Whoa now, uncle," Danny Baker said. He broke off a woody hydrangea shoot and met the bird halfway. The turkey stretched its naked skull toward him, and the man stood tall and whipped the stick through the air so it made a whistling sound. "Shoo now, chief," he said, and the bird bobbed and flounced and retreated into the trees, its ostrich-like legs muscular and springy.

"They have to know who's top dog, is all," Danny Baker said.

In the morning Allison called to tell him that Declan's fever had spiked again overnight and they'd repeated the cooling baths. He had a rash and made no tears when he cried, so the doctor had ordered intravenous fluids.

"They couldn't find a vein," Allison said. "They poked him and poked him, and they finally had to go into his neck." Her voice was monotonic and exhausted, but their conversation was less than a minute old when she asked him if he'd spoken to Danny Baker.

"Not yet," Thomas said. He put down his coffee and rubbed the sleep from his eyes. "His pickup's still in the drive." The line buzzed with a reproving silence, and Thomas looked out the window to see the marshal and his son hoisting a portable generator onto the truck bed. "Oops, there he is now," he said, and hung up before she could respond.

Pregnancy had lifted Allison to the top of a green hill – her fears lightened by anticipation – but the birth itself had pushed her into a helpless, tumbling roll down the other side. Labor was a bruising, thirty-six-hour grind, and when Declan's head got stuck in the birth canal the doctor gripped it with forceps and yanked the boy so violently into the world his cheek was bloodied. Thomas woke to find himself on the tile floor, a nurse swabbing his forehead with a cold towel and his son's squalls in his ears. And though friends had told him how wonderful the moment would be when the boy was laid on his mother's chest, Allison began to hemorrhage, and the room filled with shouting medical staff. The baby was hustled away and Thomas was sent – still in gown and mask – to a couch in the waiting area.

When mother and child finally came home, Allison slept in Declan's room every night for three months. Even after nighttime feedings tapered off and she'd joined Thomas again in their bed, she continued to check the boy four and five times a night.

Once when they lay sleepless in the early dawn, she told Thomas about being a child and learning for the first time about glaciers. "I thought they were like rainstorms," she said. "I thought you'd wake up one morning and there'd be a glacier on the horizon where a day before there was just sky." She'd dreamed about her father picking her up and running, while behind them a wall of ice tore houses to pieces, gouged sidewalks from the earth, shredded trees.

"I've started having that dream again," she said, pressing her damp face into his shoulder. "I'd forgotten about it, and now it's back."

Thomas pulled her to him and smoothed her hair and listened to Declan's clotty breathing on the baby monitor, turned to full volume on the nightstand.

Now he stepped from his yard into Danny Baker's gravel driveway and watched the man and his son wrestle the generator to the back of the truck bed and strap a gasoline can against it with a bungee cord. Only after they'd finished and jumped to the ground did the marshal acknowledge Thomas's presence.

"How-do, professor," he said, wiping his forehead with the back of his fist. He wore a sleeveless flannel shirt half open to his chest, and his biceps were round as softballs. "What can I do you for?"

Thomas told him that Declan was in the hospital, the doctors were trying to pin down what was making him feverish, Allison had spent the night with him there.

"That's no good," Danny Baker said. "I'll tell Helen. We'll be sending prayers your way for sure." Mitch stood beside him and stared at Thomas. His hair was cut short to the same length all over his head and was so blonde it was nearly white.

"Anyway," Thomas said. "The doctors think it might have something to do with the turkeys, with their droppings on our patio."

"Is that right? That's what the doctor said?"

"They think it's a possibility. That's correct," Thomas said.

The man leaned against the truck and rubbed the stubble on his chin. "We're sorry to hear the boy's sick. Declan, is it?" He glanced at Mitch. The boy's gaze hadn't strayed from Thomas's face. "I don't think it's the turkeys though, do you?"

"Probably not," Thomas said, "but I have my orders." He smiled, but when the marshal looked at him blankly he hurried on. "We're going to try to keep them out of the yard, just to be on the safe side."

"Shoot, man, that's easy," Danny Baker said. "Get you a tennis racket and run them off."

"No, that's not what I mean." Thomas felt hot blood in his cheeks. "I'm teaching Drivers Ed this summer, and I can't expect my wife to be chasing wild animals from the yard. Not with a new baby."

"Wild animals," Danny Baker repeated, and then his face brightened. "I tell you what. Get a dog. Turkeys can't stand a yapping dog."

Thomas sighed and gripped the truck bed rail with both hands. He leaned to and fro, making the pickup rock gently. "Allison doesn't like – "

He felt the silence, then a breeze rustle high in the pines. "We're not dog people," he said.

Danny Baker glanced at the sky. "What is it you need from us, Tom?"

Thomas stepped around the wheel well so his back was to Mitch. He stared into the man's eyes and spoke rapidly. "Look, it's probably nothing, but my wife…we think it would be better if you didn't spread corn in your yard. The birds are losing their fear of us, and if there's the slightest possibility they carry disease – "

"Done," the man said. "If that's all you need, we're glad to help. More than glad." He bent to retrieve a spade and pickaxe and threw both into the truck bed so they clattered heavily. "Is there anything else your wife needs? Anything Helen can do?"

Thomas stepped away from the pickup. "No, nothing else," he said. "Thanks for understanding."

"It's nothing at all. You tell your wife she needn't worry about turkey turds any longer," Danny Baker said. He laughed, and Mitch smiled and unsmiled quickly.

When Thomas returned to the house he found a push broom and swept the patio clean of a fresh collection of gray-green droppings. When he turned to enter the house he saw Mitch watching him from the deck. Thomas nodded, but the boy stepped into the lawn with a rake and began scouring fiercely through the grass, sending naked corn cobs flying into the trees.

At the hospital Declan was sleeping open-mouthed, each inhalation a squeaking whimper. A tube snaked from an IV bag to a bruised place at his jugular. The pediatrician sat with Thomas and Allison and told them their son had a virus, most likely the flu, and would probably be better in a few days.

"What about the turkey droppings?" Allison said.

"That's our conundrum," the doctor said. "We've ruled out bird flu, of course, and the symptoms aren't consistent with E. coli or salmonella. It's possible he has a case of West Nile, and that's no laughing matter." The rash, the high fever and the dehydration all suggested the mosquito-borne virus.

Thomas stroked his son's hot forehead and looked at Allison. "So it doesn't come from the turkeys after all," he said.

"On the contrary, it might," the doctor said. "A mosquito bites an infected bird and then it bites us." West Nile usually disappeared on its own, he continued, but in rare cases it turned to encephalitis, especially in infants. He asked if they had any standing water in the back yard – an unused goldfish pond, maybe, or an old tire swing – that might be a breeding place for mosquitos.

A cool feather brushed Thomas's heart, but Allison responded that Declan was too young for a swing, and a pond wasn't safe for a child. She looked at Thomas. "Is there anything else you can think – "

"No," he said. "There's nothing else." He felt the doctor eyeing him. "I'll check though. Just to be sure."

Allison rocked back and forth as the doctor recommended Declan stay in the hospital a few more days until they knew he was out of the woods. When the man left the room, she continued to rock, her hands twisting the waistband of her sweatshirt. "He'll never be out of the woods," she said.

"Of course he will," Thomas said. "He said it was rare." He stood and paced the room, squeezing fistfuls of hair until his scalp stung. He told her that Danny Baker had agreed to stop spreading corn in the yard. He'd seen Mitch raking the grass clean. Soon the turkeys would learn their place. "I'll call off from Drivers Ed for a week," he said. "I'll show them who's top dog."

"We can't keep our baby safe," she said softly.

"Yes we can," Thomas said. He knelt and grabbed her shoulders. She stared past him, and her bleakness nearly moved him to panic. He took her face in his hands and forced it to his. "I'll fix this," he cried. "I promise."

Thomas drove from the hospital to a strip mall near the house. Allison had refused to go home to sleep, so he told her he would pick up a toothbrush and shampoo and return soon. Instead he went to Home Depot, where he bought one hundred feet of chicken wire, two dozen rebar stakes, a mini-sledge hammer, five citronella candles and a propane mosquito fogger.

He arrived at the house and went immediately to work. Since the turkeys had become aggressive he had stopped gardening, and his galvanized metal watering can and bird bath were full to the brim with rain water. An amber film coated both surfaces, and he dumped the watering can into the impatiens and flushed the bird bath clean with a hose. He climbed a stepladder to inspect the eaves troughs and found them full, choked with sodden pine needles. He circled the house with the ladder, scooping crud from the gutters with his hands and snaking the hose into each downspout until the clogs gave way and water flowed freely into gravel beds. He retrieved a leaf rake from the garage and swept the back yard clean of droppings, flinging them far into the pines. He used the mini-sledge to drive the rebar at intervals along the property line and stretched the chicken wire from stake to stake, anchoring it with ground staples.

He looked up once and saw Danny Baker watching him from the deck. The man called to him, but Thomas bent again to his task.

In the end the fence stood four-feet high and wove tautly from one corner of the back yard to the other. It spanned the width of the pine woods and sliced through the hydrangea bed. Thomas's clothes were fouled by pine sludge, his hands nicked and bloodied from the wire, but he unpacked the citronella candles and placed one on the outdoor bistro table and the other four at each corner of the patio. The sun was low in the trees when he unboxed the fogger and filled the reservoir with insecticide. He lit the pilot light and walked from one edge of the yard to the other, sending clouds of poisonous smoke into the grass, the bushes, the trees. The fogger made a wet, throaty sound, and the breeze wafted the smoke skyward, where it disappeared into the green-black gloom.

When he was finished Thomas turned off the fogger and stood in the gathering dusk. The pines pressed in on him like a wall, the oldest more than eighty feet high. The woods extended a mile behind the house to wetlands beyond, and as the noise from the fogger died Thomas heard in the trees the drone of a billion crickets and katydids, peepers and toads. A flock of crows assembled in the uppermost branches and heckled him. Sand cranes called from the marsh.

He put the tools in the garage, then sat in the kitchen to call Allison. Declan was better, she said. His temperature was almost normal. They'd removed the IV from his neck. It was the flu all along.

"Oh, god. Oh, sweetheart." Thomas sagged into his chair. He sucked in a huge lungful of air, and as he released it he began to cry and babble like a child. He described the fence, the candles, the fogger, and when she didn't respond he gripped the phone and sobbed. "Did you hear me? Did you hear what I did?" His heart was full to bursting. "I won't let anything bad happen to either of you. Don't you know that?"

"I know," she said quietly. "Take it easy."

They hung up and Thomas sat for a few moments in the dark kitchen. Then he rose unsteadily, poured a scotch and walked back to the patio, where he lit the candles and fell into a padded deck chair. His eyes burned, and his bloody hands throbbed. The sun had fully set and a soft glow suffused everything. As he watched, a half dozen turkeys emerged from the pines onto Danny Baker's lawn. They pecked and bobbed, snatching at the ground in reptilian syncopation. One of the jakes neared the fence, examined it briefly, then flared its wings and sprang lightly into Thomas's yard. Soon another followed, and then another.

Thirst

Kelly McQuain

From Mexico I brought you a silver and red heart:
  a tin *corazon* to decorate our Christmas tree.
    And after a night in a luckless bar—*El Gato Negro*—
a cocktail recipe: tequila and grapefruit soda—*Poloma*,
    the Spanish word for 'dove', the same pale name
as the stubborn horse I rode
          through Guanajuato
    without you by my side.

          I don't know what I drank
that other night, an even unluckier bar in old San Miguel.
    Tecate? Negra Modelo? Some other cheap local beer?
La Cucaracha—the Cockroach dive that would not die,
    where Beats like Kerouac and Cassidy loved and fought.
And where local drunkards sighed at my American jibes
    as doe-eyed *jotos* sized me up from the back wall.

I missed you then, like I did this summer in Shanghai
    on wild Nanjing Road drinking Heinekens with a Hawaiian
named Billy, who never met a bottle of *baiju* he didn't like
    —it helped him chase hookers along the city's neon strip.
Baiju: rotgut Chinese white lightning distilled from sorghum,
    barley or millet. One swig from Billy's tiny green bottle

and I quickly had my fill of it.

Never brought any home from the trip —only stories:
of strange fruits, fried scorpions, whiskered fish.
Of the giant Buddhas carved from the Yungang Grottoes,
of the ancient monastery clinging to the Hengshan cliffs.
    I climbed the Great Wall, sang karaoke in Pingyao,
made a friend or two over a bottle of Scotch—but for three weeks
among strangers in dirty coal-burning country
                    it wasn't just blue sky I missed.

                        On my way home
I bought you a bottle of Crown Royal from Toronto,
        duty-free and flavored with maple,

because I liked to imagine the sight of you in your boxers
        bringing pancakes to our breakfast table.
            Something new to slake your thirst, I said,
handing the brown bottle over.
        You told me to add ice cubes and keep the drink simple:
                "We'll call it a Mrs. Butterworth."

These days,
        it seems I'm always returning from somewhere far off,
                even if it's just back to our conversation at the table.
Our lives drink up the years, I want to say.
        They burn like a dragon, they sing like a dove.
    Don't hate me because I can't keep still
            and need to fill my cup up to the brim—
                I'd drink your heart right now if I could,
            even if it were silver
                    and red
                        and made of tin.

How to Make
A Baseball Player Cry
Dana de Greff

First, tell the gringo baseball player how your husband, Roberto, always knew he was going to die young. If he has no reaction, tell him about what was on the plane: fresh water, plantains, rolls of gauze, baby shoes, powdered milk. Hundreds and hundreds of chancletas. And even if he doesn't ask, tell him those things were for the earthquake victims in Nicaragua. This player, Roberto's teammate on the Pittsburgh Pirates, will look surprised, and you know it's because he never bothered to ask where your husband traveled, why he'd go anywhere that wasn't here. Take his hand, lead him away from the living room full of mourners, and out to the balcony where it's quiet. Because he comes from a farming background, tell him about how Roberto cut sugar cane, all the places that hurt after

hours bent like a curveball. Explain the first time you met, the first time
you saw him play in Carolina, Puerto Rico. This was when he was skinny,
palms full of splinters, hair combed out like thick black cotton.

It was a Sunday morning in June after church, 1949. The boys' nice
clothes—starched white shirts, navy pants ironed smooth, cloth ties—lay
in neat piles on top of a piece of a tarp to keep them clean. They changed
into their uniforms on the field behind the high school, the grass crisped
from the summer sun. Sometimes you watched them, admired the folds of
skin as they bent to pull up thin socks, the small bumps of their spines, how
their chests, necks, and arms were different shades of brown. They were
your patchwork boys and you loved their bodies leaping over each other,
turning, and throwing balls like releasing prayers. You loved their blistered
hands, the tight belts at their delicate waists, waists of boys not quite men
yet, something fragile and in between.

Roberto was special, even at fifteen. In his eyes there was something
good—not pure—but good. Eyes that had seen enough for two lifetimes,
that had seen into the future. I won't be here long; I need to hurry. But that
would come later. For now, he was in front of you, and this was the day
he would be signed. You wore a white lace dress and tight braids held in
place with white ribbons, the frayed ends brushing your shoulder blades.
Even though you knew your mother'd get mad, you took off your shoes
and socks and leaned against the wooden fence next to all the boys from
the barrio, watched Roberto step up to plate. He rolled his neck, tapped
the bat against the inside of his shoes, old black trainers covered in orange
dust. At the neck of his shirt were several holes; you wanted to put your
fingers there, touch his skin.

The first swing was a strike, the second a foul ball, but the third? The
third was mythic. The sharp crack, a sound that made both teams stand
up in unison and Roberto's team jump like children. Later, that sound was
something you'd associate with love, then anger, and finally, an acute sense
of drowning. But on that day, the crack shot ran through you and up your
legs to the tips of your fingers, hands shaking as if it was you holding the
bat. As he ran the bases he kept his face passive, and before he could put
both feet on home plate his teammates lifted him to their shoulders. In
the air he took a necklace out from under his shirt, a key on a thin strip
of leather, and that's when he looked right at you and brought the key to

his lips: a promise of things to come, of leaving and returning home, of dreaming of this moment again and again.

Stop talking now and wait for his reaction. If he pats you on the shoulder and offers his condolences once again, shrug his hand away. You're not looking for pity. Everyone sitting in your living room, standing in your kitchen, has bestowed pity. If he sighs and tries to give you money, politely decline and say you need to be by yourself. If his shoulders slump, if he has the face of a man who's struck out with the bases loaded, take out the cigarettes, accept his light. He'll ask, Do you think if he hadn't come here he might still be alive?

There's no way to know, you'll say.

While you smoke, fast forward to the part about moving to America. This is where it gets interesting. (Yes, there are good stories from Montreal after he got signed with the Brooklyn Dodgers, but you really want to emphasize the America part.) Make the baseball player feel included, even though he never tried to include Roberto.

On April 17, 1955, Roberto made his debut with the Pittsburgh Pirates. You remember being confused when he told you that spring training was in Fort Myers, had to borrow a map to figure out where it was. Florida, you assumed, was a land of flowers, of hibiscuses and gardenias, roses and wild azaleas. You imagined Roberto and his teammates eating supper in delicate gardens, him practicing his English, admiring the burning sunsets. Of course, you could never have imagined what actually happened because he never told you, not until years after you'd already bought a nice house in Pittsburgh with air-conditioning, a room for the boys to grow up in. Years later, on the yellow couch in the living room, he put his head on your lap and reached for your emerald earrings, a wedding gift. The green reminds me of the grass in Florida. He told you about Fort Myers. He told you how he couldn't stay in the hotel with his teammates because of his dark skin. How he had to live with a black family in Dunbar Heights. How he had to eat his meals on the bus when they were on the road. How once, he went inside to buy a Coca-Cola and was told they didn't serve his kind before they kicked him out. They all watched. They all just ate and watched.

It was in Pittsburgh that you first learned about colors, about people crossing the street when you approached, what a rope really meant, how important hair was. You didn't know what to do if you were neither color, if you could pass, if you'd ever want to.

Tell him about the party that was thrown for Roberto when he won MVP in 1966. The players, managers, and donors (all white), the waiters (all black). Roberto joked that he should join them in the kitchen. He was always joking, but you knew it bothered him, made him feel helpless. In Puerto Rico people didn't see his skin, they saw him, the person; in America he had to start over, but with the weight of useless questions: Was he Caribbean? Latino? Black? Brown? Afro-Latino? When he was interviewed, reporters made fun of his English. In the papers, they quoted him word for word not because they cared about accuracy, but because they wanted to see him fail.

The party was a joke. Little pieces of cold vegetables, crystal glasses of flat champagne, dull, soft music. In Puerto Rico there would have been salsa music blasting, people sweating, pigs roasting, movement until the next morning, the smell of coal and pernil in the air. The gringo party was stiff, a show put on for the sake of the press and when Roberto was dragged into a photo op with the owner, you slipped off to the bathroom. Inside, everything was pink: the towels, soap, walls, even the toilet cover. You looked at yourself in the mirror, your almost straight hair, which was normally kinky, your tight dress that cost too much, the extra powder you applied to your face to get the right shade of light even though you hated yourself as you did it. Yes, it was hard for you too, hard to smile at people who looked over your shoulder, people who pressured you to speak English, cook casseroles, play cards in houses cleaned by people who looked like you, looked like your island.

Sometimes you wondered why he played baseball, why he put himself through the thousands of hours of training to have a chance at hitting a ball maybe twice out of ten times, three if he was good, four if he was fantastic. Where did the drive come from, especially in a place that didn't see his abilities, preferred to pick at his accent and disdain his skin. What difference did it make if he could speak English when the game wasn't in any language? These were questions you asked yourself when Roberto came home defeated or angry, when he wouldn't eat the arroz con frijoles.

Once, it was a cashier who wouldn't touch his hand. Once it was a little boy in suspenders who spit on him. Once it was his own teammate, a man with hair the color of butter who stole his shoes and threw them into a toilet filled with his own shit.

At this, the baseball player will tell you he never did anything like that. That man was a coward, he says. He'll touch your shoulder. You know that, right? Stay quiet. Look at the sunset. The sunsets in Pittsburgh are muted compared to Puerto Rico's, and this is something that brings you a small peace. Tell the baseball player that it wasn't always easy, but there were also happy moments, like your last trip together to Managua.

You went with Roberto during the Amateur World Series. When it was over, he took you to the market, several old buildings connected by walkways, where the breeze passed through in bursts. People stopped him, recognized his face from the newspapers and posters, wanted to shake his hand. He wasn't a hero in Pittsburgh, but he was a hero in Puerto Rico, in Nicaragua. You stopped at every table, picked up a green tostone maker, which he bought, tasted a bit of farmer's cheese, which he had sliced and wrapped for breakfast later in the hotel. When you lingered over a pair of earrings, wooden beads painted lavender, he carefully put them in your lobes. Roberto bent with you to smell tortillas, listened as you talked to the young girl fanning flies away from a bowl of chancho con yuca, fingertips stained red from achiote powder. She was pregnant, and you told her that you'd always wanted a girl. With a smile she said, "May the next one be a rose." Someone turned on a radio, salsa, and Roberto touched your hips. "Dance with me, flor de miel."

The baseball player knows what's coming next. He excuses himself to get a plate of food and you wonder if it tastes like sandpaper to him like it does to you. When he comes back (if he comes back), tell him a secret: Twenty years earlier, on the exact same day of the plane crash, Roberto got into a bad car accident, was hit by a drunk driver, and almost died. The exact same day. If the baseball player shakes his head, shake yours, too. If he asks what it means, say, He never stood a chance.

It's almost dark now. You feel an urgency to explain everything to this baseball player, to make him understand the life of the man he ignored, the man he left on the bus, the man he wouldn't shower next to. You want him to understand that he's going to live on for decades—not just his numbers, but the people he helped, the way he stared at the camera, eyes to lens. The man is gone but the legacy isn't—his face will be painted on walls, body sculpted from stone, baseball cards pinned to bicycle spokes.

Let me talk, you say. Let me tell you about when I went back, after the earthquake, after the crash.

When you stepped off the plane it felt walking into an oven; the winter cold in your marrow thawed and melted out your pores, destroyed the face you'd carefully powdered. You travelled alone, headed straight to the market, and didn't bother to check into the hotel. Cristobal, Roberto's best friend, had decided to dive for his body and bring him home to Puerto Rico. You knew this was foolish, but you wouldn't stop him. Grief for him was submerged, and for you it was hidden in a mess of blocks and cement, of what once stood. Every step was painful; you weren't walking through the market but on top of it, stumbling over tables, pipes, limbs. Your hand instinctively reached out for Roberto's, but where were they? Floating in the sea? Trapped inside the plane? Or maybe they were tucked beneath his head; maybe he was sleeping on an island, not dead at all, merely lost.

After Cristobal told you about the crash, you didn't leave your room for a week. Your mother finally forced you to go to church and after praying and hymn-singing, wringing your hands with other women, eyes up to the sanctuary, there was still a discomfort in your chest. Despite the communal attempt to feel something like forgiveness, like acceptance, all you felt was a hard knot like a baseball in your throat. Cristobal wrote you a poem that you didn't want and almost made you hate him for being alive instead of Roberto. A poem that he read on the radio while you, and the entire island, listened:

December 31, 1972
On this day we lost our brother.
Three days of long, hot
mourning in Puerto Rico.

Men sit around altars
of rum. Remember the days
he played pick-up games

with rocks? Remember
his favorite teams?

The Southern. Four Roses.
El Sur. Cuatro Rosas.

Women sit around altars
of sugar. Remember the days
he sewed shirts for his
brothers? Remember
his favorite foods?

Pork. Salt & mangoes.
Pernil. Mangos y sal.

Did he think of us before
the deep black? His body tangled
in the crew, powdered milk turning
the black gray. No white light.

Before the flight, Roberto told Vera:
"If there is one more delay, we'll leave
this for tomorrow."
"Si hay un retraso más, lo dejamos
para mañana, amor."

You didn't want a poem. You wanted justice, an explanation. How
could the plane have gone down? Why was it so old? Why did the pilot
come late? You stood and watched the four-engined, DC-7 piston-
powered take off from San Juan, and then Cristobal drove you back to
your mother's house. The plane came down in heavy seas a mile and a
half from shore. Hours later, Coast Guard planes circled the area, lit the
sea up with flares searching for bodies. None were ever found. You wish
it had been you instead, or that the plane had crashed on land. At least
then you'd have a place to visit, leave flowers, a place to cry alone. Instead,
Roberto was nowhere and everywhere at once, forever transient, forever in
between.

But there you were in the market that once was, searching for the past in dust, breathing in the charred air. Cristobal was diving somewhere over the site of the crash right now. You thought of him, his hard skin, the tears in his eyes when he got the news. He was with you, the only one who really understood. The rest of the team would wait for the wake to pay their condolences, white men with short hair and tar-stained teeth. Had they bothered to ask about Puerto Rico when Roberto was alive? Why did they insist on calling him Bob? He hated when they called him Bob, when they made fun of the thickness of his hair and lips. They never deserved him.

After so much talking, you're done. Tell the baseball player you're tired, go back inside. Don't listen to the string of platitudes, don't feel the sympathetic shoulder squeezes, don't look at the yellow couch. Instead, focus on the loud rush of water in your ears, the smell of salt. You're sinking. In the kitchen don't stop at the table stacked with food that makes you sick, American food with no real flavor. Mounds of mashed potatoes, creamy spinach that looks like mold, marshmallows so sweet they hurt your teeth. You don't want this, don't want their Jell-O, don't want to sift through the plastic containers, return them to people who claim to feel your pain but know nothing about you, your life, your husband.

Go to the pantry. Turn on the lights, then turn them off and sit on the floor. It's nice to be alone, no more nodding, no more fingers on your skin, no more gifts bought for proof. See? We're sad, too. Lean back and spread your body over the tile floor. Forget about wrinkling your dress or smashing your hair. Slowly unbutton your shirt, put your hand over your heart, imagine it's Roberto's, imagine the scratch of callouses. Kick off your shoes. Don't fall asleep and don't think about the first time you saw him play because if you do, you might never come up again; you might just stay on this floor for the rest of your life.

When the baseball player knocks, don't say anything. He'll open the door slowly, stumble over your feet, and turn on the light. Seeing you on the floor breaks something in him, something he didn't realize he was holding onto. He'll start to cry. You'll be tempted to comfort him. Don't. Turn your head to the side, stare at the cans of garbanzos, the bags of cornmeal. Listen and don't listen to the sounds of a grown man crying, the shuddering intake, the whimpers. Don't ask who he's crying for. You might not like the answer.

Considering Need

Shevaun Brannigan

Two domesticated parakeets will find each other
in the wild forest, the bell becomes unnecessary,
the mirror. Considering need, that binding honey, one
feels the cage bottom deep within her. Further,

so she might crack a seed open in her beak, for him,
the husk falling to the forest floor; so an unpredictable
sway in the branch, something leaps: the old

She remembers it dark like an eye. Blood-tinged
feathers can be covered by one newspaper sheet:
a sale, she saw, on mattresses. I know
bearing witness doesn't stop the days
from going on. A lifetime ago, when

I held birds on our deck to free them from
an unsafe house, and my hands were small,
I knew the feel of wings.

Hothouse Lounge

Kate Blakinger

My chest tightens as fire grazes Sam's skin, but finally he tosses the match he's let burn down in his fingers, and the pile of brush jumps into flames. Pockets of damp sap crackle and hiss.

We retrieve an armful each of empty aerosol cans from the silo, cans Sam stockpiled over many summers spent working at Ray's Auto Body. He sets them down in a row and sits next to me in the dead weeds.

He's hunched and quiet, his eyes glassy, his body tensed.

Sometimes I miss Sam, even when he's right beside me. I don't have the right, but I do.
"Teeth or hands?" I ask.

"Hands." He's been having these recurring dreams. In one, all his teeth fall out. In the other, he tries desperately to hold on to someone, but his hands are crushed, useless as empty gloves.

Sam is my brother, and he came home from Iraq with a face full of shrapnel. Hard pellets that look like blackheads cluster on his left cheek and spread in painful constellations across his neck, the skin crowded with shiny scar tissue. His body tries to expel what doesn't belong. Jagged pieces pierce the skin from inside. It's like the IED never stopped; it continues to explode from inside his face in excruciatingly slow motion. When it gets really bad, he slicks antibacterial ointment over the bleeding bumps and hides them under a cover of gauze.

"You know what I did over there, Gracie? I tried not to die. Day and night, I tried not to die." He pulls up weeds as he speaks.

"What else could you have done?"

It's not comfort he wants. He wants to rip open a space in this life that is wide enough for all the fury he feels, but there's no where to put feelings that sharp. I don't know how to make room for that anger any more than anyone else does, but I know this is what he needs. Our mother believes a person can heal by force of will. If only Sam would exert a little self-discipline, he could re-take his old life. I'm not sure we can fool ourselves, however hard we pretend.

Once I caught Sam with a look of concentration on his face, his fist held out before him, closed and squeezing. When he opened it, inside was a shard of shrapnel that had worked its way out of his cheek, its barb now buried back in the meat of him again. I got the rubbing alcohol. I pried loose the jagged metal, trying not to breathe as I swabbed away the blood. I tucked the piece of the bomb that had killed everyone else riding in his Bradley Fighting Vehicle out of sight in my pocket.

Later I looked at it in the light. It was shaped like a country whose name I didn't know. I closed my hand tightly around it. The resulting cut healed, of course, left no trace on me.

Sam lives out here again with our mother, in this backwater place where there isn't much to do besides burn things. He sleeps in his childhood bedroom, tossing in the narrow twin bed that hardly fits his adult body while the dormer ceiling, banded with glow-in-the-dark stars, presses down. I make the three-hour drive from the city to visit him and Mama every other weekend.

"You ready?" he asks me now. We stand, me in my sneakers; and Sam in his army-issued boots. We pick up as many aerosols as we can hold, and on the count of three, we toss them into the flames and I turn and run to take cover behind the door of the silo like we always do, but then I realize Sam is not beside me, he hasn't moved, he hasn't even taken a step back. The aerosol cans explode in the fire, and he just stands there while they slam into the sky, like he's daring one to firebomb him in the face, like he'd like it to happen that way, and his expression is rapturous, the fire in the sky beyond him a beautiful thing.

I tell my mother about the articles I've been writing. I make it all up and it hollows me out to tell her lies, but I can't help myself. The lies pour out of me in a chatty, cheerful voice. She thinks I write a column for the South Philly Review, my neighborhood's newspaper. She thinks I write about park clean ups and new restaurant openings.

"Bring me clippings to pin to the fridge," she says. "You never remember."

"I will, Mama. I'm sorry." A black feeling balloons in me. My mother wants me to be happy so badly she changes the subject whenever I vent the slightest frustration. I've been cut short so many times. When we talk now, I reflexively gloss over the true substance of my life. I want to ask her if I go running after something with my whole heart and don't get it, what happens then? But she'd want to know what I was talking about and I'd have to detail to her all the ways in which I'm not the daughter she planned on. I'd have to tell her about my job. I'd have to tell her I'm in love with a girl.

She fixes me a bowl of soup, and I eat it slowly, though it's getting late, and I have a long drive back to Philadelphia. The highways around here are dangerous at dusk, so empty you can press the pedal to the ground and fly forward without feeling like you're going fast at all, but in the woods that sidle up to the shoulder, deer wait, ready to leap into your headlights and explode against your car's windshield, as full as overripe fruit. I drive with my spine very stiff, and always my back aches when finally I'm cocooned in my bed. I feel like I'm waiting at the edge of something just as the deer do, like I'm just about to leap fully into my life, and either I'll cross a threshold into some better version of myself, or something in me will burst apart, some essence leak away.

My roommate's full name is Joanne Quinn Bellwin, and she wishes Quinn were her first name, because it's more androgynous and unusual, but she says Joanne is too engrained; it's how she thinks of herself, and so she's stuck with it. Joanne is dear to me, and a mystery. She's small and dark haired, with thick eyebrows she's never once plucked and fine, downy hairs above her upper lip that are invisible except in bright daylight. I'm sometimes hounded by an insistent desire to touch her there, feel the peach fuzz of her face. She has a wide, warm smile, and thickly lashed eyes, and she smells of paint thinner and lavender soap. She moves quickly for such a small person, darting across rooms, striding across sidewalks, and she throws her hands around when she speaks, as if everything she says she must convey with the force of her whole body.

In her bedroom, Joanne paints urban landscapes of squalor and ruin. My favorite of her paintings shows a crumbling, derelict gas station in West Philly, the pavement oil-slicked, the pumps grimed over and flaking rust, and beyond them, the minimart with its bright blue signs and its boarded up windows. Looking at it, I can smell the gasoline-soaked asphalt, noxious and intoxicating.

Sometimes she takes me along when she scouts for locations to paint, her searches carrying her into neighborhoods a person might prefer not to walk through alone. The day we found that gas station, I watched Joanne snap pictures, brushing her shining hair away from her face with a distracted, impatient gesture. The thought of kissing her stirred through me, soft as a breeze. I imagined her body, the feel of it: pillowy in places and bony in others, all cushions and corners. I hadn't done this before, fantasized about a woman. While she worked on that painting, she upended a Dixie cup full of the blue she used for the minimart. Now a small island of blue floats on the floorboards, and when I stop by her room, I stand in the middle of it, like I've found my place on a map of our secret life together, the life I imagine we share even though really, I'm Joanne's roommate, nothing more.

She has a girlfriend already, Gwen, a skinny art student with her hair cut in a very precise bob, the bangs a perfectly straight line across her forehead. Our apartment is so small that when Gwen comes over, just three people makes it crowded, and I bump into things, bruise myself on the furniture as I skirt around the two of them.

Tonight, Gwen isn't here. Joanne tells me she's trying to finish some new work for her first solo show next month. I'm both pleased to have Joanne to myself and vexed to hear of Gwen's accomplishment, though I can't dispute her talent. She paints strange and gorgeous imaginary landscapes: green islands suspended from pale skies like ornaments hooked into the ether; aimless picket fences punctuating terraced hillsides like bared teeth; mountains dappled with gingham flags, the peaks knifing up into dark clouds.

"Maybe I should paint, too," Joanne says. Gwen is three years younger than she is, and she's already making a name for herself, while Joanne paints and paints, and no one sees the paintings. They lean in stacks against the walls of her room. The walkable space keeps shrinking.

"Work tomorrow. It's Friday night. We should go out." With some cajoling, I convince her.

We're halfway to a bar with a beer list that can't be contained on one sheet of paper, where good music is always playing a little too loudly, but then Joanne stops in her tracks and raises her arms, grinning.

"I know," she says. "Let's go see the go-go dancers at your bar."

The bar where I work fills up with men whose gazes I'd avoid in the street. Sad and desperate men. I can tell she thinks this will be a fun adventure. I know better, but I'm helpless before Joanne's desires, and soon we are stepping inside the Hothouse Lounge.

Elena and Yvonne dance to Metallica on pedestals behind the counter, orange stickers over their nipples instead of pasties, the same sort of stickers people label with prices and slap on broken blenders, old-fashioned TVs, and all the other careworn objects they offer up at sidewalk sales. Elena is cute and chubby; she dances with her eyes closed. Stretch marks branch in silver streaks across Yvonne's belly. I wonder, as I always do, if these women like performing, or if the men's stares feel like fishhooks in their skin. I never ask the dancers any questions. I'm supposed to be writing an article about them, about what it's like for them to dance here and about their lives outside of this place. I pitched this story to a magazine, saying I'd go under cover as a dancer myself so I could see it all from the inside. The editor said, since I had no clips, I'd have to write it before he'd know if he wanted to run it. I came into the bar asking if they needed another dancer. The owner, an old Italian lady everyone calls Mom though she's no one's mother, looked me up and down and said, "Honey, no we don't, but we could use a bartender." She was right about me, that I'd die up there half naked in the light with all these sad, hard-drinking men gathered round to watch.

I can see Joanne is shocked by how dingy it is inside, the air stale from decades of smoking and the sweet and yeasty smell of spilled beer. We find an empty table and sit. She looks at the dancers in quick glances, like she doesn't want to be caught staring.

I fetch us rum and cokes, which Nadine, who trained me, gives to me for free, waving away my money. "I can't believe you work here," Joanne says. She is waiting for me to explain myself. I don't know how. Working is unavoidable. It's the stuff our lives are made of, but I could be up in an air-conditioned cubicle in one of the skyscrapers in Center City, earning four times as much an hour. I could be doing something fit to go on a resume. I no longer type up notes when I get home, but I still call my bartending research. I can't bear to think of it as just my job. A reporter needs to talk to people but I'm intimidated by the dancers I meant to write about, too timid to pry and too awkward to endear myself. I'm certain I want to be a journalist, but I still don't know how to be the kind of person who goes after a story, who dives into a conversation, who wins a source's trust. I'm unsuited to my own dream for myself.

I sip my sweet drink, and I tell Joanne how, out in the country, everyone knows everyone else, and rumors spread fast as the flu, but you don't do your living in public. There is a privacy built into the spaces between houses that dissolves here in the city, where conversations float through shared walls, where windows stare into other homes' windows, where people take buses and subways instead of climbing into the enclosed bubbles of cars. People startle me, and in the city their lives are right there to scrutinize. Their grievances, their kindnesses, their unfathomable choices. All I see and hear sets me to wondering. Wondering turns to writing, or it did anyway, and so here I am.

Joanne is not so different from me. She loves to know all the dirt on everyone, even strangers. She thinks of herself as a non-judgmental person, but she gossips with an unrestrained glee. "Tell me about your coworkers," she says now. "Tell me what you're going to write." I talk about Antoinette, the owner we all know as "Mom," how she's 73, and I once saw her brandish a pool cue at the ex-boyfriend of one of the dancers when he came in and started making threats. "You got to treat my beautiful ladies with respect," she said. "They dance for you, and you treat them right, and everybody's happy. You want to be happy, don't you?" The pool cue left a cluster of blue chalk marks on the front of his shirt.

"Being publicly dressed down by a fierce old lady gets people moving out the door," I say. "I practically left too, Mom was so fearsome."

Joanne laughs, her bright eyes tugging heat to my skin. I want to hold her gaze fast, so I tell her about Yvonne. I describe the tattoo of a bottle of Tabasco sauce she has on the small of her back, with HOT! written in all caps above it. Then I talk about Yvonne's two-year-old son, and how Marcus's father ditched them both for Yvonne's younger cousin, and isn't paying child support like he should. I would betray any confidence to entertain Joanne.

She starts telling me about the twin sisters she befriended when she worked at a bakery during high school, but right then my brother calls. He's been so uncommunicative lately, I'm sure something is wrong.

He tells me he's in the city.

"With Tricia?"

"No. She bailed on me."

Tricia is the widow of the man who'd been sitting next to Sam in the Bradley. Sam fixes things around her house, and drinks with her, and loves her, I think. They drink until they are sick as dogs, until Sam's sweat is enough to knock a bystander into a black out drunkenness. And then they curl up like puppies, and Sam drifts into sleep and wakes up screaming, and Tricia throws him out, weeping. They have a screwed up interdependence. She looks at Sam, and she thinks why him and not Ryan?

"What are you up to?" he asks. "Can I come by your place?"

I tell him I'm out with a friend.

He hears something in my voice. "What kind of friend are we talking about here? I don't want to be in the way if you're on a date with some guy."

I try to think what to say, and there's a brief pause, a hiccup in the rhythm of our conversation. "I'm not out with a guy."

"Well, where are you?"

My muscles ache suddenly, as if I've been exerting myself. I don't want to give up this time in which Joanne is mine alone. I do though. I give it up. Barely ten minutes later, Sam pushes through the door. He crosses the room and heads right toward us, borrows an extra chair from our neighbor, sits, and stretches his long legs under the table. He glances around, eyeing everyone, and scoots his chair to the left so he can see the door. His face is creased across the forehead, and pale, and flecked with those hard bumps of metal. When he smiles at us, some of them create little divots, like misplaced dimples.

Sam was so close to dying. Shift him left or right during the blast, a few inches either way, and he'd be gone.

"This place is kind of a dump," he says.

"I don't know how she cares to come here every day," Joanne says.

Sam looks at me.

I look away. "I tend bar here." I think of my mother, waiting for those clippings I promised, and I envision myself cutting other people's stories out of a newspaper, typing my own name in a matching font, taping this over the real byline, going to Kinko's, and photocopying these lies into something that looks real enough to hand to her, and I feel so tired.

"No way." He eyes Elena dancing. "Here? I thought you were doing some newspaper thing."

Joanne reaches out under the table and squeezes my arm.

When I tell Sam Joanne's a painter, he says he doesn't understand art. "Why would you want to spend hours making something that has no use?" he asks her. "Isn't the pleasure of making something the fact that when you're done, you can do something with it?"

Joanne starts talking about how art explores what's mysterious in life. "Art lets us perceive meaning in our experiences. Nothing else gives us that ability the way art does." She keeps going, saying something about making the senses serve the mind, her hands up and emphatic as her words tumble together.

"I don't feel like I've answered any questions about life by going to an art museum," my brother says. "I really don't." I kick him under the table but he ignores me, a thing he's always been good at.

Joanne bites her lip, irked. "The beholder has to be open to the art. Otherwise it is useless." She finishes her drink, rises, and weaves through the tables to the bathroom, dark hair swaying down her back.

I glare at my brother. "Why do you have to ruin things?"

"People need to be honest with each other," he says.

"Can't you be honest in a kind way?"

"Do you really work here, Gracie?"

"Please don't be honest about that to Mama."

"No. You should though."

He shifts in his chair, drumming a hand against his knee. His eyes coast around the room again, monitoring everyone's position. "So much of what I see people doing with their days, it seems so pointless. If these people really knew that they could die at any moment, they wouldn't be here in this shithole bar. You have to know it with your body, your cells."

"I don't think people can live like that."

His restless hands go still in his lap. "I'm in trouble then."

"Why don't you ever talk about it?"

"We're talking right now."

"You know what I mean."

"Talking doesn't help anything."

As a child, Sam had a shout always on his lips. His knees were perpetually scraped. He was forever ready to take a dare. He'd helped me egg Michael Jawlowski's house after he called me an ass-faced slut in third grade, words I hadn't understood but had recognized as terrible and wounding. He'd swum out into the center of a lake to rescue me when I'd climbed into a canoe while our mother's back was turned and drifted away without a paddle. He'd been obsessed with magic tricks, and had amazed me when he made coins and rings and small pebbles disappear from his closed hand, so that for years, I was convinced he had the powers of a wizard. He's not that headlong-leap-into-it boy anymore, but surely some of that person lives on inside him still. I want to pull those parts of him to the surface and make him remember. Or make him forget everything that came after. One of the two.

I bring up the vacation in Maine, ask if he remembers the lake.

"Yeah, sure. There were those huge spiders in the cottage we rented. Big as fists. You cried whenever you saw one." He grins at me, still amused.

"Do you remember rescuing me?"

"From the spiders?"

No, I say, and I remind him of my daring escapade with the canoe, telling the story like it was hilarious, though it wasn't. Before we'd gone on this vacation, I'd taken a few swimming lessons at the Y, but still I could hardly keep myself afloat in the warm water of a pool, let alone swim to shore through the murky chill of that lake. I sat gripping the metal rim of the canoe, staring out at the cottage and the floating dock as they shrank and the distance between me and shore swelled. Sam and my mother were so far off I was struck by the sudden fear that they were strangers, that I was utterly alone in the world. I'd never before been so aware of having an existence apart from my family members. My separateness shocked me. I don't think I called out once.

My brother has no memory of any of this. "I vaguely remember canoeing around the lake," he offers.

Sam is the one in the canoe now. He is looking across a gulf at his old life, and realizing his separateness from everything he'd known before he'd known war. I'd like to swim out to him. I'd like to drag him back.

Joanne returns with a fresh drink. She sits very primly in her chair. Sam is in a better mood now, and tells her stories of our antics as children, and after a bit, her shoulders relax. She still drinks her rum and coke fast though, like she needs to occupy her hands.

A man comes in. I notice him because he's wearing all white: baggy white jeans, too-white sneakers, a huge white hoodie that pools around him. He slumps onto a barstool near us, right in front of Elena, and he stares at her bared stomach and her breasts. As if he feels me looking, he turns his head and he grins at me, revealing weird transparent teeth, his mouth stuffed with chips of ice. He raises a quarter, holds it up to shine in the haze of light and smoke. This man wants an audience. He keeps looking back and catching my eye. All at once, tipping his head back a little, he slings the quarter at Elena. The coin ricochets off her belly, clangs against the bar, drops to the ground, and rolls away through the forest of dirty sneakers and stool legs. Elena yelps and stops dancing, looking down at the red welt marking her.

"Hey!" Yvonne yells from the other end of the room. She sits, scoots on her butt to the edge of her pedestal, and swings her scary spiked boots down to the floor. She is around the counter and in the guy's face in moments, fast even in towering heels. Elena stands on her pedestal, eyes wide, arms folded tight over her chest, while Yvonne beats at the guy's ribcage with her fist. "You pig," she says over and over. He's got his hands raised, surrender style, and says, "Whoa, chill. Just tipping the lady." Nadine is doing nothing but staring. It's like she's watching a television screen.

Even though I'm not working, I rise to help, because Mom's not here tonight to swoop in with a pool cue and the Hothouse Lounge doesn't employ a bouncer. I grab Yvonne's wrist so she'll stop pounding on the guy. The man, his lips pulled back to reveal those nasty teeth and his wet, gray gums, eyes me up and down and says to me, "Sweetie, you going to get up there and dance for me, too?"

My brother comes at him from behind me. He shoves him off his stool. For a second the man lays still, stunned to find himself on the floor. "What the hell?" he says. He hoists himself up. He dusts off his sleeves. The back of his white hoodie is grimy now, the butt of a cigarette stuck beneath his shoulder blade. Yvonne pulls free from my grip and puts her hands on her hips. In the back, the Vietnamese men circled around the pool table lean on their cues, watching, cigarettes smoldering between their fingers, and the patrons seated at the counter crane their heads. Nadine, too intent on our corner of the bar to take an order, holds a hand up to the oblivious customer asking for another drink.

"You're talking some dumb shit," my brother says. "I've got no patience for dumb shit." Sam looks younger then before. The tension around his jaw has evaporated. He seems more relaxed now in a bar fight than when he is parked in front of Mama's TV.

The man with the ugly teeth swings wildly, and it's like all of us watching breathe in at the same time and hold that breath, that's how still everyone goes. Sam doesn't react to the man's fist in his gut. He just stands there, braced, the hub our attention swirls around. And then my brother is all motion. He steps up and punches the man in the jaw. He tips his whole weight into it. It is only one punch, and it breaks the man's face. He falls, and when he lands the air woofs out of his lungs. His nose leaks blood. Beaky before, it's concave now, a comma. More blood dribbles from the corner of his mouth. Everyone is either staring, or carefully averting their eyes. The only sound is Bowie's "Oh! You Pretty Things" playing on the jukebox. The man lies there on the floor without moving, and I think, please don't be dead. I squat next to him and hold my hand in front of his face, and I feel breath.

"I'm calling 911," Nadine warns us from behind the bar. "You need to get out of here." Joanne heads for the door, stumbling, tipsy. I tug my brother's sleeve, pull him in the direction of the exit, and the three of us spill out onto Broad Street.

"You want to crash with us?" I ask Sam.

He's panting, and when I touch his shoulder, he flinches. He shakes his head. "Better I just hit the road."

"You were drinking. I'm not letting you drive all the way home right now."

"Two beers," he says. "I'm fine." Sirens sound, their wail circling in on us. "We shouldn't just stand here. My car's right around the corner."

We run. Joanne begins to laugh and soon I am laughing too, laughing so hard it's difficult to keep moving. I didn't know fear could feel like this. I clutch my stomach as we hurl ourselves into Sam's beat-up Impala and he drives, keeping to the speed limit, one hand on the wheel and one arm resting on the frame of the open window. The wind the car's movement stirs up sails around the interior, carrying all the smells of the city with it: meat on a grill, exhaust, the clean scent of dryer sheets. Joanne and I are crammed in the backseat, where Sam is enacting a small rebellion against the army's orderliness, a hodgepodge of tools and trash taking up all the legroom. Our hair cyclones around our heads and our bellies ache from laughing, and all at once, with the warmth of Joanne's leg pressed against my own, a great, invisible weight lifts from me in the breeze and is borne away.

When we reach our block, my brother parks, but he won't get out of the car. He keeps shifting around in his seat, keyed up with leftover adrenalin. I tell him he should really crash on our couch, and he gives me a dead-fish stare. A couple passes on the sidewalk, arm-in-arm, and he mutters something about needing to get out of the city, "away from all these fucking people."

Joanne stands so close to me, I can feel the heat coming off her body. Sam wants to be tearing down the highway in the dark, and I want to be alone with Joanne in our apartment, so though it's clear Sam's shaken up, I let him go.

"Your brother pulverized that guy," Joanne says. "Did you see all that blood?" She leans on me going up the stairs, and I put a hand on her back, feel the swish of her hair across my knuckles. At the top of the stairs, in the landing in front of our door, she turns, reaches up, and touches my face. She says, "You've got a pretty face, Grace. You shouldn't hide behind your bangs." She smoothes my bangs to the side, and then half-falls half-leans toward me. She is so close, I can smell the faint odor of cigarettes that has entangled itself in her hair. I help her catch her balance, and I'm not sure what else to do or say, but then I do what I want: I kiss her. Her mouth tastes like alcohol and sugar. I pull her close and she is laughing wildly now, her mouth open and busy with its laughing when I kiss her again. Our teeth bump with a tiny click. I don't know where to put my hands so I hold them in the air behind her, hovering and uncertain, and I press my mouth against hers, and for a moment she kisses me back. She sways, and steadies herself by grabbing my arm. She is too drunk. I pull out my keys, and she hangs on me while I open the door. She rubs her face against my shoulder, back and forth like a cat wanting to be rubbed.

Inside though, she groans and scrambles for the bathroom. I hear her vomiting. I get a glass of water for her from the kitchen and return to find her sprawled on the chipped tile floor by the toilet. I hold out the glass and she shakes her head, so I set it on the lip of the sink. "I'm fine," she says. "Please go." I back up and she pushes the door shut with one foot. She stays in there for a long time and she doesn't open the door, so I go to bed without brushing my teeth. I lie under my covers hoping she will come into my room in the night and crawl into bed next to me, which I know she won't do, and yet I keep picturing how it will happen, the longing so acute, I can't sleep.

A set of elevated train tracks run above the city streets just a short walk from our apartment, and in the middle of the night, the whistle of the freight trains that rattle through is the loneliest sound to hear in the dark. I think of Joanne alone in her room and me alone in mine, and all the people alone in the boxes of their apartments all across this city, stacked on top of each other, each building attached to the next, connected but so separate. I look at the shadows of my furniture, and slowly, the outlines of my dresser and my tiny desk crisp up as light begins to creep into the sky and push through my curtains, and sometime after that, I finally drift off.

Joanne sleeps even later than I do. She comes into the kitchen with her hair flattened on one side and wild on the other and fills a mug with tap water. She drinks it intently, leaning back against the counter. She is still wearing the purple tank top she was wearing the night before. I ask her how she's feeling and she shrugs. "I'll live."

I sip my coffee and burn my tongue.

"About last night," she says, and stops. Jangly with nerves, I can't help myself, and keep drinking my too-hot coffee. "Even if I weren't dating someone, living together creates boundaries. I don't know. I don't know how to say what I'm trying to say."

Her affection for Gwen is real, even though it may not last forever. I know that. I know kissing her was a trespass.

"We drank too much," I say. "That's all."

"Maybe."

"And there was a crazy fight."

"True."

"Emotions were running high."

"The circumstances don't matter. That's the thing." Joanne makes an expression I find inscrutable, a mix of remorse and defiance maybe. She turns and refills her mug at the sink, and with her sharp shoulder blades pointing at me, she says, "Gwen asked me to move in with her. I told her no, but maybe it's a good idea." When she faces me, she's holding the mug oddly, with both hands, as if it's a prop and she is posing for a picture. Or as if holding onto this object is what is allowing her to stand upright, and she must grip it for dear life. "Maybe it would make things less complicated." The coffee burns a hole in my gut. She starts talking faster. "I wouldn't go right away. I'd help you find a new roommate first. I might even know someone who's looking."

"You should do what you want," I say. This I didn't expect. I sit at the table for a long time, and then I go back to my room and get ready for work, each action mechanical, requiring no thought, and only the most basic effort.

I'm behind the bar at the Hothouse Lounge when my phone buzzes in my pocket.

"What's wrong?" I ask, because Mama sounds strange, rattled.

"I'm at the hospital," she says.

My heart kicks in my chest. "What happened?"

"Sam burned his hands. It's bad."

Mama tells me how, when he got back to the house, Sam didn't put himself to bed. No, he went to the silo, where he had a stash of fireworks, real ones, not homemade aerosol firecrackers but Smokin' Aces and Moonshine Cocktails leftover from the Fourth. It was 3:00 in the morning, but something in him needed noise, and so he tore a hole in the quiet.

As Mama talks, I picture all that brilliant color flowering in the darkness. The smell of gunpowder drifting, the showers of embers falling, winking out, the staccato bursts of sound, not quite like gunfire, but close. I see Sam standing too near, reaching out a hand as if to pull those colored sparks from the air.

One of the fireworks slanted off toward the silo instead of up, banging as the flash powder ignited, spraying blue sparks as it collided with weathered wood. The silo caught at once, and Sam beat at the flames with his shirt, then his hands, but when the weeds in the field, withered by drought, went up with a sigh, he knew he couldn't extinguish what he'd started. Fire crawled toward the house, gusted along by a westerly wind, and he raced the flames across the field, bursting in through the back door yelling for Mama, who was up already, awakened by the noise.

They watched the house burn. "It was eerie," Mama says. "The house I lived in for twenty eight years on fire before my eyes." By the time the fire trucks pulled up, there wasn't much to save.

"Why did you wait so long to call?"

"I don't know, Grace." Mama sounds so tired.

"I'm coming," I say. "I'll meet you at the hospital."

A terrible agitation takes hold of me. I retreat to the back room, the place where the dancers get ready, where we store packages of napkins and cases of beer. I should be gathering my things, but I just stand there. Yvonne has her son Marcus with her. "His daddy never came to pick him up like he said, so here I am, bringing my baby to work with me," she says. "That man. Just about good for nothing." She puts on lipstick. She does this so expertly, she doesn't need a mirror. "Your brother really banged up that guy last night. He get into a lot of fights?"

"Not like that, but he's a soldier. He just got back from Iraq."

"He knows how to handle himself. It was kind of scary."

My hands shake, so I stuff them in the pockets of my sweatshirt. "Can I ask you something, Yvonne?"

She looks at me expectantly, eyebrows arched in a go-onand-do-it way.

"Is it terrible dancing here? Do you hate it?"

"Hate's a strong word," she says. "It's a temporary thing. I'm in school for my associate's degree." She pulls her son onto her lap, and he settles against her, running his toy sports car along her leg, making engine revving noises. "You're the center of everyone's attention. Sometimes that feels good. Other times, I try to feel nothing but the music, try to forget myself in the sound."

I tell Yvonne I'm writing a magazine article about go-go dancers, that I'm doing research. Right now though, this isn't research. I tell her that. This is something else.

She helps me get ready. She tells me to breathe slowly, reminds me to keep my eyes up, on the lights. To avoid faces, no matter what. As I pull off my sweatshirt, I tell myself it'll just be for one song. Just three minutes.

I climb onto the pedestal in my bra and underwear, feeling just about as stupid as a person can feel. I realize too late I still have my socks on. Shabby socks, the heels worn thin—they surely ruin the look. Yvonne puts a Black Sabbath song on the jukebox. I told her I wanted to dance to something angry. I close my eyes. I see Sam, hands plunged in fire. The back of my throat burns. Maybe I'm trying to punish myself, shame myself, I don't know. I feel like my body isn't connected to me, like it's an unflattering outfit I just happen to be wearing. Eyes shut, I pretend I'm alone in my bedroom, but I'm sick in the pit of my stomach, and can summon nothing of the abandon I feel when a song I love gets me dancing. Opening my eyes, seeing people stare up at me, is even worse. There is a man chewing gum with his mouth open, looking at my breasts. I can see the hairs on his knuckles, the spots on his fingers. Sam's hands will be uglier than this man's hands now. I look up at the lights. The song seems to go on and on. I can smell my own anxiety, the nervous sweat under my arms. My humiliation is like a hot, dark well opening inside me. I am falling and falling.

But then, some other emotion stirs. Alongside the mortification and fear, something else. This feeling has nothing to do with sex, with the men's hungry looking. It rises through me, a feeling as though all the doors in the world have opened.

The song ends, but the feeling goes on.

I step down from the pedestal and return to the back room. I pull on my shirt and my jeans. I fish my keys from my purse.

At the hospital, the overhead lights are too bright. Sam's hands are swaddled in gauze and lie at his sides, a plastic hospital bracelet clasped loosely around his left wrist. An IV pumps fluids into his blood. It's like Sam's body is something that doesn't want to stay together, every muscle ready to tear, every bone ready to shatter, his skin ready to burn away, expose every nerve. He stirs at the sight of me, sighs, blinks slow blinks. He is swimming in morphine. I reach out, touch the scar tissue on his neck. I can feel all the hard bits that were once flying through the air. Sam looks hazily up at me, and then beyond, at the ceiling. The room feels cramped, like our worry is tightening the air around our faces.

I move away from the bedside to the window that overlooks a parking lot. The sky is still lit, and yet I see the moon, a white thumbprint on the blue. Sam once pointed out to me that Neil Armstrong's footprints are still up there, a disturbance on the surface of the moon. In interviews Armstrong has said he wishes someone would go back and sweep them away. Don't we all want to go back and sweep so many things away? I feel around in my purse for that twist of metal I kept, that I carry everywhere. The scar it gave my brother went all the way into him, deeper than flesh. He'll carry that mark until the end, until he isn't carrying anything any more.

I throw the piece of shrapnel away in the wastebasket in the corner. I just open my hand and let it go.

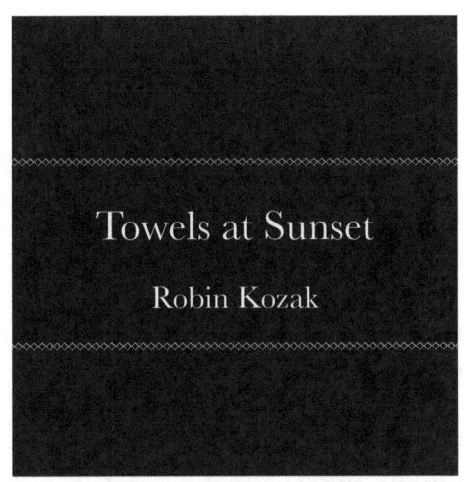

Towels at Sunset

Robin Kozak

They must bear no stain,
they must come perfect

from the dryer—cotton
fresh from Turkey, bright

olive stripes, or amber
ones, or blue. They must bear

no crease, must take the folds
from my hands obediently,

tags tucked underneath them
like the legs of calves,

as meek as sheep. They
must limn the linen chest like poppies,

coral and gold, or else the pale green I like
in bowls of roses on the table, or

the blue of hydrangeas, a bit
mysterious, shadowing the wood

when I open the doors. They must
conform, conform now to my vision

of perfection, because my father
would wipe himself with one

when he was done with me,
and I remember. Love,

when I see you again,
will you forgive my trespasses?

I am hell to live with for a reason.

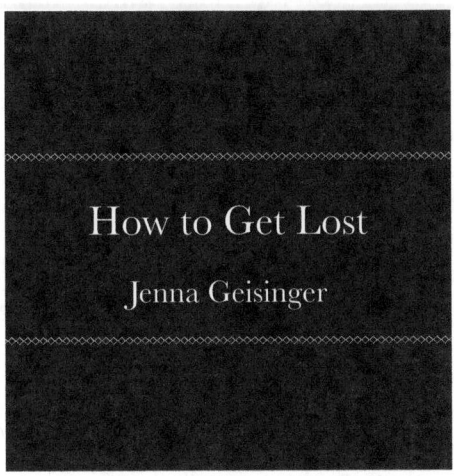

How to Get Lost

Jenna Geisinger

The first step is to fall in love with the only boy that ever remembered your name. His charmed smile and kind eyes wage a coup against reason and you don't even notice. Ryan snakes an arm around your waist and your heart flips. "I like that you have some meat on your bones," he whispers to you, pinching your side. "The girls I date are usually bony." You automatically hold your breath, sucking in the fat that cleaves to your hips and middle. Martina, the last girl he dated, boasted a 00 jean size, and his summer fling, Steph, had collar bones that could be registered as lethal weapons in all fifty states. The Rice Krispie Treats your mom snuck into the side pocket of your backpack churn in your stomach. You wish she put weights in there instead. Then, at least, studying would count as exercise. But you hate sweating. And celery. Your t-shirt feels like a second skin, clinging to the valleys of your stomach. His grip is too tight and you feel the fat pinch between his long fingers. You try to leave, "Math homework," you say. He tells you to do it later and leaves a trail of kisses down your neck. One assignment won't affect your grade that much.

You haven't done homework in a month. That's fine because math can't kiss you back. The tests on the fridge slump, curling from time and lack of achievements. Your mom asks if you've gotten any of your tests back, cracking a mom-joke about the fridge looking bare. Except that every grainy inch of it is crammed with magnets from each state your dad went to rehab. "The Rehab Tour" your mom had joked. Good one. You mumble that your teachers are swamped with work in the middle of the semester. She puts another batch of cookies in the oven. You tell her that you're going to the library to study. Your mom puts chocolate chip cookies from the cooling rack in a tin for a studying snack, but you throw them in the garbage cans out front as soon as you're out of sight. Her cookies are pillows of chocolate and your breath catches as they arc into the trash. Pull your shirt down over your hips and take a detour to his house. He kisses you the way they do in movies: his face crushed against yours. His lips are slow and smooth against you, while yours are clunky and inexperienced. But in that moment, cradled in his arms in his unfinished basement, it feels like love. The warmth of his chest envelops you like an old blanket protective and safe. Did your dad ever kiss your mom like that, before he started drinking?

She brings him Tupperware containers exploding with Mexican Wedding cookies when she visits him. They are gunked with too much powdered-sugar, messy and over-the-top, like him. Can kisses do that? Lock you into his gravitational pull until you're too far gone to turn back? More dust collects on your books and in Ryan's arms you can't recall what a prime number was even if you wanted to. The midterm is tomorrow. The library closes. You are still in his arms.

You won't notice yourself changing, not at first. But it's inevitable, like your dad's tenth relapse. Don't fight it. Ryan makes an off-handed comment that you never do anything he wants to do. At the first hint of disappointment, your heart rate skyrockets and cold sweat beads down your back. So you agree to go to his boring car meets even though you tell him you hate going, they always reek of weed and none of his friends so much as acknowledge that you're there. But you need him. You need him and he doesn't need you. So you tag along, following him around like a baby duck and coo at the lowered, rusty GTIs and Jettas haphazardly parked in the vacant lot. Bro enters your vocabulary more than you'd ever hope to hear, let alone say. You even start dressing to fit in, which mainly consists of hiding greasy waves under a snapback and wearing Calvin Klein underwear with low rise jeans so the band winks overtop. You ignore the push up bra effect for your side fat. You haven't eaten cookies, but they hang around your hips like an over-protective brother. You hope he notices how hard you're trying. You hope it's enough.

Next, wait for your best friend to leave. You think this is impossible. A ten year friendship can withstand anything. You've endured Lizzie McGuire getting cancelled and Sarah Pratt taking Derek to the formal instead of Lisa. You've huddled together in matching ugly Christmas sweaters and smeared mascara because your dad was rushed to the hospital. That trip—there would be many others, but this was the first--your mom baked every cookie in her Pillsbury recipe book arsenal, the flour seamlessly fused with her pale hands. That time was the scariest.

By the fifth time you and Lisa had the drill down. You ride your bikes to get pints of ice cream, paid for in quarters from your piggy bank. It was always Chocolate Therapy, two spoons, and two heads pressed together. When Lisa got her wisdom teeth out, her face was bloated and drooling. Chocolate Therapy. Your mom's face was flour white with red blotchy eyes. She made another mom-joke that Chocolate Therapy was cheaper than real therapy. She dug her spoon into the container and swiped a mountain full of ice cream, fitting it all in her mouth and choking on it.

Lisa buys Chocolate Therapy tonight. A solo bike rides down a wet road. A single pair of tires sloshes through puddles, kicking up mud on her faded jeans. One spoon peeks over the top of the container. One spoon and four servings. She takes a deep breath, preparing herself for the density of the pint. Lisa hopes that each spoonful of melting therapy will evaporate the image of her long-term boyfriend underneath a freshman cheerleader. That freeze-dried brownies and congealed dairy could erase his smug face when she walked in. Or worse, her best friend walking away. You were at Ryan's, watching a documentary and snuggling your face deeper into his chest.

It ends with a walk to the car. You walk out to your car with Lisa and there are daisies tucked under the windshield wipers. Ryan steps out from behind your shitty Hyundai armed with your favorite candy. You squeal and run to him. He sweeps you into his arms and you never imagined anyone could lift you off your feet. Ever. Lisa rolls her eyes, a habit incurred from years of sitcoms and two older sisters. The eye roll was an imperative currency in her household growing up; for the bathroom, the last cookie, and the remote. While you are flying above her in Ryan's outstretched arms, she rolls her eyes so hard they nearly leap off of her face. "We get it," she mutters. Ryan drops you to your feet, wrapping his arms around you. You both laugh, his smile presses into your cheek. Lisa slams the passenger door, visibly frustrated with her arms crossed. Ryan brushes a stray tendril from your eyes. "Frozen yogurt tonight. Me and you. Documentary on Netflix. What do you say?" Lisa leans over and honks the horn repeatedly until you finally break free of his touch. "JESUS! Of course, but can it not be the Banksy one? We watched it like ten times!" You giggle and kiss him, running to the driver side with your hands over your ears. Lisa angrily slumps down in her seat, knowing that you won't remember the plans you made a week ago for a movie and Chocolate Therapy. Knowing that you'll blow her off. Again and again. And she wonders if ten years can replace dignity and loyalty.

Mom gets the call. Dad relapsed. Again. His sobriety is as fleeting as time. The hospital begins to feel like a family reunion. Your mom sends the nurses Christmas cards, and all of them know you by name and are armed with an ample supply of awkward hugs. Your mom paces outside of his hospital room. You call Lisa from the payphone. No answer. No Chocolate Therapy. You call Ryan. You sputter into the phone all of the things you've been too afraid to say in person. The Rehab Tour, your mom's cookies, Chocolate Therapy. You wish you didn't have to leave it in a voicemail where it can be quickly ignored and erased. But what choice did you have? You never go into your dad's hospital room. Seeing him from the hallway, slumped in a backless gown with tubes sprouting from him like particularly fragile weeds, makes it real. He is always in and out of the house. Mostly out. You honestly cannot remember the title of his last job or the last time he even had a job. Your mom is more ATM to him than wife. If you never go in, he is still the guy that rented It Takes Two and brought you Reese's Cups. He watched it with you three times because you kept falling asleep on his chest at the exact same part. You sit in the waiting room and read bad magazines. This one is fifteen years old. You think you remember reading the horoscopes a few hospital trips ago. There was an article about Mary-Kate and Ashley Olsen; you read that one before, too, but this time you could have cried right then and there, big, ugly tears that leave ruddy splotched-cheeks and turn your nose red. Lisa is never going to call you back. You chose Ryan over a ten year friendship. You aren't even sure if he is going to call you back. Or if he was worth it. How do you deal with this by yourself? You never had to be alone with it. In the waiting room or at home.

This is the final step of getting lost. Ryan says he found a new girl that's different from anyone else he's ever met. He met her at the car meet when your dad was dying. When the nurses tried to resuscitate him. When the heart monitor bleeped over and over like gun shots and your mom collapsed from shock. When you took the bus home because you couldn't face it. Apparently Ryan hardly checks his voice mail these days. He says that you and he have too much in common. It's too boring, he says. He talks about her bouncy blonde hair and how she paints. She's gorgeous, he says. He talks about how cute she is with paint-stained fingers. And she's a vegan. You bite back rage. He prattles on about her and you wonder if he lifts her off the ground or brushes hair from her face. Maybe he kisses her in way that makes her hold on beyond a reasonable doubt. You wonder if she likes documentaries. He kisses you on the cheek and you pretend that your hair doesn't smell stale and oily. Does her hair smell like that? Do vegans use shampoo? He speeds out, his car scraping the lip at the end of the driveway. The snapback feels too tight and you spent a paycheck on underwear that he won't get to see. You wonder if he'll bring you up in conversation. Will she be jealous? Probably not. You slink into the house. Your lower lids act as a dam against the threatening tears, but it bursts when you walk into Disney re-runs of Lizzy McGuire. You want to call Lisa. Tell her about the hippie Ryan dumped you for. Tell her about your dad. Dead. Lifeless. Devoid of Life. You still can't get your head around it. Can ice cream fill a vortex swirling in the center of your chest? Blood thumps in your ears. Good. At least you'll have a new pain to focus on. There are no cookies waiting for you when you walk inside. The air is cool, rather than its usually oven-related sticky heat. Your mother is sitting numbly on the couch. This time her arms are not pasted with flour up to her elbows. They are clean. Spotless. You haven't seen the freckle on her forearm in years. A new magnet is added to the collection. This one from the funeral home on the corner. New wrinkles crease her eyes and a new vein bulges from her forehead. A black dress with tags is draped over the kitchen chair. You sink to the ground, wishing you felt your dad's flannel pressed against your dreaming cheek. When you felt safe. For the last time.

Firestorm: Checagou

Nancy L. Davis

In the tall stalks of plenty where prairie meets plains
a city is born. Wild onions, wild fantasies.
Rivers run through it. Strident streams of Great-Lake
       currents
steady the flow of New-England merchant men:
princes and paupers, land pirates build the inestimable
sprawling of sweeping horizons.

Pelts fall to planks
warriors to mayors
dreams to currencies
forests to sweatshops.
Steam horses spar
with human life.
A river reversed
a pestilence delivered
downstream.

Necessity being the mother of invention,
steel structures rise, trains loop and dip
and the disassembly of beasts foretells
the Second Coming: lean iron horses feeding
scrap yards. Meanwhile,
the torpid transmigration of souls transpires:
dumped into Bubbly Creek later washed
down the mighty Mississippi, generations later
the river choking on silt.

The Negro Speaks of Rivers. "I've seen fire and
I've seen rain."** I've seen a lakefront open to parks
and people, wetlands overfed with fill. The vanishing

and the vanquished. Trains, planes, automobiles:
the confluence a gritty grid of asphalt angles and granite
canyons. Boats carrying the hopeful across the
Great Dixie Divide. Mechanical men stacking flaxen
into elevators of wealth. Driven creators the brilliant
architects of modernity.

Flash forward to grim brick smokestack-like Habitats
for Humanity. Distinctive Projects. *Progress*. Native Sons
also rising. A Metamorphosis: onion fields to fertilizer beds
to killing parks slashed to the quick
with modern-day scythes and sickles;
drug-sick shepherds keeping watch on their flocks to part rival
weave from neighborhood chaff: flushing out futures like grouse
in the grasses, flesh falling from bone; sacrificial lambs, our heads
bowed to the heavens. *Our Country 'Tis of Thee.*
The ages echoing one into another,
aging with heartbreak, of thee I sing.

Rapid-fire consumption our
Gross National Product.

Metal scrambles, screams through tissue;
just another Stormy Monday, the papers say. Strange Fruit falling
from the popular to arms. *Farewell.* Hand to hand combat. Friendly
fire. The gun runner wailing with the gospel choir.
"O, here's the shoe my baby wore, /But, baby, where are you?"***

A most uncivil war. Urban unrest. City of Big Shoulders, gangly
     adolescence.
Oh holy

night. Violence begets violence. O say,
can you see, by the dawn's dimming light.
The rocket's red glare the bombs bursting in air
gives proof through the night that our hearts are not there.
For the land of the free and the home of deep strife:
unsettled, unhealthy, unbidden. Rife
with sorrow.

I speak of rivers
fire and rain.

*Native American term meaning skunk weed, smelly onion
**James Taylor, "Fire and Rain"
***Dudley Randall, "The Ballad of Birmingham"

When the Leaf Bug Bites I'll Be Looking Out the Window at You Smoking in the Rain

Rachel Howe

On the hotel room balcony, Luke stood smoking cigarette after cigarette as I put the kids to bed. Their excitement at being in a hotel, at sharing a room with us, had them popping up like the moles in that arcade game where you hit 'em with a mallet. I can't deal with this, he told me as he closed the sliding glass door behind him. I watched him as he leaned against the railing, his hip pressing into the soft, splintering wood, his long torso leaning out into the crickety night, rain falling softly behind him, drops catching the light of the bare bulb every so often like falling stars against the black sky beyond.

Esme fell asleep on my arm, which began to prick with pins and needles after a while. She always slept with her mouth open like a goldfish reaching for air. Every time I tried to move my arm, she stirred. Eventually I gave up and lay there, staring at the stained popcorn ceiling. In sleep as in life, Henry fidgeted, which was the reason I'd never let him sleep in bed with us at home. It always meant getting kicked in my belly or my back, and being half awake all night. Now he made little noises as he tugged the stiff floral bedspread on the opposite bed. Was he imagining himself a superhero? Or were his dreams as mundane and frustrating as my own, wrestling with toothpaste tubes that never released their goo or continuously sharpening pencils which would never write?

I wrestled my arm free from Esme and went over to kiss Henry's smooth forehead. He smelled of baby sweat, damp and sweet. I could smell my own body, too, as I leaned over, a deeper, pungent smell that comforted me in this strange environment. Luke, being what my parents call a real American– which is their way of saying an Annie Hall kind of WASP, is afraid of body odor. In fact, he is afraid of any odor. He generally strives for the neutral in his life - except in me. But maybe he strives to have it in me, too.

The hotel called itself a resort. It had an indoor pool housed in a room so over-bleached all the white was yellowing. There was a game room with checkers and a pinball machine, a bar that actually played Frank Sinatra (no irony) and only Frank Sinatra the whole time we were there, and a swing set with a slide in the back. It was Labor Day weekend, we had driven up from Philly to the Poconos on a whim, and this was the only room available for miles around. Our original plan had been to stay home Saturday and Monday, but spend Sunday at the Jersey shore with friends. At the last minute, Luke had suggested the mountains instead. I really preferred the beach, but I didn't say so. I was afraid it would lead to yet another fight and ruin the weekend. Our fights were usually about how I always had to get my own way. "I just have to get out of the city, Liz," he'd said, and I had agreed, tired of looking at my grimy basement filled with mismatched toys and socks. But we both knew what we really meant was, "We have to get away from each other."

There were a million things left unsaid between us these days. We used to argue like all get-out. There were broken glasses, spilled cans of paint, even a vacuum cleaner down the stairs one time. I still didn't have all the attachments. But we'd started to hold it together when the kids came. Luke was never a fan of direct expression; he preferred the silent treatment. And all my screaming just made me seem like the crazy one, so I started to pull it together, to hold it together, to hold it in. And when Luke reached out for me - when his father died, when he got layed off from the bank - I was too busy holding myself in to reach back.

In the morning, Henry captured a leaf bug on the balcony and brought it inside where it pinched him. Surprised, he dropped it and it floundered, panicked, around the synthetic brown/orange carpeting. It was still drizzling and fuzzy outside, but the sun was peeking through the clouds and beginning to burn off the blur. Henry ran back to the balcony to show Luke the drop of blood jeweled on his finger, and Luke let him lean against his leg awhile, the smoke from his cigarette mixing with the rising mist.

We had taken the kids to the pool as soon as we got to the place the day before. They drank in the chlorine like sugar and had emerged only for dinner, eyes red as potheads, drowsy and cranky from their efforts. Now, they wanted to go back. Once they got in, I knew we'd never get them out. "It looks like it's clearing up," I said. "Let's hit that waterfall I was reading about last night. It should be really close by."

Esme's knees started to buckle as she braced for her oncoming tantrum. "No Mommy, noooo!"

"Come on, Liz," said Luke in his timbred voice that meant he was going to win and he knew it. "They can go for a little while can't they?" It was a cool sound, an unworried sound, such a contrast to my clenched one whenever we had a standoff, which lately was every day. He sounded like he was flicking a cigarette away and it turned my mind hot and red. The kids jumped on the beds, squealing.

Luke was the good parent now, but I knew what would happen. I'd spend the day inhaling chlorine as my hair frizzed while Luke watched TV in the room, smoked on the balcony, and made a quick appearance to dunk them in the pool just as I would be about to lose my mind refereeing yet another fight over whose turn it was to wear the goggles. Meanwhile, the world outside would become beautiful and sunny, a perfect day for a late summer hike, and I'd have to watch it fade into pink from inside the peeling, steamy room.

"It's going to rain later," I tried in a practical voice. "I think we should go now. You know how they get once they start anything. Anyway, we can hit the pool when we get back, before we leave."

"Noooo!" yelled the kids from the beds.

"Come on, Liz. Why do you always have to be such a hardass?"

Now, the whine crept into my throat, clawed at it like a little troll that lived in my larynx and had made its way up to my vocal chords. It wanted out. "We drove all the way up here. We didn't go to the beach. I want to get out of this crappy place and see some goddamned waterfalls!" I turned to the kids, trying to win them over. "Who wants to see waterfalls with Mommy?"

"No!" They yelled in unison, the traitors. "Swimming!!!!" But they were joyous, tossing their heads back, their hair flying in the air as they descended back to the mattress from the air, the rough sheets pooling at their feet. "Daddy! Daddy!" yelled Esme, "Tell Mommy we want to go swimming!"

"That's right. Mommy doesn't always have to get her way, right guys?" He looked at me as he said this.

"Yeah, yeah! Mommy always gets her way," Esme cried delightedly, punctuating each jump with a single word, but Henry, though he kept jumping, gave me a sad look, his eyes tender. I pinched my mouth into a smile for him, raising my eyebrows to show it was okay. He smiled back an unsure smile that broke my heart. I turned to look at Luke hard. "Later," he announced. "As soon as we get back from seeing the goddamn waterfalls." He looked right back at me.

We struggled the kids into all manner of clothing and sandals and sunscreen. Packed a knapsack with water and granola bars and an extra pair of underwear for Esme, just in case. We were walking out the door, the kids rushing ahead, racing down the hallway when Luke said, "You know, I'm kind of tired. Maybe I'll just stay back and rest. Then I can meet you down at the pool." His hand went up to his hair, his nervous move. He knew he wasn't going to get away with this one.

"This is supposed to be a family weekend. I don't want to tramp around the Poconos alone with two kids. God, sometimes I feel like I'm already a single mother."

"It was your idea to do this stupid hike," he shot back.

"It was your idea to come up here!"

"Shhhh!!!" he scolded. We were standing in the orange carpeted hallway. It wasn't even 8:30.

I said it again in a whisper, the kind of yell whisper whose peaks are tinged with throaty anger. "It was your fucking idea to come up here! I would have been very happy to go hang out with the Shermans and eat crabs and swim in the ocean. At least I would have had another adult to talk to." I turned away from him then and ran after the kids who were arguing over who could press the elevator's down button. I didn't even look behind to see if he followed.

Luke and I met in college. He wore flannels and bobbed his head to Pearl Jam, pumping the keg and handing out red cups, rarely taking one himself. By the time Nirvana would be wailing away in the background, and everyone else had either hooked up or had passed out on dirty couches, Luke would be ready to go take a really good look at the stars. He'd get a Mexican blanket. He'd take me by the hand. He'd say the names of the constellations: Pleadies, Cassiopea, Saggitarius. He'd point to them, he'd kiss me, the ground would be wet under the blanket and seep into the seat of my pants, go cold beneath my shoulder. I wouldn't care, not even if there was a rock under my hip. He would kiss me, and I could see the stars.

Despite being called the Nature's Wonder Resort, there was no breakfast included or available, so we grabbed food from the gas station across the street. In the car, the kids munched on their stale soft pretzels, and I sipped hot, bitter coffee that burned my tongue in a not unpleasant way, the steam fogging up my glasses. Luke had followed, grudgingly.

From his booster seat in back, Henry told a joke. "What does an elephant get when he sits on a marshmallow?" he asked, already giggling at the answer.

"What?" I turned around in my seat, smiling.

"A mushy tushy!" Henry announced, and he laughed so hard that pulpated pretzel fell in a wad from his mouth, into his hand. He held it up with a big grin as we passed dark green trees, a Girl Scout camp, a boat launch, posters announcing state game land. This got Esme going, and the three of us couldn't stop laughing.

"Ewe!" I said finally, "Give that to me."

I held out my hand for the sticky bread and knew I was his mother in an intimate, physical way. I plopped it into the plastic bag with the rest of the wrappers and straws and sugar packets from the gas station.

"Isn't that funny, Daddy?" Henry demanded when he realized Luke was silent. But Luke was lost in his own world. "Daddy? Daddy!" There is no cover from children, and Luke was forced eventually to join us back in the car. "Daddy – a mushy tushy! Isn't that funny?"

"Hmmmmm…." Luke nodded, his eyes still focused two car lengths ahead. I shook his shoulder, and he gradually turned to me, his face changing rapidly. It reminded me of this doll Esme had; the head spins around to show different faces, each with a different emotion. His face settled into an expression with flared nostrils on his aquiline nose, his ears cocked, making the wiry gray hairs at his temple stick out, as if he'd smelled something bad. His eyes locked into mine, I sucked in my breath at the hate I felt radiating from him in that moment. "What?" he finally asked, his voice like metal.

"Henry told a joke," I managed, but I turned my eyes to the trees, the leaves, the trees, the leaves, the forest for the trees. I wanted to say something, say anything, but no words came to mind. I knew it was not his fault that our marriage was falling apart. It was my silence and my fear. I was trying to hold it together by not arguing back, to make each moment okay, but it was all rotten underneath, and I knew it.

Luke sucked in a breath, and that seemed to flip a switch. He became Dad again. His shoulder straightened, a playful smile came to his lips, his eyebrows raised inquisitively. "Tell it again, son," he prodded in a warm voice as he turned around slightly in his seat, his hands still on the wheel. "I wasn't paying attention." Son - what a WASP-y thing to say. I could hear my mother in my ear – Oy! Americans! Everything on the surface.

As we trudged up the hill towards the stream, each of us with a child, and then switching children, we hardly had to talk to each other. I squeezed Esme's fat little belly and her skinny bug legs wiggled around in glee and that was enough. The sun went in and out, changing the light dramatically as we made our way beneath the canopy of Eastern trees, blackberries still ripe on the vines just beyond the edges of the trail. The children ran up ahead as they began to hear the faint trickle of water. I smiled, and in my gentlest voice pointed out how lovely the mountains were, even as the summer was fading. Luke just made a guttural sound to indicate he'd heard me, but otherwise didn't respond.

When we passed a side trail, Luke announced, "I think I'm going to go off this way for a bit. I want to be by myself for a while."

"Really?" I couldn't keep the anger out of my voice. I stood sweating and stunned, gnats buzzing in my ear. I swatted them away.

"What's the problem, Liz?" Luke's shoulders sank. He asked the question not, of course, because he wanted to hear what the problem was, but because this was the routine.

I felt my throat clench and the voice that came out sounded high pitched. "You're going to leave me alone? With the kids? Now? Again?"

"You seriously can't handle them for half an hour in the woods? Jesus, you'll be fine. They're not babies anymore. I've got a lot on my mind." He turned to walk onto the green trail.

You always do, I thought as I started to turn my back, to walk off without explaining. I was the demanding, control-freak wife who had no sympathy for a man who'd lost his job and was just getting back on his feet at a new one with a salary reduction. I knew I was being an overgrown brat, but something in those woods, something about being in that run-down motel that my husband and kids seemed to enjoy so much, something about being away from the piles of dishes and laundry and bills and dust bunnies and birthday parties and deadlines at work and phone calls that Luke was going to be late again and issues with the day care and the kindergarten and passive aggressive phone calls from his mother and wet beds at 3 in the morning and crayon all over our newly painted dining room walls and a back turned away from me in our giant, lonely bed made me face him and call him back to me. "Luke!" I shouted.

"What?" His voice like a razor, he turned his face back to me, but his body still pointed up the adjoining hill, into the darkness where the trees swallowed the path.

"It's not about the kids." I tried to keep that horrible, whiny sound out of my voice. I took a breath. "It's about me." I looked at my feet, at the mud drying back into dirt and a fuzzy red and brown caterpillar making its slow way to a leaf just beyond the toes of my worn out sneakers. My face felt hot and my fingers were prickly. I tried to take another breath, but my chest felt blocked. When I looked back up, Luke had turned fully back to me. "I don't want you to go. I want you to be with me. To be with me. Here, together."

He looked wistfully up the trail, and I looked away. I said what I needed to say. I breathed in and out, sending oxygen to the places in my body that were gasping for it. I wiggled my fingers and turned to go toward the kids and the goddamn waterfall and the crowd of people surely photographing it and daring each other to dunk under it and eating hummus and peanut butter sandwiches on large flat rocks next to it. He was beside me suddenly, his long arm caged around my shoulder. He pulled me into him, and I let out a breath I hadn't realized I was holding as my narrow shoulders crushed into his ribs. He didn't say anything and neither did I. We just walked in step down the trail.

Driving back to Philly on the highway, we passed over the state park. "Look down there - I think that's where we were hiking," I announced. The kids sucked on candy and stared out their windows. Luke nodded. Satisfied with what I could get out of him for the moment, I looked at the cars parked below, the incredible green of the trees. The other trees, the ones lining the highway seemed dusty, lighter, tired, closer to being ready to shed their leaves for fall, to rest.

"Take a look at this," Luke said suddenly, handing me his iPhone. "I signed up for this thing; it's a service. You pay 10 bucks a month and you can program in any album you want." He touched the app and an array of choices popped up. You could look by artists or song or genre. I had a radio feature on my phone, but you could only choose one song on it – then you were stuck with whatever the invisible DJ in the device chose next. This, he explained, would allow you to choose whatever song, whenever you wanted to hear it.

"Neat!" I said, handing it back to him.

He put on The Steve Miller band. He liked to point out all the jazz influences. "Listen to that bass line," he would normally say. But this time, he surprised me. I was half listening, half wondering what we were going to make for dinner, when he said, "When this song is over, do you want to pick something?"

"To listen to?" I turned toward him.

He smiled back at me, "Yeah, to listen to." He said it gently, and I remembered him kissing me under the stars all those years ago. I took the phone back from him as Steve Miller finished wailing away. What did I want to hear? It had been the better part of a decade since my musical choices had ranged beyond "ohn Jacob Jingleheimer Schmidt" or the local alternative station as default aural wallpaper as I drove to my job as a social worker. Usually, I just listened to the news and numbed out.

Now, with the gadget in my hand, I felt electrified. The hairs on my arms perked up. My fingertips tingled as I scrolled through my choices. I glanced at Luke, who was responsibly looking 10 seconds down the road. The sky was again dreary. The answers were nowhere around me. And then it floated to me: Julianna Hatfield – that's who I wanted to hear: her blunt lyrics, her raw voice, the bare guitar behind her. That was how I had felt in college. The yearning, the anticipation, the new connections to people, ideas, art. I had been truly myself then, interested in the world and eager to join it. I was unapologetically angry: at my parents, at God, at men who called to me on the street, at the idiots in Washington. I used to picture myself on a kibbutz, in the deserts of Arizona, swimming in the rocky blue grottos of the Baja Peninsula. And then I'd met Luke, and for a while, we were alive together, talking through the night and making love on dirty bedspreads or a couch in the hallway, it didn't matter. Once we stayed up an entire night together, each reading a novel – and they weren't even novels for class. I read Trainspotting, flipping back and forth to the Scottish-American glossary. I don't remember what Luke read, but it didn't matter. We lay head to toe on my long, twin, dorm room bed, our legs wrapped around each other. In the morning, we skipped class and listened to The Pixies.

Julianna crooned about about hating her sister through the speakers as the early evening sun fought its way through the clouds. I had forgotten how breathy she sounded, how like a grown baby. "God," Luke looked over at me, smiling, "remember her?"

"Yeah, I know. Remember all those baby trends – the little barrettes, the pacifiers?"

"Oh my god, yeah," He drew out the last word and looked off into the distance, but his hand found mine on the center console as the opening cords of the next song crashed and popped on our puny car speaker. "Sleater-Kinney," Luke acknowledged the band. "You really liked these guys, didn't you?" The kids were crashed out in back by now, and I checked briefly to make sure the heavy bass didn't wake them. Esme drooled, openmouthed onto her car seat. Henry's head hung down, his blond curls bobbing with the rhythm of the car and the occasional lift from the air conditioner.

The singer's staccato lyrics rang through their angriest song, "Monster," the anthem of all the fights I'd once had with my mother. I listened for a minute, letting the pure thrill of her anger wash through me.

"I was so angry with my mother then. With both my parents, I guess, but mostly with my mother. I always felt like I could never be good enough for her. I don't know. I guess everyone feels that way about their parents." I thought a minute as the beat pulsed through my whole body. It felt so freeing, just as it had back then. "It's funny, you know?"

"What is?" he asked. And it felt so good to be asked. To feel that he was really listening. Lately, he always seemed to answer any of my deep thoughts with "Uh-huh," before going off to make himself a sandwich.

"Well, I think they still have all of these expectations of me, and they are disappointed in me for not becoming a lawyer and marrying a good Jewish doctor. They'd never say that, of course, but it's there. It's funny because it just doesn't make me angry the way it used to. I guess they've softened. I guess I have, too."

Luke appeared to consider this. He'd always had such a mild relationship with his own parents. Not a very deep relationship, but a pleasant one. I wondered if he could understand. I squeezed his hand as the song ended. "When we get home," he began as a new song started. I leaned in, wondering what he would propose for us. Maybe ordering a pizza and watching a Disney movie all together before bedtime. Maybe getting the kids to bed early so we could hang out together. "I gotta run into the office for a bit."

I sat stunned, my hand still under his. I pulled it out and my chin jutted forward. I looked over, but all I saw was the long side of his face. His eyes were on the road. "What? Luke, it's Sunday evening. And tomorrow is

Labor Day. Can't it at least wait until tomorrow? I thought we were having a family weekend."

"Calm down," he answered, ducking my question. "It's no big deal. You can handle one night of bedtime." I hated when he told me to calm down. I felt the pulse of "Monster" in my blood again. "You know I have to get my numbers up. I'm the new guy there. I need to get back at least to where I was." There was just no arguing with that. I wanted to pull him out into the middle of the pulsing crowd and get him to jump, jump, jump! But he wasn't that guy anymore and the crowd had long since gone to law school and gotten 401K plans. I stared out the window at the high sun, which hung like a yellow egg in the sky. Luke kept looking at the road, barely in the car at all.

Sanctuary

Patrick McNeil

Frank Ewing only ever lets me into his place because he has to. It's right there in the lease.

"I ain't ever signed off on that," he tells me through the crack of his door the first time I knock. "You show me where it say that."

I pass a copy across the threshold and point to where the Housing Authority mandates monthly visits from me, his new case manager.

He looks at the paper for a long time. In a few months, he'll start to let me help him with his mail, and I'll come to understand he can't read.

"Boy they kill you with the small print," is all he says about the lease. He never learned how.

He is seventy-five and has a long enough history of homelessness that the city pays me to provide whatever support he needs to stay housed, now that he's finally housed.

"It's not like an inspection or anything," I add. I'm not here to get him in trouble.

He opens the door and lets me in. The place is always the same: clean enough, with some cowboy show on the TV, mattress on the floor, unopened condoms on the windowsill, and nothing in the fridge. It's hard to tell how thin he is under his too-big clothes.

"Want some help with food?" I ask. "There are some places I know about that could help you out a little."

"Don't need no help. See you next month. Seventeenth, right?"

On the seventeenth, I bring back a loaf of bread. One of the pieces of mail I help Frank read is from the Housing Authority, threatening eviction. He hasn't paid his rent once in the six months he's lived there. I ask why not.

"How much I owe?" he says. "I'll pay them next month."

He doesn't. I explain the situation to the housing authority, and at first, they assume Frank's using, but then when I mention the condoms, the pieces fall into place for them.

"So he's tricking, too."

Next time I see Frank the lights don't work. He lets me call PECO and work out a payment plan, but the thing about it is he has to actually pay. Both the rent and electric payments are so small it's like they're symbolic. It's like:

You want this place? Give up something for it. We know your pension is modest, we understand things are hard. We're not asking for much, just give us something.

He doesn't give them anything. Maybe it's symbolic for him, too.

On the day I visit Frank to tell him he's being evicted, I meet the woman he's been spending all his money on. She's leaving just as I get there, and in lots of ways, she's not what I expected: she's older, in her sixties maybe, and beautiful in the way that mothers and grandmothers are, wholesome. Her hair's done up, she's wearing scrubs, she's off to work, she tells me. We talk for a minute, and she calls me baby in that way that older women sometimes do that I love. Her name is Prudie.

"So that's her," I say to Frank once she's gone. I've been coming to see him for almost a year at this point, so I should know better, but it's the wrong thing to say. He darkens, says it's none of my damn business, and points to the door. I read him the notice to vacate.

At eviction court, the lawyers compel Frank to either submit to a representative payee--someone to handle his finances, pay his rent, budget his spending--or vacate the unit in thirty days.

"Please," the lawyers appeal to me in private. "Try and talk some sense into him. You know how many people would kill to have what he's about to throw away?"

I do, I get it, people wait five, ten years for a Section 8 voucher, but for the whole meeting, all I can think about is Prudie in her powder pink scrubs. I don't try and convince him one way or the other.

After he's evicted, I go and see him in the shelter, see what he's paid back this month. When the balance is zero, he will get his voucher back, judge's ruling. Three months pass and he doesn't pay a cent, and shelter staff let me hear it.

"Every month it's the same thing. He leaves out the first--payday--and comes back on the fourth or the fifth, broke as a joke. Not a dime has he paid, it's like he doesn't even care about getting back home. And it's not like he's even getting high—we've tested him. Addiction we can at least try to treat. There's funding for that. But this? And don't think we don't know exactly where his money's going."

"To love," I say, and it helps, they laugh. Now we are on the same side, but I'll never tell them about Prudie, and Frank will never give her up. I do try and press him a little, though. The shelter is a hell of a place to be seventy-five years old.

"Just give them a little bit. I mean don't you want to get the hell out of here?"

He laughs. "I sure do get the hell on out, every first of the month, don't I?"

I don't know where it is he meets Prudie every month, but by now I know better than to ask. Wherever it is, it's the one place that none of us can touch.

Before I leave we play a game of chess in the day room. I've never played anyone as good as Frank. He seems to wake up when we play, like he's thirty years younger, moving quickly and slamming the pieces down, "There." He talks smack, he laughs at most of my moves, and he uses his queen in ways that would make me nervous.

"You putting her on that pedestal ain't doing you any good, neither," he tells me.

I smile, he's right. "I'd just be scared of losing her."

"Shit," says Frank, and he darkens like he does. "That ain't love."

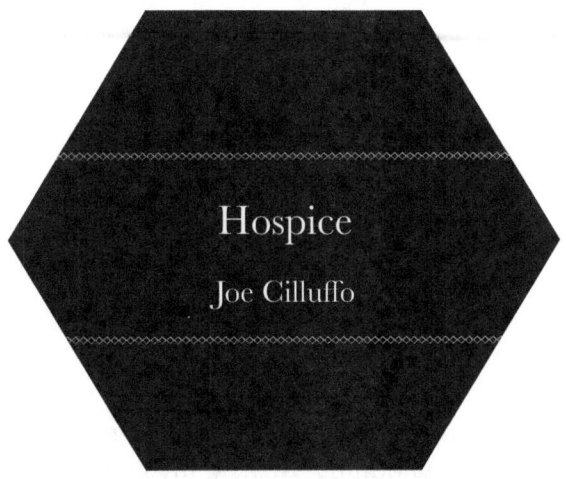

Hospice

Joe Cilluffo

My son says the garden is dying.
Every August, it's the same.
The cucumbers, which had clambered
so fiercely up the lattice
and across half our garden square,
begin to yellow and wilt.
The peppers brown. They soften.
Tomatoes explode across their vines, manic –
they bear more fruit than the days can hold.
Look there, I tell him, see that space?
Next year's garden is already growing.
Seeds are in the ground,
gift of the fallen.
We could do nothing
and, by June, there would be more tomatoes.

He sees, I am certain, in only two dimensions
– what is before him, and what he remembers.
We could do nothing. Nearby, my mother
dies in slow motion, surrounded
by four walls, a window
she doesn't look through,
cut flowers. All her words
from these last, long months
wouldn't bend a blade of grass.
We could do
nothing. My son and I
uproot the cucumber plants,
the peppers. I wish I were strong.
Eyes will open to the green and new.
I try to picture
the garden to come.

Like Nothing Happened

Dennis Lawson

It's an hour drive from our office in Wilmington down to Dover, and my colleagues wanted to carpool, so I'm praying something goes wrong. Getting pulled over speeding is the most likely possibility—lots of state cops patrol Route 1, snagging cars that are just over the speed limit. Maybe John could suddenly feel ill and cancel the whole thing. He's the owner and founder of the firm, but he's on his way out. He's finally retiring in a few months. He's sitting in front of me, in the passenger seat. Harris, my boss, is driving his leased BMW. The back seat is uncomfortable. It's raining outside. Everyone on Route 1 is driving sensibly, including Harris, except for this little Kia that passed us a little while ago. And then, there it is, pulled over on the side, with a cop standing in the rain at the passenger's window. Harris slows down to fifty-five as we go by. I'm stuck here.

The good thing is, I've taken the afternoon off. I knew this morning would be exhausting. I can maintain my friendly, charming, professional face for only so long before I can't do it any more. This is an hour down, probably at least an hour meeting, and then an hour back up. My only saving grace is that Harris has an early afternoon meeting, so we can't do lunch.

"See that, Thomas?" John says. "That's what I was talking about. As soon as I saw that little heap fly by, I knew he was a goner."

"He had an appointment in Samarra," I want to say, but that's too weird for these two.

"Especially in this rain," I say instead.

A lot of people in business question the value of the arts. I learned to act in the theater club in school. If not for that, how would I be able to act like a normal person?

\#

Delaware's Public Archives are in a large brick building with a striking, glassy cylindrical façade. We're there to deliver a presentation on a potential marketing campaign. The Division of Archives had put out a request for proposals, and John thinks it's going to be easy pickings.

We hurry in to get out of the rain. Harris signs in for us, and the girl at the desk tells him that it's going to be a few minutes. I walk around and look at the current displays.

It turns out that the Director of the Archives has a meeting with the Chief Deputy Secretary of State, and it's going long. Harris and I should've spent more time on the presentation.

At the same time, I like it when John is revealed to be out of touch. He thinks he can just bank on his past reputation, but he can't keep up with the present. We recently lost a client because, at an event, John took credit for some creative that the client had actually designed in-house. The conversation got back to the client.

Finally a staffer leads us into a conference room, and then the Director and two more of her staff members join us. All women. I can already hear John complaining about it. On the way home, he's going to say that it used to be that you'd sit down with some government guys at Fraizer's Restaurant, have some beers, and hash out a contract.

We would've been better off bringing John's wife. She's number three for him. She'd been previously divorced herself, and she went into this marriage with eyes wide open. She has a fun sort of cynicism about her. I used to flirt with her at staff parties. She ignores me now.

The Archives staff has all sorts of insightful questions that we're not remotely ready for. At some point, I tell a lie about doing research there in college, for no other reason than to make it seem like we aren't completely clueless.

As we're walking out of the building, a young woman comes striding in. She's a tall, thin redhead in a long black coat and black rain boots. I hold the door open for her, and she doesn't acknowledge me. I recognize her from somewhere, but I can't put my finger on it.

"Let's get out of here," John says.

In the car, Harris tries to put a positive spin on things. He says that the Division of Arts has just put a request out, and that we'll have a better idea of what state agencies are looking for in the "present climate." I want to tune them out and figure out how I know that redhead. But I know that if I do that, I'll end up staring out the window and seeming like a nutty spacecase. So I force myself to make occasional contributions to the conversation.

I'm going to drop dead if I don't have some coffee.

\#

Harris and I chat for a few minutes at the office and then he takes off. I go through my emails while eating lunch at my desk. Then I'm out. I stop at Dunkin Donuts for a coffee. The weather has improved, slightly. The rain has stopped, leaving us with a miserable, gray December day. Maybe my therapist will brighten things up. I have a one-thirty appointment.

I hop onto the highway because it's the quickest way to North Wilmington. Right now I'm driving a black Acura. I prefer the feel of my previous car, a V6 Accord, but the Acura has better looks. I roll along the Concord Pike and its various strips of retail shopping. I'm starting to relax.

I sit in the waiting room, reading an issue of Sports Illustrated and drinking my coffee. Dr. Flynn calls me in, right on time.

I sit down on the couch. Dr. Flynn makes some notes at her desk and then sits on the leather chair that faces the couch, with her white pad of paper on her thigh. She is in her 60s, older than I usually go for. She's taller than me in her high heels and meaty.

I take stock of today's outfit. Blue blouse under black sweater, black pants, no socks or stockings, two-inch black high-heels. Faint eyeliner, red lipstick, an odd assortment of rings and bracelets. I believe that over the course of the year or so that I've been seeing Dr. Flynn as my therapist, her clothes have gotten tighter and tighter.

"How would you describe your mood today?" she asks.

I can feel a smile pulling my lips along. I show Dr. Flynn more of myself than I show most people. "I'm pretty excited," I say.

"Why is that?"

"I had a meeting for work today, and I saw a woman who I know I recognized from somewhere. It took me a while, but now I remember who she is."

Dr. Flynn crosses her legs. I detect a faint bounce in her aerial foot. More and more, I feel compelled to ask her to join me on the couch. I think she would—if I asked her. What would I call her during sex? Dr. Flynn? Lisa?

"And who is she, Thomas?"

"She's a go-go dancer. I saw her in small club on South Street in Philadelphia. She wore a leather vest and denim skirt, and she danced to 'I Wanna Be Your Dog.' That's an old Stooges song."

Dr. Flynn watches me for a few seconds without speaking. Then she asks: "Do you think that's really the case? Or were you having a fantasy?"

"John and Harris saw her too. I held the door for her."

I realize I sound defensive. Dr. Flynn waits for me to say more.

This reminds me of our conversations about John's wife. I get the sense that Dr. Flynn only believes around half of what I tell her, maybe not even that, which is a big part of why I feel so relaxed around her. I don't think she takes me all that seriously.

"I'm not planning on making a big thing about it, if that's what you're thinking."

"What would constitute a 'big thing' to you?"

I enjoy her repetition of my words. I lean back and cross one leg over the other. "As in, I'm not going to go hang around the Archives to try to bump into her again, and ask her if she dances in Philadelphia."

"I think that's a prudent decision." She looks down and writes something on her pad.

"I'd be more inclined to go back to that club the next time I get to Philly. I could tell her she's very memorable."

"Do you think she would appreciate that?"

"Wouldn't you?" In a movie, Dr. Flynn would stride across the room and slap me, and the tension would electrify the air.

Instead, she says, "Did you ever go back to the woods? Where Jillian disappeared?"

#

Candy—not her real name, ha ha—is in a bathrobe when I get to her place. She lives in an apartment over a convenience store in Claymont, a couple exits up I-95. I found her in the back page section of an alternative Philly newspaper. She tells me to wash up while she gets ready. This is the downside to going to her place—the shower is not a pretty sight. I wonder if she takes baths in there? I shudder at the thought.

I'm not going to let my visit with Dr. Flynn prevent me from having a good time. Dr. Flynn brings Jillian up fairly often, often enough that I shouldn't be surprised when she does. But when she does, she does so gradually. She asks my permission: "Can we talk about Jillian today?" She's never come at me out of the blue like this afternoon. It feels like a new step in our relationship. It's in the open: She wants to dominate me. Perhaps she believes she can provoke me into saying more.

Later on, when Candy and I are in bed, I ask her if she could bring me a little whiskey. She takes heavy steps into the kitchen and then practically drops the glass on my chest. Once she's been paid and we've had our visit, she wants me to get out. But the lounging is one of my favorite parts.

"Next time, I'm going to ask you to dance a little bit for me," I say.

"Drink up," she says.

I can't stop imagining her submerged in her bathtub, her dead face just below the surface. Like this is a movie where I can see the future, and my awareness of the possibility of her death allows me to prevent it.

It wasn't a movie that put that image in my head though. It was the police, back when Jillian was missing. They questioned me for hours. I was twelve. My mother was fine with it—whatever it took to find Jillian.

I remember the names of every detective who spoke to me. Franklin was the worst. "You watched her drown," he said calmly. "Her face was under the water, but her eyes were open. You kept her down there, and then her eyes were closed." I give him credit for being so poetic about an awful incident. In hindsight, he couldn't have been that bright. You don't close your eyes just because you died.

I get dressed while Candy fixes herself something to eat in the kitchen. The rain has picked up again, tapping at the windows.

"If the police found you dead here, do you think they'd suspect me?" I want to ask, but I know I can't. I keep trying to come up with some variation on that that I could get away with, but nothing doing. The silence is getting weird, so instead I say, "I'm thinking of getting a Breitling watch. Do you think I could pull it off?"

"I've got another appointment sweetie, so we'll have to chat next time." She taps my cheek twice with the palm of her hand, harder than I like, though I'd be laughed at if I called them slaps. "Oh, by the way, my rent is going up. So my prices are going up."

I knew I shouldn't have mentioned the Breitling.

\#

I have around an hour before my extremely pregnant wife is going to get home from work. Ideally, I'd like to sit in front of my stereo and drink a beer and let the day melt away. But on days I visit Candy, I try to step up my husband game so Kate doesn't feel ignored. I stop at the grocery store to buy lobster—one of Kate's favorites—so I can cook dinner for her and surprise her.

I kill the lobsters with compassion on the cutting board in the kitchen, with a knife through the head. Quickly.

Kate used to have a job working for a nonprofit, but then the money dried up. There are too many nonprofits in Delaware anyway. So then she registered for this program in Wilmington, where you get intensive training on programming for several weeks. Now, she's programming for one of the big banks in Wilmington. You better not criticize the banking industry around her. She was always a little more conservative than me, but it shows more now. We had some political debates this past year. She likes Trump. I don't really care anyway.

It's nice and bright in the kitchen as it gets black and dark outside. I turn on the lights in the living room, and downstairs in the family room. I hate it when I'm home alone without Kate and the darkness is all around. For instance, and there's no way I can ever tell her this, I think our house is haunted. I can feel the presence when I look out at our backyard. Sometimes, when I'm mowing, I have to stop and pretend like the machine seized up, because I can't bear to be out there.

The presence seems to be female. Sometimes, when I'm downstairs alone, or if I'm up in the middle of the night to go to the bathroom, I can feel her beside me.

\#

Kate waddles in, eight months pregnant. She looks exhausted, but not unhappy.

She gives me a quick peck on the cheek, and then she notices the kitchen.

"Lobster!" she says. "Oh, honey, thank you. I'll be down in a few minutes."

She goes upstairs to put on her pajamas.

We talk about our days while we eat. She reminds me that the following Thursday, we're going to her ob-gyn after my weekly appointment with Dr. Flynn. I'd like to talk about Breitling watches—should I go for a dressy one, or maybe a big chronograph?—but I decide to wait until after the baby is born.

Later on, Kate lies down on the couch, and I rub her feet before applying nail polish. I think that what I love most about her is that if I told her too much about myself, she would leave. She gives me a normal, pleasant life. From what I've read, I think I'll feel normal when I'm in my mid-fifties. And I'll have a wife of 20 years and a kid just out of college to help me enjoy being alive. I'm looking forward to it.

\#

That is, if I can keep this life going for the next 20 years. It's ten o'clock and Kate is asleep in bed. She used to sleep on her stomach. Now she sleeps on her side, and she snores. My tableside light is on and I have a book open. I'm wide awake, as if all the coffee I drank today is hitting me right this second. I've already had a large tumbler of whiskey, so it looks like I should pour another.

Kate knows that a girl went missing when I was in the sixth grade. But I grew up in Massachusetts, and Kate's not all that curious about it, so that's the extent of her knowledge on the subject.

I creep down the stairs into darkness, and even though I don't want to think about it, I'm thinking about it. I turn on the light in the dining room, where our bar is, and pour myself some more Jack Daniel's.

*

Jillian and I grew up in the same neighborhood, and we used to ride our bikes everywhere. There was this big stretch of woods behind a local development, and we liked to go exploring there. The fall was better, since the poison ivy had died down by then. We would walk instead of riding our bikes, trying to be less conspicuous.

That day, I was throwing stones at a stream. It had rained the day before, so the water in the stream was rushing like a river full of dangerous rapids. I imagined being swept away by the current. Jillian hopped over the stream and kept walking.

I didn't really mind—we got separated in the woods all the time. But then I heard a weird sound. It was like a car door slamming. It didn't make sense, but at the same time, it wasn't that unusual. Sound carried in a weird way in those woods, so we'd hear all sorts of things that were actually far away. It still gave me the heebie-jeebies though, so I hopped over the stream myself to find Jillian.

I followed the path all the way to this clearing, which we usually avoided because older kids hung out there sometimes. I could hear the highway nearby.

I followed the path back out, thinking Jillian must've taken a detour and would be back on it. Still nothing. Finally I went home and told my mother.

The police found Jillian's body that night, around a mile from our path. She was in this deep part of the woods that's pretty hard to get to, because there really isn't a path. It was almost like she sailed along the stream, because she had drowned. The police never arrested anyone for it.

*

I know that experience messed me up. I try to live like it didn't happen. Just a fantasy, as Dr. Flynn says.

I get back into bed. I drink my whiskey steadily, but it doesn't relax me. I'm still wide awake, and I'm thinking of the redhead. The go-go dancer. When I don't know a person, I imagine that we can make a connection. We can have drinks, and feel that spark, and then go out to the woods, where we can be under the sky together. So much sky, and it feels like it's just for the two of you. And all of the things that you keep hidden can come up.

This part of me, it wants to connect with someone who will understand. I know that can never happen though. That's what keeps me in bed, and waiting for my alarm, and being a solid chap.

Acting normal, like nothing happened.

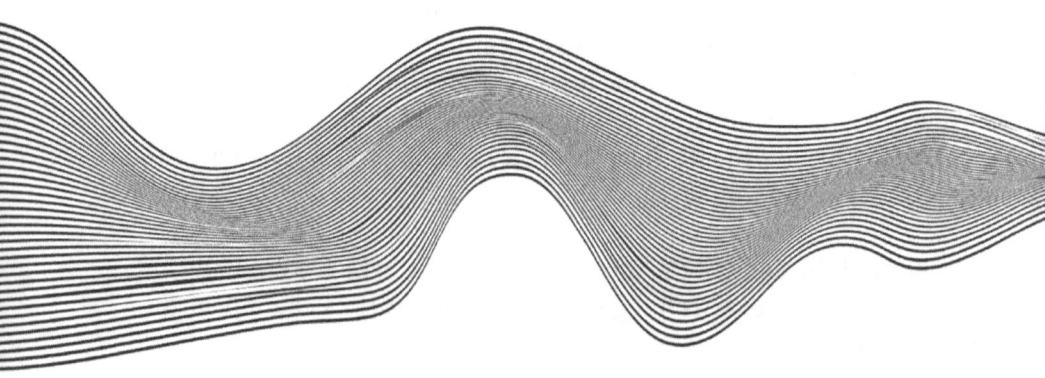

Dear Pylvia Salth

Kay Coolican

I am drunk
& listening to 4:49 a.m.
in the shower again
on repeat, thinking that

if steam handles lips
the way hands
handle match tips, then you

handle me the way
"too" handles "close"

(& there may never be enough
hot water).

Now, think of all the things
we can count on
our fingers

like the certainty of
smoke:

when it fails to leave a
burning thing behind,

we choke.

The Fix

Jennifer Rieger

Nestled in the back corner of my classroom, perfectly adjacent to my much nicer, high-back teacher chair, is a tattered, blue office chair. Before the chair's sad and shabby state, it lived in my extra bedroom, the room I temporarily deemed an "office," while patiently awaiting a whitewashed cradle, changing table, and pastel rocker that were never needed. The chair comforted me and took a beating as I immersed myself in the life of an English teacher and was transported from new house to new house before permanently residing here, in its cinderblock, academic abode, for the past fifteen years.

It's a comfortable swivel chair—cushioned and adjustable, with just the right give for teenagers rocking themselves into a state of peaceful, if somewhat resistant, contentment. That chair has held students struggling with college essays, and students fighting with parents. It's heard stories of learning disabilities, failing grades, unexpected A's, and unplanned pregnancies. The dingy armrests and faded upholstery have supported the most confident and most vulnerable—those reveling in their teenage years and those contending with them.

Somehow, I became a mother to many of the chair's inhabitants. Give me a kid whose problems I could solve with the skills acquired through my English degrees, and I'll give you my new project. Family struggling financially? Have a seat and let's open a Google Doc. We're going to have fun writing scholarship essays. Math teacher giving you a hard time? Let me take a trip downstairs and schmooze him a bit. First love break your heart? I have tissues, chocolate, and a free afternoon of grading procrastination. I hold their hands, wipe tears from their eyes and snot from their faces, and love them as my own. This is the side of teaching they don't tell you about—the side that makes the headaches, heartaches, and the dual caffeine-wine addiction worth it.

My own son, Evan, a grown man now, spent many childhood years watching me compose research papers, literary analyses, and later, lesson plans in that very home office and from the tattered, blue chair. He recently graduated from college with a degree in vocal performance, and he's trying to adjust to the life of a young, struggling artist. My husband, Ryan, and I, having had him at the oh-so-grown up age of nineteen, sometimes wonder where this child came from. He was a funny little kid of intellect and creativity, but also possessed an introverted nature that embraced the adult world, dismissing childhood frivolities.

As he got older, Evan became increasingly contemplative. He's a skeptic—a thinker and a worrier. He holds his cards close and most days you need a chisel and a pickaxe to reach his softer side. But, it's there. In moments of either sheer happiness or extreme disillusionment, when only a mom can suffice, he lets me in. And I love it. These moments are rare though, so when I come across students who I connect with, students who need me, students whose doubts and fears spill out from the safety of that chair, I can't help but make them my own.

I never believed I was supposed to be a mother. How I got pregnant in the first place, the odds were ridiculous! I don't know whether to laugh or cry when I hear of all the fertility treatments my friends have had to endure, while Ryan, in his dashing potency, barely sneezed on me and low and behold, it's a boy! As we juggled the new and peculiar responsibilities of young parenting in a sea of our own college antics and anxieties, we treated Evan as more of a sibling than our child. He attended concerts and parties with us, watched Friends and Seinfeld on Thursday nights, insisted on calling us Jen and Ryan during his entire second year of life, and learned to tap a keg at the age of three. Even in our youthful naiveté, he was loved, intellectually stimulated, and a tad spoiled. But I was also the mom who forgot about show and tell, felt frozen chicken nuggets qualified as a suitable dinner, and spent more time on my career than playing in the yard.

Despite our unconventional parenting style, Evan was still a sweet boy. I read everything to him, from Mother Goose to Shakespeare. He'd climb onto my lap as I worked, sucking his pacifier, curling my hair around his fingers, and ask me to read what I was writing. "Well, you see Evan, once upon a time there was an old king, King Lear, who really wanted people to tell him how great he was. Two of his daughters lied about how much they loved him so that they could get his land, but the third kind and lovely daughter remained loyal and true." His brown eyes would glance up to my face to gauge my seriousness. I'd wink, and he'd go back to weaving his chubby fingers through my hair.

My career progressed and years seemed to merge, along with many student faces. I devoted the majority of my time to them, whether it was helping with assignments, attending their games, or listening to their problems. Time passed. At the age of thirty-four, my window was closing. I knew if I wanted another baby, I couldn't wait. I read books, I talked to other mothers, and I went off the pill. But instead of a baby, doctors found a ten-pound tumor in my uterus—a mass slowly taking over my body, and destroying a decision I had put off for years.

It hasn't been until recently, after turning forty, when I started pondering that closed window once again, paying attention to this older body, hearing the whispers I've tried to block out—aged eggs that I still possess haunting me from the very ovaries I decided to keep when the surgeon took my uterus. I can hear them, small baby voices, ticking off every hour, every day, every year, trying so hard to team up with errant sperm. Those baby-ghosts love to whisper, hypnotizing me every time I smell a newborn's head or look at Facebook posts of toddlers splashing in bathtubs and playing in pumpkin patches. But the truth is, those whispers are small echoes of a life that wasn't supposed to be, a life I unknowingly abandoned when I stepped foot in a classroom and used my time to start caring for other people's children.

Those whispers taunt from some innate, ancestral, maybe even mystical place of wonder that, surely, I'll never understand. What I do understand is the transformative value—how to use those voices to repair others and bring meaning to my life. For every Chloe, Anna, Brian, Andrew, and Alex rocking in that blue chair, I have purpose. I am able to fix the naïve transgressions of young motherhood with a kind of cosmic redo. I take in their doubts, their pain, their love, and relish their comfort and happiness when I console and dole out advice. They hug me, and thank me, and tell me that I'm the one who got them through.

I laugh. If only they knew.

If only they knew that at night, when I contemplate all of my inevitable graduation goodbyes, all of my children who will leave me, I wind up curled in Ryan's arms. He strokes my hair and reminds me that I'm loved, that there will be other kids who need me, that this isn't the end. If only they knew that in the dark hours of sleepless mornings, I sometimes find myself sitting in my home office, the room I had hoped would be a nursery, and I stare out the window thinking that while I do love my students, all 2,323 of them, I'm no hero. I'm just a mom looking for a way to quiet the echoes.

Content Warning: Pantoum

Alejandro Escudé

We warn you this video may contain graphic images,
the man is a blood-chalice, the woman is saying sir
and the uniform stands firm as the camera captures
the road, elbows and hands, the zip-zip of cuffs.

The man is a blood-chalice, an alphabet of red, sir
you shot my boyfriend, she says, don't tell me he's gone.
The crying baby is somewhere suspended in dread
over a road of hardened elbows, hands, zip-zip of cuffs.

You shot my boyfriend, she says, don't tell me he's gone,
the uniform stands firm, the woman is saying sir
on a road of interlocking elbows, the zip-zip of cuffs.
We warn you this video may contain graphic images.

We warn you this video may contain graphic images.
The policemen approach from angles, spider-like,
the camera to the woman's face, her voice unravelling
as she summons the facts, "You shot four bullets…"

From angles, the policemen approach, spider-like,
saying "sort" and "out," as if death were not final.
The man is a man no more, a head-tossed savior,
his body like a white bloody blanket over the seat.

Saying "sort" and "out," as if death were not final,
the uniform stands firm as the camera captures
his body like a white bloody blanket over the seat.
We warn you this video may contain graphic images.

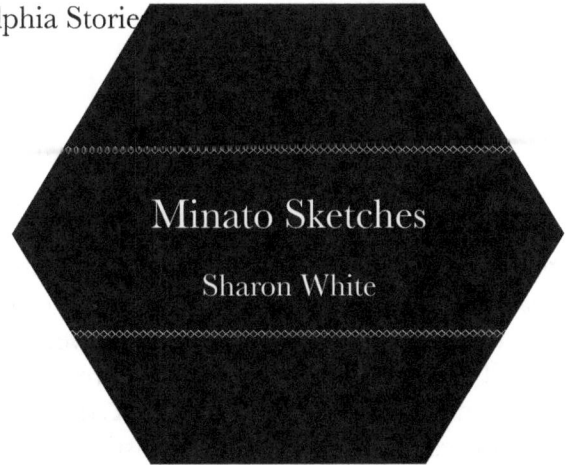

Minato Sketches

Sharon White

1.

She kept reading about how all the paper houses had burned. But as she came down out of the clouds, she saw shiny fields, wet with a sheen of green water and the spikey hills she remembered. The villages tucked into crevices between the islands of trees and rocks and fields. There were certainly paper houses hidden along the shining river. And more were folded in the curves and lumps of the hills. Long white birds announced their presence with their silence and the squat bodies of cormorants raced down the dark rivers once she got to the city. Everything was different. The last few years replaced with concrete that somehow seemed more alive than she remembered. So the woman who told her about the fires was right. The houses had vanished. In the morning she watched as armies of pedestrians marched to work. Their faces placid with sleep. One eyebrow raised here, another foot placed there. Such precision and pizazz. Every now and then someone would break rank and get a coffee at one of the cafes, mildly folding and unfolding a paper. Picking a white cup off a table and then putting it down.

2.

She ended up on a street with noodle stalls. None of them had any faith. She knew, after all, that they had to kill Jesus for him to be a savior. Military men were at every corner. And the large blue fish in tanks displayed along the walls slept. She could see them breathing in the dusk of their containers. Men in white shirts and black pants jostled against each other, banging their brief cases on their thighs. Everything was lit with a burning core. These men had been at work forever. Toting their bags from home to trains to the office to the narrow streets where the food was displayed on plastic cards or in bowls with plastic wrap. Old women beckoned costumers in at the doors. Huge signs with beautiful letters hung from every open window. So many drunk men rubbing their bellies, dancing in knots close to each other just about to fight. No English here, one sign said. Inside the stall it was quiet. A cook cocked his head and looked away. It was cool, so cool she pulled her sweater closer. She'd left two grown boys and a husband in a country far away, governed by an idiot in a red coat. Everything was alive around her and no one was quiet.

3.

Her new boss said I'm part Cherokee and part Quebecois. I have great friends all over the world, some from my youth hanging out at Johnson Pond. I have many more friends than you do and have held important positions. I'm a denizen of this place, a wow guy, why do you think I got this job? Look at my desk, my legions of pictures of families close to me, for sure I'm close to my brother and sister, too. We get together every year in Maine. I've lived most of my life away, but you know Maine is certainly what I call home. An old house on the green, the view of the ocean from the porch, the sound of gulls in the morning, the children skating on the pond in winter, the smell of woodsmoke. My history goes like this: I, like you, have moved from institution to institution always here, mostly here, but bigwig positions, nothing less. Have you had a stroke, he asked, I know I may have seen that in your documents. Are you sure you haven't had a stroke? She adjusted her smile and said, it was a mild one, a mild one. I have no visible residue. But she knew residue was not the right word. Visible signposts, perhaps, a certain look, the way her family inserted one word or two when they had a chance, the way her little dog looked at her with distrust. It all got to be too much. That country so far away, their loving hands guiding her down stairs, past beggars in the street and gangs of motorcycle thugs prowling the boulevards where they lived. They went to a place in the north one winter soon after her stroke and stayed in an inn where the sheets were very white and they left chocolate on your bed at night. So sweet. They ate in the dining room and she brought her little white dog with her. The dog slept under the table and she could see other holidaymakers snatching looks at her from their beautifully set tables. There were people singing in another room and lights twinkling in the trees outside. Her husband and sons were happy, skiing during the day, and she could sit on the little porch in the sun with her white dog and think about nothing, nothing at all. There was no struggle to find any words. She was in the first months of her therapy and it was difficult to say anything. She could hardly smile. Don't worry darling, her husband said, we'll get you back to normal in no time and she would shake her head. She knew there was no normal around the corner. Her therapist had her draw a clock and she knew from her face, even if she said that's great Gigi, that's great, that she had somehow gotten it wrong, terribly wrong. She studied flashcards and did homework for what felt like hours. She was instructed to substitute one word for another, but she'd never been much of a poet and isn't that what they did? She used to love to tell stories and she could see the painful look on her younger son's face when they were all silent at the dinner table, her boys back from one college or another. One job or another and it was her husband, who used to be the quiet one, who carried the conversation like a suitcase.

4.

She had days before the program started so she went to a garden. She had admired this garden in books for years. When she was in this country years ago she was more interested in the mechanics of love than gardens. A brief affair, a few weeks of doing nothing but fucking on the floor in a narrow apartment where everything was miniature. It took her weeks to realize she wasn't in love at all, just enamored of the idea. It was so far away, so far away from the kind of life she normally lived. And she loved the burning bite of sake and how it made her feel. How loved he made her feel, split off from the self she thought she knew, even if she didn't know what she was capable of doing. She didn't know that later when she had her stroke, years later, she wouldn't know who she was at all and the sorting chambers of her brain would disintegrate so she couldn't even talk to her little dog. Her little dog who she sometimes thought she loved above all else, her little dog with the pure white paws.

It was a garden of Waka poetry. The paths circled the pond in the middle of the garden like a magic incantation. Each viewing spot was a bell. A way to inspire memory. A key to the locked room where the words lived. Precious Seaweed Shore. Her days at the Cape with her mother and father and her brothers and sisters. The days burning to a crisp on the sand, cold as hell in the water. Those hours playing in the brook that went down to the sea, the horseshoe crabs moving so slowly along the bottom, waving their blunt spears back and forth. Her brothers stoning the rabbit to death one day when they went to visit cousins two towns away.

Ebb Tide Harbor, her life now.

It took her months before she could draw the clock on the blank piece of paper correctly. Now she watched a man measure bamboo stakes precisely and then saw them off and then hammer them with a wooden mallet into the ground along the edge of the mossy verge of the lake. He measured three times and then cut. She watched him happily. She was definitely happy, sitting on the wooden bench in the old garden. Very old, she knew, early 1700s. Two of the ponds were gone now, but the impression of the water on the surface of the earth remained.

5.

She wanted a resurrection. She knew that was blasphemous to want to so much. She wanted to be struck new with life. Instead God sent her lightening in her brain. And even if the doctors kept saying she'd be fine, she didn't think this state was fine. She was such a talker. She could talk the ear off anyone, couldn't she? Her sons knew that. And as she traveled more and more with her husband and they could do anything they wanted, she had so many stories to tell.

When her mother got sick it was up to them to take care of her, first in her older boy's room and then in the facility down the road. It was a place with trees around it. The only place in miles with a grove of trees. Her mother didn't care at that point that the two rooms looked out at trees, but she did.

It just seemed too much some times. The world was crumbling at the edges. A tyrant had taken over the country and the government was in shambles and then her mother started to say less and less. A kind of imitation of Gigi's stroke, but much worse. She wouldn't come back from this descent into silence.

She brought her meat sauce in a silver thermos. Morsels of chicken in foil. Beautiful sweet ripe clementines. Armfuls of farmer's market flowers. Her mother stopped eating, her mother stopped moving, her mother stopped doing anything at all. And what was there to do? Her mother didn't remember the soap operas she'd spent her life watching or the news at 6:30 or anything really. She was afraid she would forget who her daughter was. But she didn't. Her sister came and stayed with her those last months. Her mother took forever to die. She's just doing it on her own time, the kind nurse with the polished copper skin and tiny eyes told her. The books can only tell you the average time. The average time was two weeks, her mother wanted ten months and she took it.

6.

She'd had a bitter fight with him before she left. Her husband said, "I sacrificed all my waking hours to your rehabilitation and this is what you want to do now that I've got you back?"

"I was still myself, when you thought I wasn't here," she said. "I was still myself all those hours when you were away. I was with the boys in my heart, wasn't I? I fought hard to get back to what you thought you wanted me to be."

But it was all so dramatic, she thought. The simple thing was there were two of her now. The woman he'd loved for so many years and the one who went away. Went away in her head, all the words mismatched, unavailable for the moment. Not useful.

"You're not the same," he said, "not the same at all if you keep this cockamamie idea in your head and leave us again."

"I can't believe you said cockamamie," she said and then they started to laugh. Everything was so ridiculous after all. There was the tyrant as president, the marches in the street, people with different kinds of hats parading in every town, marching and chanting. Flags waving on every corner. The terrifying blasts in even places you'd think would be safe. Knife attacks on subways. It was a relief to be somewhere like where she was then. Military men, and sometimes women, stationed at subways and street corners and outside of train stations to guide your way. The soft patter of rain, now that the monsoon season was warming up. She was not in the same world, but it didn't matter. No one knew who she was before and she'd gotten the job on her own without the help of her husband or sons or even her little white dog, who she missed terribly.

She'd taken the train to a part of the city with twenty temples. Arched wooden temples with deities who might be sympathetic to her. It was kind of Zen to walk slowly around the village on her own through the vast cemeteries and narrow streets that were spared war and fire and bombing. The hydrangea were in bloom. Delicate lace bright blue like the sky. She met a girl with an owl. A pet owl, three months old. A baby, the girl told her. For a few yen, she could pet it. But it was enough to look at the owl as the bird swiveled her head back and forth. The soft whirl of spotted caramel feathers around her face. The owl's deep black eyes shining as she looked into them and the owl didn't flinch. The bird was perfectly calm. There was a world there that was very different from the one she'd fled. Serene, astonishing, filled with peace.

7.

She talked to a man at the faculty meeting who told her she should get a car, borrow someone's to go to the big international store at the edge of the city. She could get chairs there, you could get anything really. It was stupid to take a train or a bus there, it didn't make sense. After all what were cars for, if not to transport people to places where they could buy things, he laughed. He was thin and wore a white tunic. He had beads around his neck and his hair was as white as his clothes. Everything about him was impermanent, a little foggy. She could hardly hear him when he spoke. I used to teach physics, but now I teach music and yoga. Like the music of the spheres, she said, so that makes sense. He leaned in close to her, yes. The room was filled with men. There were hardly any women. She followed a man with an umbrella out of the building to an annex across the narrow street up the elevator. Are you one of the faculty she asked, or a parent and he said quickly, I'm the CFO. You're a bigwig, then, she said. When the door opened he vanished down a corridor and shut the door.

A woman in the business office opened a brown packet filled with the first edition of her pay and fanned the money out on the desk in front of her. The solemn faces of someone famous in this country glared at her from the surface of the gray desk. There were so many shades of gray in the city.

She was making a garden on her balcony. It was just big enough for several small pots and it looked out at the canals. Someone had planted a spring garden along the paved walkway that ran along the bank. She was on an island of concrete in the concrete city. One man at the meeting told her during the last earthquake everything swayed and then was still. He likes to wear women's clothes, another man told her.

8.

At one of the temples she visited she put coins at the foot of several minor gods who wore pink caps. They were standing guard along the fence to the temple near their leader, a much larger statue with a pink apron around his neck. There were crows the size of eagles carrying pieces of toast and little birds who flew through the towering trees faster than she could imagine. She missed her husband. He would have laughed at the pink hats. He was pretty irreverent about everything. A woman was pushing a cart filled with willow brooms and wooden buckets marked with black calligraphy. For holy water, she thought. Bouquets of fading flowers defaced the graves. Why didn't someone take them away once they started dying? Bundles of wires crisscrossed the sky above her head as she walked into a tiny alley where they were selling juice and puffy buns with cream. She hadn't been hungry in such a long time, but the buns were soft and warm in her mouth. It was a relief to be alone. She didn't have to search for the words she wanted, she could let whatever came to the surface be what she wanted to say. Penguin. Pigeon. Parrot.

9.

Men with white gloves drove the cabs in the city. The seats covered with white lace. The white ghosts followed her when she went to the 100 yen store where the checkout person, a lively woman, told her there were so many foreigners in the neighborhood, or took the little bus to the hills north of where she was living. When she was watching her mother die all those months, her little white dog came with her. She waited for morsels of food her mother dropped on the rug or the crumbs from the tiny pieces of bread her mother ate. One day her dog noticed something on the ceiling. Her son thought it was angels. The angels come to lead her mother to heaven. She laughed, "Really" she said. "I didn't think you believed in any of that stuff."

"Really mom," he said, laughing, "look at the way Tinker's acting."

She was acting strange circling her mother's hospital bed, sniffing under the covers, whining at the ceiling. It was comforting in a way that angels were there to help her mother, when no one had been around when Gigi'd had her stroke. She was making lunch, something heated up in a pan. A strange thing to do, but there it was. Lunch was in her hand, she was walking across the kitchen, her beautiful white kitchen with jars arranged on the shelves, and the shining silver refrigerator, and then she fell. Lightning and then nothing. When she could see again she dragged herself across the kitchen floor to the hallway and then to the living room. Her phone was on a table in the immaculate room. It took her hours to reach her phone and when she got through to her husband all she could do was make a noise, a simple noise that she thought sounded like help me, but her husband said much later, months later, was more like a croak.

10.

It was hard to go a day even so far away from where most of her life had been without her mother appearing in some way before her eyes. She'd been persistently haunting her for her whole life. A woman who wanted perfection in everyone but herself. Gigi took the little bus to hills north of where her apartment was in the largest city in the world. The librarian at the university had told her about a museum with a small, perfect garden. She walked aimlessly in the direction of where she thought the museum was past women with their perfect faces, their gloved hands clutching bags from expensive stores. Each one accompanied by her mother. A woman who was an older version of themselves, but just as perfectly dressed in shades of cream, or gray or delicate floral.

On the bus, she'd met a woman who told her how to get to the museum. I'm going that way, I'll show you, she said. Her English was impeccable. They walked quickly along the wide boulevard. "And you live in the dormitory of the university?" the woman asked.

"No," Gigi laughed. "I live near the bay, in an apartment."

"How nice," she said. "But you're very brave to spend the summer in Tokyo."

"The heat?"

"Yes," she said. "The heat, the humidity. It's really quite terrible."

"What do you do?" She asked the woman, who was wearing navy. Her short stylish hair framing her face.

"I'm a guide," she said. And she laughed. "I'll leave you here, I'm going to the market. Have a wonderful summer. You should really stop at the market after the museum. It's my favorite museum."

She wondered if everything in her life was an echo of her mother and if, since her mother's death, everything was a shadow of that same echo. In the museum she spent an hour studying many hanging paper scrolls with squares of poetry framed by paper, adorned with gold flecks. Saturated with the color of the sky or the moon or the sun. In another room there were tea bowls with names, famous tea bowls celebrated for their misshapen beauty.

There was a Buddha in the garden sitting quietly when everyone else was circling the garden, taking pictures. The Buddha sat on the edge of the flowing stream, before it cascaded to the pond where two turtles overlapped on a rock. Stretching their green streaked necks out, sunning. It was much cooler in the garden, she wished she'd worn a sweater.

11.

She met her new boss again in the street when she was looking for lunch. He was pushing a bike. A young woman, very beautiful, was trailing behind.

"How are you?" She asked.

"Great. I'm going to work out and she's going home. You know they're here to review me. I thought I'd look for a putter. When those meetings are taking place on Friday, I'll be playing golf with Fred Olson. But I need a golden putter. When I played with Tony Mashimito he had the putter to end all putters and he beat me like that. He gave a ton of money to the school. I want to be ready this time. I've got to step up my game."

There were children all around them as the young woman smiled shyly. She was dressed in a silky flowered frock. He was in a polo shirt and shorts. His bike was black. His teeth seemed to be broken, or cut off at the ends.

Such an unfortunate mouth. She couldn't imagine him kissing the young woman who walked behind as he pushed the bike. But you never knew about these things.

12.

She knew her mother's body too well after those months taking care of her. She would guide her into the shower, turn the water on and then hose her off with the handheld shower. Her mother's skin was still firm. The pounds she'd accumulated over all those years of life gleaming on her bones. After those months in the facility when she refused to eat, things changed.

She wakes to bright light, almost burning white here, very early in the morning. At the Cape when she was young, not so young, just after she graduated from college, the first time she had a hard time calling up words, she would visit her aunt and uncle and stay in a bedroom in the basement. Right on a marsh. It was the light then that called her to the ocean. A brilliant burning on the waves, the salt spray on her tongue in the morning. A kind of crystalline definition of the birth of the day.

The city presses down around her after her days in the foreign country. The ambulances politely calling out to pedestrians to please move away from the vehicle, the women in the department store showing her all the attributes of the pillow she wants to buy anyway. They instruct her to try it out, her head on a piece of gauze covering the pillow, her feet placed on a sheet of plastic at the foot of the bed. When the transaction is finished the two women dressed smartly in tailored clothes, like a uniform, bow and thank her over and over again.

It's the time of the year when trains are delayed in the city. The electric screens in the subway announce passenger injury several times a day. Or antelope on the tracks. Gigi thinks it's a problem with translation. Could there really be antelope in this country? The term passenger injury means someone has jumped. It's just a euphemism for death, several people at the faculty meeting told her. It's a bad time of year for that. The raining season coming up, the brutality of the spring. Everything blossoming. New life. She'd read in the news that pigeons had been arrested for carrying little backpacks with pills sewn into the fabric. The backpacks were miniature and fashioned to look like their feathers. The pigeons didn't know they were drug mules. They just loved to fly.

13.

In a prefecture north of the city there were radioactive wild boars. Thousands of animals with blunt noses and fierce eyes. Hundreds of hunters had tracked them down and killed them but not enough to clear the cities. She was curious. Her days in the sparkling city were lining up into something she couldn't define. It was the first day of classes. Someone was pounding on the floor above her apartment, shaking the ceiling.

A friend had lost her husband once in in the aftermath of an earthquake. She was visiting a place where they were building a beautiful resort on the sea. Her two girls were with her. She and her husband had gone to take a look at the resort. The girl's godfather was part owner. The girls were up in the hills with a friend exploring. When the tsunami hit, their parents had to run for dry land and their father spotted the skeleton of a building. He led a group of people wearing only their bathing suits to the top floor. It was too much for him and he died there, already prone to a weak heart. Her friend had to cover him with someone's flowered wrap and leave him there while she searched for her daughters. She thought she'd lost her family to the water.

"I didn't know if they were alive," she told her. "Until I heard from a friend who I met days later that the girls were with another friend, safe and well in another part of the island. It changed everything for me. And then we all went back to the place where Andrew died and brought his body into town."

14.

One of her students, a solemn boy from India, told her he almost died climbing the sacred mountain. You were supposed to be able to see it from the city, a perfectly shaped cone with snow on the top. But she'd been lost in the concrete caverns for days now and couldn't understand how you could see the mountain from the city. It rose up, she knew, from the plains below. A stark reminder of the majesty of geography.

Her student, Goreesh, was climbing the mountain with six friends. They were ill equipped and cold by the time they got to the shoulder of the mountain. There was a hut where they paid a huge amount to sleep on hard pillows and wrapped themselves in one thin blanket. He was not feeling well. Maybe it was the altitude, he thought, and his friends wanted to give up. But he went ahead in time to see the sunrise. He was so tired, he told her, that he slipped at the edge of a ravine and was almost never heard from again. And he was so young. His mother would have been bereft and his friends very unhappy, but he caught himself and they all went on to reach the top. It took them 18 hours to climb the mountain.

She was thinking perhaps she should tell the man she'd met at the faculty meeting that she would take him up on his offer to find a car. She wanted to go somewhere, anywhere out of the city. Was there something wrong with that? She was thinking she wanted to go to the prefecture with the wild boars. There were deer there and hawks and other animals gathered in a place with lots of grain and fruit trees and tender shoots to eat. A ripening away from human habitation. She thought it would be interesting to catch a glimpse of that. The authorities were trying to convince the people who'd fled to return to the place they'd left.

Her husband had been calling her, trying to convince her to come home. "You can use your health," he said, "as an excuse. Tell them you didn't realize how stressful the trip would be."

"But I'm fine," she said. "And I don't want to come home yet. This is important to me even if you think it's stupid."

"I'm not important to you?" he asked. It was his night and her morning. There was no way they could talk about this. It was yesterday there and today here. They were not even on the same globe, somehow. She heated up the water on the stove. Watered her collection of plants on the tiny balcony while it heated and looked down at the canal flowing in and out of the bay. The bay was once barricaded from foreign ships.

Her long rehabilitation had seemed like it would never end, but she was passionate about being able to talk again. And she did, but not in the way she thought she would.

15.

If there was a story to tell she couldn't remember it some days. And what of the man with the white hair and the white stones around his throat and the white clothes. What was his story, she wondered, as she walked past the temple and then up the hill that wound pass the Friends

School and the expensive looking houses and tiny gardens to the boulevard
that led to her apartment. Everything was miniature in her place. The
chairs, the lamps, the glasses, the forks. That's what her mother's life was
like those last weeks, something that had spread out to several houses and
states and countries and shrunk to one room. A bed, a chair, a TV she
didn't watch anymore, a sink, a toilet, a brush.

Sometimes there was music that came out of thin air. Like the words
she lost all those years ago. Or was it so long ago? There were children
with pink hats holding their mother's hands as she came up to her
building. A monk kneeling in the garden, touching the roses one by one. A
man feeding two cats by the canal. Was everything a gesture of something
else? Her mother's hand fading in her hand as she watched. Her eyes
disappearing. Everything sinking into the white sheet of the bed, until
finally even her teeth seemed to have disappeared.

17.

What are you doing up? She texted back to her son.

Woke up. No reason, he texted back.

How are you?

Fine.

Just fine mom?

Great. Really great, she texted and added a heart.

Love you mom, he said, miss you.

Miss you sweetheart. Nite nite

Nite, mom.

It was her sons she thought of when she thought she was dying. She
wanted to go back to the time just after the lightening. Just fall back into
blackness, but the thought of her sons pulled her across the floor and into
the bedroom where she'd left her phone. Just that thought. Her love for
her sons. She didn't want to leave them just yet. And though she loved her

husband dearly, it wasn't the thought of him alone that pulled her back to the living. Not that at all.

18.

He'd always wanted to go off to the wilderness. When he was in high school it was the west. He'd talked a friend into driving with him to Oregon. They took three days driving nonstop. And it was wild out there. Trees packed into the land along the ocean as thick as thieves. They camped near the beach even though it was illegal. What did they care. They'd grown up in a town not far away from a place with perpetual underground fires. The catacombs of coalmining. He studied physics because it was a language he could understand. It translated the wilderness into numbers. There was something comforting in that. Evidence that there was still mystery in the world. Why did he fall out of love with that language? He supposed the woman he met at the faculty meeting was right. It was just a continuation of his obsession with the music of the spheres that pushed him into yoga and dance. He fingered the beads around his neck. You're just an old hippie, that bastard Bryan, had said to him yesterday. He could hear the big headed jerk telling a student even though he had a letter that said he could miss as many classes as he wanted, it wouldn't stand up in his class. Anxiety was no excuse.

He'd been in this country now for how long, Bryan had asked him, and he still hadn't achieved enlightenment.

It was the path that mattered, Richard thought, the path was the only reason for anything, wasn't it? Right now he was hell bent on getting to see those radioactive boars and the wilderness grown up in the prefecture. He'd heard that Chernobyl was the same way. The animals taking over the landscape, even though the radiation was off the charts in their bodies. His tea was cool now and he placed the cup on the low table in his apartment. It was the beginning of summer. The morning light blazing at 5 on his face as he sat on the narrow balcony and looked down into the water of the canal.

19.

She woke every morning with all her molecules lit. That's what it felt like. Her body more alive than it had felt in years. The whole city was on fire. Fire bombed, fire forged from disaster at one point or another. And then shaped again with concrete. When she walked along the canal she saw men sitting on benches before they went to their offices. Their eyes closed, leaning against the back of the bench or bent forward, the slim egret and brave heron slicing past them in the air. One man bent over his dark trousers fanning his legs with a paper fan spread wide, picking lint off the dark fabric, another fed two cats crouched by the edge of a building. On her way to the university she passed a shrine. She could hear the monk beating a drum with a stick, a ringing sound that filled her with peace.

It was such a long time before she could put a sentence together after lightning struck her that time. After her stroke. Her therapist had sheet after sheet of exercises for her to do. Filling in sentences like a fourth grader. Dredging up grammar from the depths of her brain. Sometimes it felt like there was nothing there anymore. No word for key, or apple, or car. The trick was to search for nearby words that might give someone else some idea of what she wanted to say. It was a game. A trick. A way to pretend she was normal.

She stopped teaching. It was difficult enough to remember the word for son or husband, let alone plinth or column. But here she was teaching the history of art to five students from all over the place really. In the city for one reason or another.

"It's such a short course," she said to her husband and sons. "I'll just be away for a couple of months."

"That's a joke, mom," her older son said. "You'll be most of the way around the world."

"You're so bored with us you want to get that far away?" Her husband asked and laughed. He was stirring sauce on the stove. Her older boy was setting the table. Jobs she once did without thinking.

When the occupational therapist had her make tomato sauce, she couldn't remember how to use a spoon and picked up the smallest knife to stir the pot. This interchange of one thing for another was maybe not so bad. What did it matter anyway? In this country you used chopsticks.

20.

She passed a green phone booth almost every day. You could make a call there to someone in this country or internationally. She couldn't remember the last time she's seen a call box in her country. Country of ignorant men, country of tyrants and cars. Country of hate, country of bores. She wanted to make a celestial call. Every day she thought about her mother. What a strange thing to do. Her mother had been a pain in the neck, really, but still she was her mother and she missed her like she'd miss a hand or a foot or an ear. In all the stories she'd read there was a way to get what you wanted. And even if you failed, the story was the challenge. She wasn't sure what she wanted anymore. For so long it was to talk again, to be part of the conversation.

Even if she opened the door to the phone box she wouldn't know her mother's number wherever she was. It was unlisted surely.

She passed a little girl with a pink hat as she walked away from the phone. She passed a man playing a song on a harmonica, something from a Broadway musical. She passed a little dog with soft pointed ears and bent to pet her. She's six, her owner said. She was the first person Gigi had encountered on her walks who spoke English. She's so cute.

She could feel the dog's bones through her shining fur.

She passed a woman with orange shoes walking two dogs on two leashes who had bright orange booties. She passed the gray birds quarrelling in the trees along the canal and a woman picking berries from a bush.

If she picked up the phone and heard her mother's voice what would she say? There were so many things to tally up as mistakes or losses. But here she was in a country that had lost so much. Whole cities obliterated, wiped clean in the war.

21.

"I just like reading," her student said. "I don't watch TV. I'll be reading and the tea will boil or the dog will want to go out and I just can't put the book down. The phone will ring, I still have a landline, or the doorbell will chime and I just can't put the book down. The house will shake, or I'll have to go to the bathroom, and I just won't put the book down. Even when my father died, I couldn't put the book I was reading down. It was about a princess. She'd fled to the mountains with her brave samurai general and a loyal handmaid. Her father had raised her like a boy instead of a girl. She was real swashbuckler. Prancing around in the mountains, her gold hidden, her dynasty in ruins. The samurai had offered up his sister, disguised as the princess on a platter, to save the royal line. The revolutionaries thought they had killed the princess and let down their guard. This was in oh, I think, about 1600, so it was cold in the mountains and the princess was hidden in a cave. She wasn't content to stay there, though, and spent much of her time thwarting her own attackers, two peasants who had stumbled on two bars of gold in a stream. It all ended happily. That's what I'm most worried about. Will everyone make it alive out of the story and get back into their lives."

The student was from somewhere in England, somewhere in the north, Gigi thought. She was round like a ball and her head stood on top of her shoulders framed by blond hair. One of the other students, a boy, was her friend. He had tattoos down both of his arms, an insignia like an anchor on his neck. They needed the course to fulfill their art requirement, but they weren't really interested in the subject. Gigi tried to make it interesting by showing movies and slides in elaborately constructed powerpoints. Her husband had helped her put things together before she left. Just follow the word on the powerpoint and you'll be fine, he said. They don't know the difference between a portico and a plinth, so it won't matter if you mess up now and then.

She knew she didn't tell her husband enough how much she loved him. That was the problem, wasn't it? She was afraid he'd wake up some morning and realize he had poured so much wine into her chalice and all she did was drink and drink and never distribute the goods to the congregation. She didn't say thank you enough for the hours he spent drilling her on vocabulary or the walks up and down the corridor of the rehab place until she could walk straight and not list to the side. Until she could get up off the floor on her own and the director said she was certainly ready to home.

Her student pulled a flowered kerchief out of her bag and wiped her face. Her friend laughed. Just like the woman on the train, he said. Not quite, she said, and tucked the piece of cloth back into her cotton tote.

Gigi had watched a mother and daughter share a handkerchief on the train, too. It was something people seemed to do in this country. The had shared hand lotion and then used the cloth to wipe the excess off of their hands. It was such an intimate thing to do. She had never had that kind of relationship with her mother. Her mother was always the princess. Her sister the handmaiden. The night before she'd dreamed of her mother, young and beautiful on the arm of her father. They were going to a party. She smelled of the spicy perfume her mother always wore. Her lips were painted bright red. She wore slim shoes. Her father smelled of aftershave. They were all glitter. Her brother had a tantrum after they left, and she told the babysitter to just ignore him. He'd turn blue and then settle down. He wouldn't choke to death.

22.

She found, by chance, a small shrine tucked into the corner of a lane. It was a surprise that there were still these crooked lanes in a city that was so big you could drive for hours and still not escape it. She'd had a conversation about escape with Richard, her colleague who taught the music of the spheres. He really looked angelic, she thought. Spare, white, robed in the lightest of clothes. A kind of Zen impression of a catholic angel. He was one of the few people who seemed at all interested in her. Which was just as well. When she was anxious it was harder to call up the words she wanted. Her students were an incurious bunch of kids, so she hardly ever had to answer questions. She just walked herself through the information on the slides and pointed out the important details of whatever piece of art she was talking about and everything went smoothly.

The shrine was reinforced with concrete, covered with wood. Incense was burning. It was in the cool corner of a shady place. She'd read that the deities with the pink caps and pink bibs were in memory of lost children. This deity had a stained bib, the same kind she used on her two boys when they were babies. There were fresh flowers and sticks of incense in a little box. She slipped a coin into the slatted box at the foot of the shrine and picked up the slender stick of incense. She had lost a baby before her two boys were born, one and then the other not long after the first. It was a surprise to get pregnant so easily when she was not that young and then it was a loss so great she thought she wouldn't recover for an instant when she sat with her husband in the waiting room and the doctor told them that the baby was gone, the slip of child just disappeared on the ultrasound.

Richard had told her he wanted to drive north to see the wild boars in the prefecture that had the earthquake and tsunami a few years ago. It was sort of a wacky thing to want to do, he told her, but then he never had much of a liking for normality. Even growing up. That's probably why he ended up leaving the country even before things got so bad. He thought if he had stayed he would've ended up in jail, certainly, since that's where most of his relatives worked. The huge buildings that took up so much space near the town where he was born.

23.

He only wanted to write about himself, her student told her, how his brain was on fire. How he couldn't escape the thoughts in his brain, like someone hitting on the wall in his room and shaking it minute after minute. He wanted to clear out who he was and become someone else. He'd thought he would be a filmmaker, but that didn't look like a good idea. He just didn't get along in groups. He couldn't talk.

"But you're talking to me right now," she said.

"Yes, but it's just you and me."

He wanted to be screenwriter, he thought, then he could work alone. She didn't want to tell him at that point, the fluorescent bulbs in the classroom humming, shades tilted to let in the blazing light of noon, that everyone had to talk to someone unless you were a hermit and what chance was there of doing that in this place or this time?

She had gone to a poetry reading with her older son not long before she'd left the country and the poet told a story about his boyfriend who was living for a few weeks in a community of people who raised their own food, meditated on their lives, and went off into caves now and then to think. It was in the southern part of the country. A place where she was afraid once hiking in the woods and she had to avoid a man with gun who followed her for miles. Tracked her like a deer. The police called the poet, who wasn't as famous as he would become, and told him his boyfriend had committed suicide. It wasn't anything the poet expected his lover to do, so he called the coroner's office and had the report sent. Suspected suicide, but several irregularities, the report said. Someone at he sheriff's office said, No, it was definitely a suicide. The poet was even more suspicious and composed poem after poem about the tragedy. Years later filmmakers got interested in the case and read the coroner's report and then interviewed the coroner. The poet's boyfriend had been tied up, beaten, and then burned. It was certainly not a case of suicide.

Outside her window she could hear the blackbirds chattering on the trees below the balcony that lined the canal. They were squeaking and whistling, arguing over the berries that looked like mulberries. She had read the last empress of the country had raised silkworms and had her subjects spin silk. The empress also wrote 30,000 poems.

When she told her son, he said, "But mom, they were very small poems, weren't they? It's not like she was writing epics."

When the
Music Ends
Barbara Daniels

Years after your death a magazine
emailed: "We want you back, Viola."
Today, a little morning rain. You told me
before you met Dad you walked sedately
past the bank where he worked, turned
the corner, took off your shoes, and ran.
Why he married you: that blazing hair.
When I looked like an egg, no eyebrows,
no lashes, some people laughed at me.
Just last night a waitress said, "Sorry, sir,"
mistaking my tousled hair and androgynous
shirt. My streaming service wrote me:
"When your music ends, we will continue
to play music you should like." Hair
doesn't grow in the grave, but it should,
shouldn't it? As you were dying, your friend
said, "You have the best hair in the building."
Still red in your ninety-ninth year. When I die,
my atoms could leap into fingers and feet.
I might be somebody's shining hair. It's raining,
but softly. Mahler's third symphony plays.

The Lucky Ones

Kara Daddario Bown

On my last day of radiation, I sat eagerly awaiting my release from six months of treatment. In anticipation, my eyes scanned the fluorescently lit, crowded waiting room of Abramson Cancer Center. As I waited for my name to be called for the last time, I thought about the young girl—about five years old—who I noticed in the waiting room the prior week. Her head was bald, and a yellow mask protected her small face. She sat in a wheel chair, which was too big to accommodate her tiny frame despite being made for children. The ill-fitted device called even more attention to what I was thinking: *She shouldn't be here*. None of us should be in this waiting room but especially not her.

I thought about how lucky I was when I was six. The humid Philadelphia summer evenings of my childhood had been spent eating cherry popsicles in my parents' backyard and running through the sprinkler, feeling wet, squishy grass beneath my feet. When dusk settled into darkness, I would walk around a white flowered dogwood tree and catch lightning bugs.

I hoped the little girl I saw spent more days playing in her backyard than confined to a waiting room filled with yearning. All of us were waiting for the day we didn't have to feel scared and uncomfortable anymore. We were waiting for life to resume. She didn't appear to be burdened by this same longing, I realized, as her eyes connected with mine. She sat serenely in her chair while I impatiently tapped my leg, wishing I could be anywhere else. I knew I couldn't have handled a cancer diagnosis at her age with as much grace.

I remembered the girl's mother had wheeled her towards the exit of the waiting room. *Please let her ring the bell. Please!* I held my breath as she passed near the silver bell that hung from a wooden pedestal. Ringing the bell was a rite of passage for any patient who completed their treatment. The girl's mother stopped at the bell, and I saw a small arm reach up and forward to grab the wooden clapper that was attached to a string. *Thank God.* Sound permeated the room, and everyone applauded. The girl's eyes hinted at a smile under her mask and her body sat a bit taller in her chair, projecting the same pride as if she were the winner of a spelling-bee contest.

My name was finally called, breaking my train of thought, and I walked back to the changing area. Once I was gowned, I stepped out into the patient waiting room and stood in the doorway, peering out into the hallway periodically to ensure I wasn't missed for treatment.

In the emptiness of the room, I wished for the company of a woman with breast cancer who had become a familiar face and a comforting maternal presence. When we spoke, deep lines hugged the corners of her mouth, suggesting she laughed often. We met on my first day of treatment, and I recalled our conversation when she glanced at me as I sat in a chair facing her.

"What are you here for?" I asked.

"Breast cancer," she replied, "full mastectomy."

I winced. "You look good," I told her. This was one of the only compliments many of us paid to one another. If you looked good, your treatment was going easier than most.

"What are you here for?" she asked.

"Lymphoma. Non-Hodgkin's," I replied.

"How old are you?" she asked.

"I'm thirty-one."

She shook her head vigorously then stopped and fixed her eyes on me again.

"My daughters are in their thirties. I'm so glad it's me here and not them," she moved back further into her chair.

I realize now that the look I saw in her eyes on that first day of treatment is the same look I must have given the little girl weeks later. She was relieved she wasn't me. She was relieved her daughters were not me. How lucky, she must have thought, that she was healthy as a young woman.

The definition of luck evolves after a cancer diagnosis. What used to be a simple dichotomy – lucky or unlucky – stretches into a continuum that is flanked by the number of blissful moments before cancer and the number of moments to be lived after cancer. Luck used to be finding a quarter on the ground or free parking in the city or winning anything more than a dollar on a scratch-off lottery ticket. Now, luck was a good day feeling like you used to or that moment when you first wake up and, for a few unburdened seconds, forget what has happened to you. It is lucky to see a sunset or feel the embrace of someone you love. And, it is still very lucky to catch a lightning bug.

A woman in her mid-forties entered the waiting room, returning from her treatment. She had thick hair that fell to her chest and was pinned haphazardly in the front with a small clip. I looked with envy at her as she passed through the room. *How lucky is she to be done for the day. How lucky is she to still have her beautiful hair.* Although I lost my hair months before radiation, feelings of discomfort would rise every time I caught my hairless reflection in the mirror or a car window. I would have given anything in that moment to experience the sensation of placing my hair behind my ears or threading it together carefully into a braid.

My name was called again, and I was ushered back to the treatment room to receive radiation. Technicians secured me to the hard, cold table with my radiation mask and placed a breath hold tube in my mouth. The breath hold apparatus mimicked a snorkel with goggles, a mouth piece and a nose clip. Every day during treatment, I pictured myself diving into clear blue water searching for fish to ease the claustrophobic panic that set in when my entire upper body was restrained. As my treatment began, I thought about how luck's definition becomes even more complicated when examining its relativity.

Cancer is generally classified as an unlucky disease yet even that is relative. Some people find luck in having a particular type of cancer or early disease staging. It can be lucky to have fewer side effects from treatment or have the support of loved ones on good days and bad days. Luck can also be measured by quality of the time before and after cancer. Luck can be remission and luck can be acceptance. Relativity shatters the dichotomy - it seems you can be both very unlucky and very lucky at the same time.

To prove my own theory of luck's relativity, I turned towards another recent memory. Midway through my chemotherapy treatment I lost my dad who had been a steady beacon of light in this world. Extended family and friends approached me at his funeral with teary faces and said, "How unfair this is. How unlucky you must feel dealing with your treatment and your father passing." What they didn't know is that I am the luckiest person in the world. My cancer was caught accidentally and early, and because of this, my treatment plan was shorter than most people diagnosed with Non-Hodgkin's Lymphoma. I would also rather embrace every moment of grief I experienced from the loss of my dad than spend one day not being his daughter. I had a wonderful dad for thirty years. When I was six, it was my dad handing me a popsicle in the backyard on a warm summer evening and my dad holding me close when a game of hide and seek became too scary. Our memories together play like a montage through my mind and soul every day. How many children in this world never know that kind of love? How many children, like the girl in the waiting room, experience a childhood with undeserved hardship? I am a lucky person.

My treatment ended unceremoniously with the technicians freeing me from the radiation mask. I thanked them and walked down the cold, white hallway back to the changing rooms. As I dressed, I rationalized that luck is always with us, we just have to want to find it. Even in the darkest night, if we search the horizon until our eyes are strained, we might find a small beam of light in the distance to guide us forward.

After I changed out of my gown, I walked slowly into the general waiting room and made my way towards the bell. I paused to take in the room exactly as it was that day. I wanted to remember what it was like to be there in that capacity, in that moment. I reached for the bell clapper and pulled it towards the mouth. The quiet room erupted in applause as the first sound of the bell pierced the air. I stood facing the bell, listening to its echoing sound, and felt both relieved and guilty. The bell only rings for the lucky ones.

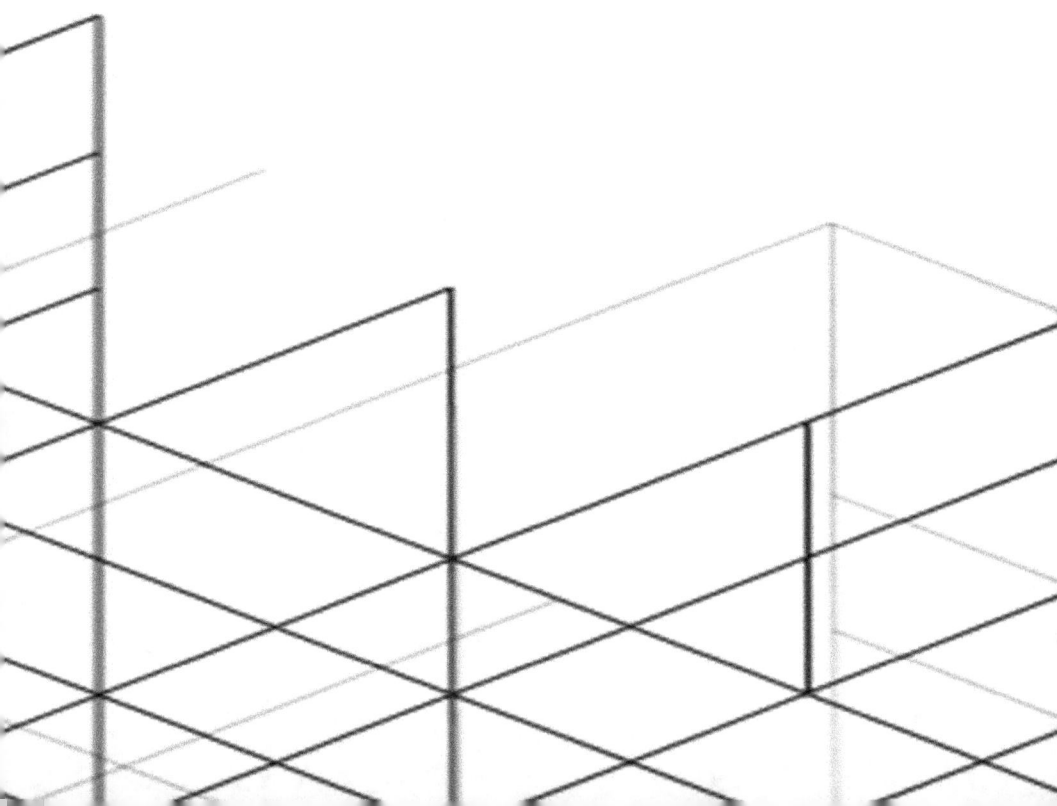

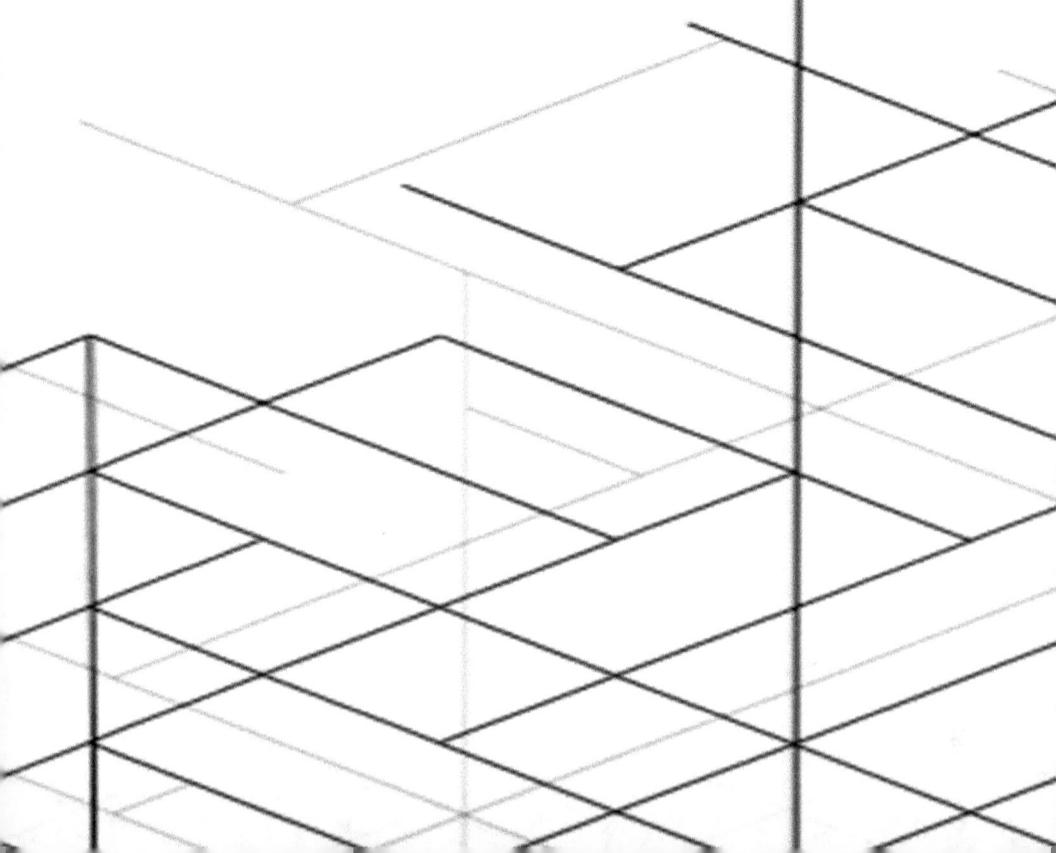

Coal

Sara Graybeal

Ángel works at a print shop, casting logos onto sweatshirts, white letters on black tees. TGIF. LONG HAIR DON'T CARE. YOLO. KEEP CALM AND…

He's been in hiding from pop culture for a while and this is a crash course he feels unprepared for. "Get back on Facebook," his sister recommends, but Ángel enjoys the mystery. WORK WORK WORK WORK WORK. I GOT HOT SAUCE IN MY BAG, SWAG.

He sometimes gets orders from organizations on shoestring budgets, asking for five hundred shirts by the end of the week. "C'mon, buddy, it's for the cause." Though his boss discourages it, Ángel does his best to meet these last-minute deadlines, stenciling RAISE MINIMUM WAGE and NINGÚN SER HUMANO ES ILEGAL late into the night. It's a strange, satisfying loneliness: fluorescent bulbs, sweat pouring down his chest, shirts hot-tumbling into boxes. The dark parking lot outside occupied only by his bike, a Suzuki Supermoto with chipping yellow paint. At the edge of the pavement, crickets. And beyond them, the bright snake of highway where cars roar in and out of Philadelphia.

Occasionally there is a different kind of order to fill: ALL LIVES MATTER, BUILD THE WALL. He worries, pushing paint across the screen. This is how it feels to be a cog in the wheel. A slave to capitalism. The chemistry post-doc who plodded wearily toward the creation of the atom bomb. Who can predict with what hatred these shirts will be worn, what anger they will incite? Who can predict who will shoot, who will die?

His bike has a broken rearview mirror, but after orders like these he takes the highway anyway, revving up to eighty, ninety. He keeps his shirt on so as not to attract attention from cops, though he'd like to feel the wind on his skin, sweat droplets flying, a cartoon shower of sparks behind him as he burns up the pavement toward home. He stops before he hits a hundred despite his clawing adrenaline, his muscles' ache for higher speeds. It's a promise, made to his mother back when she caught him racing. He tried to explain the necessity to her: It's not about winning. It's about driving his body to the burning core of its capabilities, a place of nerve and smoke where one thing snaps and he's dead. Seeing himself, from that place, reborn again and again.

She didn't understand. "I don't want you reborn. I want you alive. Promise me."

He did. It's been ten long years since then.

At home, early mornings, his mother serves him last night's dinner with coffee. His sister sings along with Beyoncé, getting ready for work, and his daughter Mariángel knocks on the door. Her mother brings her by every morning on the way to kindergarten for a kiss, which is allowed, and a sip of coffee, which is a secret, dark and sweet, gulped just inside the front door. Then Ángel says, "See you later, mi reina," and sinks onto the couch and sleeps, until the alarm goes off and it's time to get back to the shop.

On sunny days he plays old salsa, Hector Lavoe and Jerry Rivera. "This is some music," his boss says, smoking and tallying up numbers at his desk while Ángel leans over the Spider, a metal stand with six hands, one for each colored screen. He makes ten pink bridesmaids' shirts: I WOKE UP LIKE THIS. Then thirty cheerleading practice shirts: FLAWLESS. "Do girls listen to anyone besides Beyoncé?" Ángel wonders out loud.

"Huh?" says his boss, then shrugs. "Hey, you got me."

Fall is coming and they're printing logos on Varsity jackets, blue onto red onto yellow, the colors sinking perfectly in place. Like sculpting a sunset. He wishes Mariángel could see. She likes pastels and watercolors already; "definitely your baby," his mother says, taping up pictures of flowers and rainbows.

But not all the orders are colorful. #ERICGARNER. #FREDDIEGRAY. He has started predicting it by the tone of the caller, a brittle focus, an almost-deadened attention to detail. "The name has to be spelled right," the callers say. "Please make sure the name is spelled right."

He doesn't tell them that, Facebook or none, he knows how to spell these names. He doesn't tell them they're speaking to Ángel, who once marched beside them, Ángel, who stretched out in the Vine Street Expressway, stopping traffic to demand justice. The organizers waited for him to reappear once word got out he'd come home from jail, in the same way his neighbors waited for him to sit back down on his mom's steps and put a little money in their pockets. He hasn't done either of those things. He hasn't even gone back to doing tattoos. He took a job at the print shop because he thought it would be simple, far from the drama, a little like art, and sometimes it is all those things, and sometimes it is none. When the activists come to pick up their shirts, they do a double take. "My man. Where've you been?"

"Around," he says, shaking his head in a half-guilty, half-dogged way. They give him fliers and new numbers. They say they'll look for him at the next rally. He says he'll be there, but he won't. The rallies are where the cops first spotted him. A few trips to his block, a couple tapped phone calls, and that was that. Targeted for politics, arrested for weed. He's abandoned them both for good measure.

The world is an earthquake. He's keeping himself far from the epicenter.

But the orders keep coming. The worst are the calls for fifty white tees, always the same thing, a loved one shot, a grainy photo, a cursive **RIP**. He can see these women, heads bent over cell phones in dark living rooms, voices layered tremor upon tremor. He wishes there was a better thing to say than, "Yes, ma'am, I can do that for you." A greater reassurance than, "It'll be ready by tomorrow." He says nothing sympathetic or inviting. The women weep anyway.

In October a customer comes in, bell tinkling, a gust of smoky autumn air. Ángel is six months free and still breathless at old smells, his mother's quiet smile, the things he hadn't known he could lose so fully until he did.

"Our order with someone else fell through," the woman says. "You come recommended. We're marching this Saturday. We need three thousand shirts with an assortment of hashtags. What do you think?"

Ángel looks around the shop. His boss is out for the day. "I can't do it," he says. It's like standing at the top of a chorusing waterfall, deciding not to jump. His arms slacken with disappointment. "I'm supposed to cut back on my overtime."

"Oh," she says. He avoids her eyes. In the old days, let a mother come to his door saying her kids were hungry, a friend whose brother needed bail. A family in deportation court without a lawyer. Whatever it was, Ángel would come up with it; he'd come up with it and if he couldn't, he'd march. He'd lie down in the street.

Once, growing up in Puerto Rico, his brother had cut himself in the leg with a machete. Ángel can still see it: green vines closing in, his brother's terror, the helpless flap of skin, blood billowing out. Ángel had screamed for help. He'd stripped off his shirt and knotted it around his brother's leg, but when even this soaked red and no one came, he turned the machete against himself. He didn't know why. Did he think it would solve the problem, his mother demanded later, and he said no. It was just what his hands did, in that sickening moment of stillness.

His father had set a hand on his back. "When the world bleeds, Ángel bleeds," he'd said to Ángel's mother. "Can't you see?"

His father is gone now, and his brother, and all that blood, and even the scar, replaced by muscle and exhaust pipe burns and the tiniest nick of a bullet and then nothing at all. "It's not about other people anymore," his P.O. says. "It's about Ángel now."

But who is Ángel, if not the person he's always been? Who else can he possibly be?

"We'll figure something out," the customer says, giving him an undeserved smile.

He tries to smile back. Late afternoon sun pours through the windows, igniting the cardboard boxes orange. The Spider watches like a pit-bull, awaiting his command.

"I got you," he tells the woman. "Don't worry. They'll be ready by Friday."

"What's wrong with your hands?" his boss asks. "Are those blisters?"

Ángel says they're mosquito bites. "Too much sitting outside."

His boss whistles. "In November? Hey. Have you been here all night? Go home and get some sleep."

No, he hasn't been here all night. And he's an insomniac, doesn't need sleep. The lies come easily.

In truth, he's been working. Typing up hashtags, printing shirts. He made three thousand shirts for that march, and then the next one, and now, though there are no more events, he can't stop. Coal in his veins, a thing existing in order to burn. Too many names that need printing, too many stories begging for fabric and paint. #SANDRABLAND. He thinks of his sister, whose car always breaks down. #KORRYNGAINES. His mother, at home alone. #AIYANAJONES. Not his daughter. Not his daughter. He prints until his skin rubs raw against the wooden squeegee, until his palms crack open and his eyes slip shut and his body curls into itself. Cars hurtling down the highway. Crickets at the window like humans, crying for safety.

His boss hauls out six cardboard boxes, stacks them up like a police barricade and crosses his arms. "Ángel. We need to talk."

No, the shirts weren't made for pre-existing orders. No, he didn't ask permission to print the shirts. No, he doesn't have money to pay for them. No, he has nothing to say.

His boss pulls out one after another, like a crazed mother looking for proof of her child's delinquency. "Hashtag Janet Wilson. Hashtag Keith Scott. Look, Ángel. Look, buddy. I agree with you. I'm on your team. But we're talking six hundred un-ordered shirts. You bringing down the system? You overthrowing the government? 'Cause I'll tell you where you're headed, man. I make one call, you're headed straight back where you came from."

Ángel never finds out if he means jail or Puerto Rico. His boss tears up his last two weeks' check and sends him home. He understands he should be grateful.

His mother is incredulous. "Now what will you do? Sit on the couch? How can this be, Ángel, with your talent and your skills?"

He'd planned to give her a hundred dollars, the same way he does every week. Instead, in the face of her disappointment, he gives her six hundred and fifty. His last two hundred he gives to his daughter's mother. His pockets are empty.

But he's home to oversee Manhunt, setting cones at the end of the block to stop traffic and sending kids inside when the streetlights come on. He's home to help his daughter learn to write her name. MARIÁNGEL. The accent is important, he tells her. Don't let your teacher forget it. It's like the sun, falling through the middle of the word.

She doesn't like it, she confesses. Her mom's phone underlines it in red; "that means it's spelled wrong. My name is spelled wrong."

He writes his own name for her. He adds the accent. "Look, reina. It's right there, the sun, shining."

He is home, too, to hear the domestic disputes, the police raids, the fifteen-year-old killed over a basketball game. And he's home to see the gunshots nearly every morning on Fox 29. Over and over, an endless reel.

His mother doesn't serve him dinner. She's tired, she says. He eats hot dogs, pretzels, canned pears. His parole officer, believing he's still employed, congratulates him: eight months free. There is lead in his shoulders and his neck, lead in his spine, lead driving his bones into the sofa cushions, pulling his body toward the ground. If there is one thing he does not feel, it is free.

Fall turns to winter. He does odd jobs, shovels snow, patches leaking pipes. He tries to do tattoos but his hands shake at unpredictable moments. It's not worth the risk. Besides, even tattoos require tears, RIPs.

How not to try for rebirth, he wonders sometimes, when everywhere, every day, there are so many ways to die?

But his daughter is growing. She has fire-black hair and bright eyes. She can write her first and last name.

In February, on his birthday, she brings him crispy M&Ms and dandelions she pressed in summer, brilliant flat heads tipping into his palm. Examining them, he finds a four-leaf clover, unknowingly harvested and preserved.

At the print shop, one of the T-shirts said: WE ARE THE GRANDDAUGHTERS OF THE WITCHES YOU WEREN'T ABLE TO BURN. He watches his daughter's blazing smile. She is luck, he is sure of it. She is magic. She is victory.

Sometimes when there's a knock on the door, he thinks his time is up, they're coming for him. His parole officer, or the organizers, or the men on his block who are out of a job, or people who want tattoos, or his father and his brother who have been dead for years, or his sister, or his mother, or his daughter. As he gets up from the sofa, he imagines they're standing in the street, chanting his name. Their words collect and swell and break and then they're chanting something else, but he can't understand them, and he can't quiet them the way he used to, with a steady breath and a silent raise of a hand. He's trapped in the entrance. Soon they'll climb the steps, pound, break down the door.

"Ángel, qué te pasa, it's your sister!" his mother says, and his fear crumples and slides, ashamed, to the edges of the room. He rubs his eyes and opens the door.

He has this recurring dream where his phone is ringing. "We're marching," they say when he picks up. "We've shut down 95. We've taken City Hall. Come on, man. You need to be here." But he's printing shirts, a million this time. "Gotta get these done," he says. "Last minute. No one else in the shop, it's got to be me."

"But what are they for? The revolution is now. Leave the shirts. Get down here."

He can't answer, because every time he looks down, the letters blur. He can't read them. But he has to finish. A million shirts to save the world. Black tees, more black tees, more black tees.

Four months since he was fired. The sun sets over rooftops.

Mariángel watches cartoons beside him. "Bye, brujita," he says when her mother picks her up. That's what he calls her now. Little witch. She calls him monster, a playful revenge, though sometimes, when she's sad to leave, she calls him king, rey.

He's been feeling empty. Like his blood has dried up, leaving nothing in his veins. His P.O. is happy: almost one year down. Is this what he's been spared for? Watching the sun go down and up, another couple hours of sleep, another coffee?

"Rey o monstruo?" he asks as she hugs him. "Which am I today?"

"Rey. Y monstruo," she says, her breath sweet, sticky hands cupped at his ear. "You're both, Daddy."

He stares at her, startled, strangely relieved.

When night has fallen and his mother and sister are asleep, he takes his bike out for the first time since fall. He cruises down the block and onto the highway, all the way to his old exit, the dark parking lot. He rummages in the trashcan for the spare key.

The designs only take a little time. He could write these letters in his sleep.

There are two thousand black tees in stock. Then white tees, five hundred, white on white, impossible to read. It doesn't matter. #ÁNGEL, he prints. #ÁNGEL. #ÁNGEL. After a while, he switches to the second design. #DIABLO. #DIABLO. #DIABLO.

He's thirsty. The clock ticks toward one, two, three.

He leaves the shirts everywhere. In boxes, on the floor, stacked ten and twenty to a pile. Some dried, some sticky. The bottoms of his shoes soaked white. The floors, the desk. They'll find them here. Enough to plaster the world at its seams.

He gets back on his bike. Merging onto the highway, he pumps the engine to a hundred, a hundred ten, a hundred twenty. Hair flattened to his scalp. Tears flying. Each second a scorching celebration: alive! alive! alive! Faster and harder than his life has ever permitted, past his exit, past this city. As bold and as brilliant as the world is not ready, burning at his very core, at his epicenter, finally.

Your Lucky Life

Ken Fifer

In your sailor hat and peacoat, you cross
the asphalt and see what you thought
was your home is an old wooden boat.
You stand on the prow and what was
a black locust turns out to be your Jacob's ladder.
When you climb down you think
you're in Washington Crossing State Park,
but really you're on your own porch in Raubsville,
thanking Pat for the tuna on rye.
So you lean back, sip your Schlitz, look at the river,

shift your chair among the nine white pillars
which apart from being ornamental
hold up the second floor and roof.
It's as if whatever comes your way
leaves your footprints. When the locusts hunch
      over,
when the noisy green maples dig in to grow
bored and restless along the pointless Delaware,
when the paint of banisters peels from your
      palms,
when the birds leave no tracks at all
you think they all must be your countrymen.
And when moles tunnel under your home,
smacking their lips, wrinkling broad noses,
cleaning their glasses, with the river this close
they must all be your relatives. Each time
you bite into your sandwich you know
the pleasure and pain of harvested grain
in silos where the light goes down.
You can taste the gaff in your cheek,
the fishy vicissitudes, the last moments
of tuna roused from the deep
which fit so exactly into your mouth.

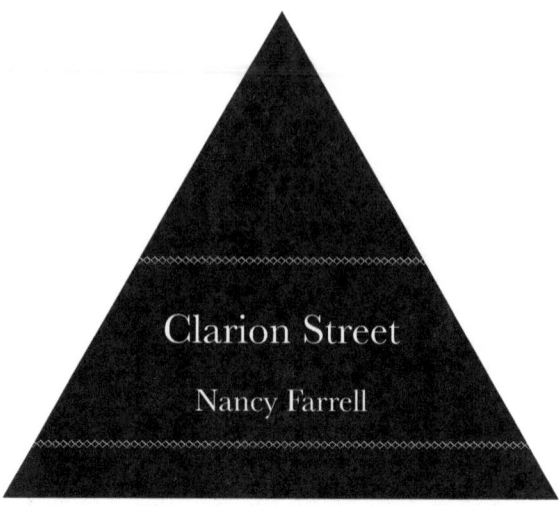

Clarion Street

Nancy Farrell

It was mid-summer, 1972, when I was 12 years old, that my parents sold our small row home on Clarion Street in South Philadelphia. They bought a finer row home in a suburban development dubbed Briarcliff, which rested in the Delaware County town of Glenolden. My father, Charles, was excited to own his first garage, while my mother, Violet, looked forward to the neighbors being less close at hand, albeit only a tad less. With the South Philadelphia and Briarcliff agreements of sale both signed, the clock began to tick toward our last day as South Philadelphians. That day would arrive in October, 1972.

My father had been struggling to keep his home goods business afloat. Progress was not on his side. My father's customers were the housewives of South Philadelphia, but their numbers were dwindling. It was the dawn of the shopping mall. The drapery that my father stored in his car and carried into houses could not compete with the variety at Sears, Roebuck and Company. In 1972, the remaining housewives continued to open their doors to my father, but it was because he was a sociable, homegrown fellow. They desired coffee and conversation with him, but his home goods, not so much.

Undeniably, it was my mother's office job at the Bell Telephone Company that enabled our move to Briarcliff. The job was a 20-minute walk from Clarion Street, and something she accomplished in sensible heels and strictly on time. The residue of my mother's stern upbringing gave rise to her handling stacks of Bell Telephone Company paperwork with speed and competency.

Once the news of our upcoming move spread, I was forced to fathom the unfathomable. I laid in bed at night as one realization after another turned my stomach. Clarion Street would never host another of our holidays. The aroma of my mother's spaghetti and meatballs, cooked each Sunday after Mass at the Annunciation BVM Church, would fade from the kitchen. The days of the overhang outside our back door sheltering my bike were numbered.

Life began to shift, as my mother collected ideas for modern decorating from *Good Housekeeping* magazine. Briarcliff would be her chance to start fresh. Meanwhile, my father declared that Briarcliff would be cleaner and safer than South Philadelphia. I felt insulted on behalf of our home, as I watched one room after another turn to dust and echo. Briarcliff-worthy knick-knacks were boxed up, while unworthy ones were placed in the trash.

The most troubling part of the move was the inescapable loss of my Clarion Street friends. There was my closest pal, Bridget, with whom I shared a birth year and every juvenile notion, such as whether a song she made up, "Little Brown Jug," might someday be recorded by The Monkees. With her perpetual pixie hairdo, Bridget had a pureness of heart epitomized by her habit of chalking "I'm sorry, let's make up" on the sidewalk outside my house following our rare spats.

And then there was Brenda, who was the same age as Bridget and me. Brenda was pretty and being hip came as naturally to her as breathing. When the bullies from around the corner turned up, Brenda remained unfazed. Always with a bottle of Coca Cola in hand, Brenda liked to deliberately spill dribbles onto the street, simply for kicks. Bridget and I occasionally hitched ourselves to Brenda's hijinks because it was exciting, but we typically favored the comfort and trust of our twosome.

There was Anthony, as well. He was one year older, and our informal leader on Clarion Street. He wore his hair long and he had a drum set in his basement, where he played Led Zeppelin songs. Bridget and I found Anthony charming, even though his rock star persona was undercut by his family's laundry, which continually drooped on a clothesline above his drum space. We believed we had a love triangle parallel to Betty, Veronica, and Archie in the Archie comic books that we purchased at Bertolino's Pharmacy.

My last summer on Clarion Street passed much like the prior ones. We roller skated, played tag, twirled hula hoops, and told spooky stories, all the while devouring cones of ice cream from the Mr. Softee Truck and Broadway Licorice Rolls from Jean's Grocery Store. We fell into bed at night sticky with sweat and sugar, confident that all of those things would be within reach again when the sun came up.

The gang knew that my family's house had been sold, but this turn of events was unfamiliar. All of us had only ever lived on Clarion Street. I longed to confess my heartbreak, but instead talked up the spacious MacDade Mall/Eric Movie Theater complex located near Briarcliff. What I should have announced was that nothing could top Clarion Street. There was the Mummer's Parade that took place every January 1st just two blocks away, and it wasn't just the lively music and magical costumes that made the parade extraordinary. It was the neighborhood families who opened their doors in welcome to all, offering escarole soup and crumb buns. Our parents lost track of us on New Year's Day, but never worried about our being cold, hungry, or safe.

There was also the 37-foot statue of William Penn, the founder of Pennsylvania, that sat atop Philadelphia's City Hall, which was visible, opportunely, from the flat rooftop outside my bedroom. And then there was the lunch counter at nearby Woolworth's, where the price of an ice cream sundae was determined by whichever balloon a customer chose from the day's balloon assortment. The balloons dangled colorfully above the lunch counter and contained within each was a slip of paper that was a price tag. When a balloon was chosen by an ice cream sundae customer and then popped, the treat's price was revealed.

In October, 1972, when my family's last day on Clarion Street landed, I felt a helplessness equal to the weight of the moving truck that rested in my line of sight. My friends watched curbside, while I leaned on our wrought-iron railing, as our forest green sofa and television were carried out sideways and stowed. I knew that my parents intended to comfort me, but were busy with last minute tasks. There were closets to be checked one final time, and keys to be collected.

With the last of our possessions amassed in the moving truck, the metal door was slammed down and the tarnished latch secured. This was my family's cue to climb into our blue Rambler Ambassador and to begin following the moving truck to Briarcliff. I rolled down my back-seat window, and my friends peeked in to wave goodbye. I sat in the car, stricken, and closed my eyes, as our car proceeded to the corner of Clarion Street. To lessen the ache, I pretended that we were headed instead to our yearly vacation at the Lamp Post Motel in Wildwood, something I treasured. "It will be okay," my mother said from the front seat.

And my mother's prediction was true. Time passed, and I did gradually become accustomed to the suburbs, and to the new friends and happenings that filled my days in Briarcliff. There were stumbles, to be sure, like when I was stung on my forehead by a bumble bee as I walked to my first day at Our Lady of Fatima School. Or when my mother signed us up at the Glenolden Swim Club, where I sat glued to the pool's ledge, filled with the terror of a non-swimmer. And then there was the ill-fated, week-long Girl Scouts camping trip I took to Sunset Hill, when I was commanded by the leader to wear a wash cloth bobby pinned to the top of my head because I had neglected to pack a hat.

Despite those missteps, I grew to accept that dipping my toes in creeks and fishing for minnows at Glenolden Park were reasonably worthwhile pastimes. And I developed a great affection for the group of Briarcliff girls who took me in. We moseyed to the MacDade Mall, where we shared pizza at Italian Delight and bought David Bowie albums at Wee Three Records.

But my memories of Clarion Street never fell away completely. One of my first visits to the block as a grownup was on a date to The Victor Cafe, an eatery that borders Clarion Street, where the servers are budding opera singers. The date was with the Briarcliff man that I would one day marry. He walked patiently alongside me down Clarion Street, past my old house, which then featured dark red awnings and a polished front entrance. Just as I had done back on moving day in 1972, I paused and closed my eyes, and I felt a tenderness borne of nostalgia, and a melancholy borne of a spell forever gone. Impulsively, I decided to ring the doorbell of my old house. Perhaps the current owner would be sympathetic to my story, I thought, and I could take a peek inside, but no one answered the door.

A decade later, I revisited Clarion Street, this time with my young daughters in tow. I held their hands, as I told them about pushing doll coaches with Bridget down the sidewalk. I told them about Brenda and her penchant for mischief. I pointed out the house where Anthony played his drums.

The friends I left on Clarion Street had never been far from my thoughts as the ensuing years rolled from one to the next. About a year after my family's move, Bridget became a boarding school student at the Charles E. Ellis School in Newtown Square, an institution for fatherless daughters. My mother dropped me off at the school to visit Bridget one brisk, Sunday afternoon. Bridget and I strolled through fallen leaves to a nearby McDonalds, where we caught up, and where we realized that our bond had not waned. Afterward, as I sat in Bridget's dormitory room, I worried that she might be lonely, but the opposite was true. She revealed that she was comfortable at the boarding school, and that the other girls were nice. Living at the Charles E. Ellis School was a continuous sleepover party, Bridget disclosed.

Thereafter, despite spans of time when we unintentionally overlooked one another, and when the tides swept Bridget in one direction and me in another, our relationship endured. When Bridget was married in 1981, I was by her side, and when it was my turn in 1984, she was by mine.

Brenda's family also moved away from Clarion Street. They bought a home in Springfield just four miles from my family's. At the time, my father and Brenda's father, Ray, developed a companionship. They were Delaware County transplants who, in spending time together, found a way to hold on to a bit of South Philadelphia. As a result, Brenda and I saw one another from time to time, and she spoke of Springfield contentedly. A decade later, I would coincidentally acquire work at the same Center City law firm where Brenda's sister worked, which circumstance renewed our families' link.

With an expanding Internet at our disposal, Bridget and I, then in our 40s, decided it was high time that we discovered what had become of Anthony. Utilizing social media, we discovered that Anthony was a professional drummer in a band called Splashing Violet, and in another known as The Flip-N-Mickeys. We wasted no time in messaging Anthony, and he wasted no time in agreeing to meet us.

On a balmy, early spring evening, Bridget, Anthony and I had our reunion at the Triangle Tavern in South Philadelphia. Open since 1933, the Triangle Tavern, with its Italian grandmother-style cuisine, had prevailed despite several bouts of new ownership and an assortment of renovations. I parked my car outside the Triangle Tavern, and I kept an eye out for Bridget, as it dawned on me that Bridget and I had chosen the ideal place to meet. After all, what was our relationship, if not something that had prevailed despite many years and many changes?

Anthony was inside when Bridget and I entered. His back was to the door, but when he heard us, he leapt from his seat. He hugged Bridget and me in a warmhearted way that belied our lost decades. Anthony, who had remained boyish in appearance, wore a black t-shirt and jeans indicative of his career, and his hair still rested past his shoulders,

Over pizza and beer, we kicked around memories of the 1960s and early 1970s. Anthony recounted the innumerable times we had been scolded by our elderly Clarion Street neighbors for misdeeds as small as dripping ice cream onto the pavement, or as big as bumping a parked car on our bikes. And we nodded in agreement over the incomparable thrill of the Whip Truck Ride that passed through our neighborhood in summertime.

Afterward, as I walked to my car, I thought about what I would say if I could speak to that girl who had sat, stricken, in the blue Rambler Ambassador in 1972. I would tell her that hurdles and teary nights spent over her diary lie ahead, but that in time her self-confidence would grow, and like the South Philadelphia knick-knacks her parents once deemed worthy or unworthy, she would discover what to hold on to and what to let go.

Present day Clarion Street thrives in the revitalized Passyunk Square district. My small row home, purchased by my parents in the late 1950s for $5,500, would sell today for over $300,000 at current market prices. The former mom-and-pop grocery stores are now trendy businesses, and The Victor Cafe is a Philadelphia tourist destination. Still, when I visit, I recognize the kids outside. They do not notice me as they play with their Barbie dolls and their Nerf Super Soakers. I sigh, and then I smile, and I know it's time to go.

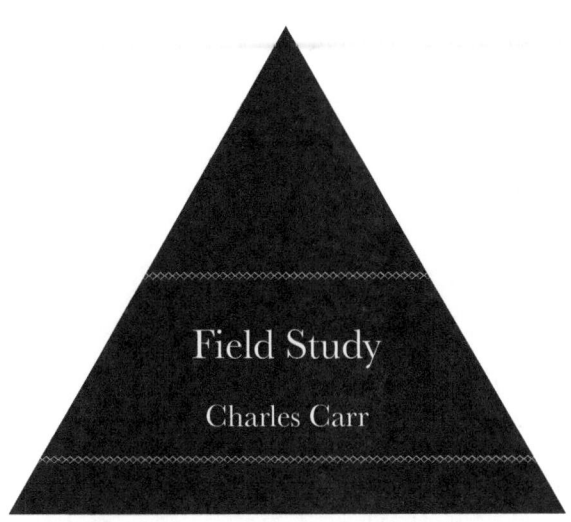

Field Study

Charles Carr

1.

E A G L E S written in vapors in the sky

A dalliance of eagles overhead

Midair clasping talons cart-wheeling down toward earth

Chant of boos at the site of the purple-winged god of the north wind,

2.

A procession of green double decker buses carrying the champs moves
slowly up Broad Street

A rage of joy screams　　　　people　barricaded swarm the parade route,

bearded player wearing a turban and Mummers costume dives into the
　　　　crowd

floats on raised arms

3.

A few clutch urns of ancestral ashes
Man wearing a jersey with number 99
circles in a ghost dance
empties ashes on the edges of a park at Broad & Oregon

4.

Elderly couple wearing fated team caps holds a sign
58 Years! The Curse Is Gone!
Wings on everything
Every shade of green expressing loyalty to the Champions
The reflective glory on the back of jerseys: names numbers of their heroes
The face of Nick Foles taped over the image of a saint

5.

Two giant marble Pylons open out to the Parkway to a roaring sea
Boys huddled together standing on the shoulders of the sculpted soldiers
on the Civil War Memorial
A cap placed on the head of The Thinker at the Rodin Museum
A ski cap on the head of George Washington at Eakin's Oval, a boy riding
        side saddle
Beer bottles stuck in branches decorate a tree in front of the Barnes

6.

Go-go dancer swivels up a light pole spins with an outstretched hand to the
        crowd
Two young men mud wrestle
Another body surfs through another mud patch
Cans of beer hurled at pole climbers
Finally one reaches the summit, guzzles a beer, directs the chorus below
in *Fly Eagles Fly*

Leslie

Lauren Green

Michael leans over to flick off the heat, catching a whiff of Rick's half-eaten apple in the cup holder. He had thought the fling with Rick would maybe last a night or two. Fifteen months later, they are driving home to see Michael's ex-wife, Leslie, who is throwing herself an end-of-life party.

In the passenger seat, Rick extends his arms overhead and begins to spell out O-H-I-O, not for the first time this trip. Michael knows that Ohio means little to Rick, who has spent all twenty-four years of his life in New York City, where Michael met him at a tacky Chelsea bar called Rawhide.

"Did you know there's a river here that's flammable?" Michael asks.

"Huh?"

"The Cuyahoga. It's so full of pollutants, it once caught fire. Literally."

Rick snorts, the way he always does when he finds something either amusing or lame. Michael is unsure which category his fact falls into. He sets his gaze ahead into the near-dark once more, where a sliver of moon lances through the lacy canopy of sycamores that flanks the side of the road.

Leslie had been sick once before, long ago. She had told Michael this on an early date—how she spent her fourteenth year propped-up in bed, teaching herself card tricks from a paper booklet while doctors pumped her body full of delphinium-blue poison. By the end of the summer, the whites of her eyes were tinted blue, like sky reflected in a corner of windshield, and she could levitate the queen of spades.

And now she is dying. Second cancer—that was what she called it on the phone. Not a recurrence but a separate entity altogether. Michael was in his office at the YMCA when she rang. As Leslie's voice floated toward him, he imagined her in their old kitchen, worrying the landline cord into a coil between her slim fingers, crossing one slick, shea-buttered ankle over the other.

"Come," she said. "I mean, if you want. If you still love me—" she said, but she did not finish the sentence.

The end-of-life celebration seemed somber and hellish to Michael, who had no desire to return to his former existence. "It's not exactly like she's ever been the life of the party," he grumbled to Rick. *Life of the party.* The words were like tinfoil against his teeth. *Jesus Christ*, he thought.

But Rick had insisted he go, and had offered to accompany him, most likely in the hopes of purloining some medical cannabis. So, it was decided.

Michael casts a sidelong gaze to the passenger seat. A deep red nick dents the cove beneath Rick's ear where he cut himself shaving this morning. His cheeks are unsullied, young. "Arizona," Michael says.

"What?"
Michael gestures to the license plate of the white semi-trailer that looms like a cloud in the reddening distance. "Arizona," he says again.

"Oh, nice."

Rick drapes his brown leather jacket over his lithe body and wriggles it up to his chin. His head lolls to one side. Blue-black twilight peeks through the lines on the window glass where he has fingernailed away the frost. "It's so boring here," he says, his voice husky with sleep.

"Welcome to Middle America," Michael answers, with a small laugh. He waits for the reward of Rick's quick snort, which does not come.

Nighttime bounds across the highway and far into the plains. Darkness spreads over the soybean fields and hoods the silver Camry. Michael lets his thoughts drift to Leslie. Leslie in the bed, late at night, waiting for him to come home. Leslie on the twig-littered drive, watching him pull away.

A car streams around them, blaring its horn, and Michael careens back into his lane. Beady red taillights glare out at him from ahead. "Maryland," he says. "Did we already get that one?"

He glances over at Rick, who has lapsed into sleep. Outside, wintry currents howl. Michael reaches over, turns up the heat, and tries to think again of Leslie.

*

The rules to Leslie's party, which she had emailed out to her twenty-five or so nearest and dearest, are simple:

1. No using the words "death" or "dying" or "cancer" or "time."
2. If you need to cry, step outside.
3. If I need to cry, you are not allowed to judge me.

*

The roads grow more and more familiar. Michael spots the Sunoco station he and Leslie frequented whenever they drove to the airport, the mossy bog they meandered around when spring fever spiked, the convention center where Michael got down on his knees for a man whose name he did not want to know.

He nearly misses the turn onto his own block, the one he took every day for twenty-two years. He passes the Claffeys, the Morgans, the Haberfields. He slows as he approaches the stone-and-stucco house that once belonged to the Fletchers. A "For Sale" sign gnashes its long, white fangs into the overgrown yard.

The Fletchers were a young couple who had perpetual, mystifying tans, which they emphasized by dressing exclusively in pastels. They lived in the house with their toddler, a flaxen-haired boy named Jacob. Michael and Leslie sometimes watched Jacob through the window as he raced his Tonka steel cement mixer up and down the drive.

"Why isn't anyone out there with him?" Leslie would ask. "Someone should be watching."

"You don't know that someone isn't," Michael would counter.

One day, Mr. Fletcher strapped Jacob into his car seat and drove to the reservoir on the outskirts of town, where teenagers would venture in the gauzy days of July to get lucky. The reservoir was two miles long and sixty feet deep—lightless and shimmering as a black snake. Later, the skid marks would indicate that Mr. Fletcher didn't even brake—he drove full speed ahead into the water, which swallowed the car in several large gulps, down into the belly of all that glimmering black.

For nights after the tragedy, Rachel Fletcher's wails kept Michael and

Leslie up at night. When they passed by her in the supermarket, her grief seemed otherworldly. Her eyes darted unsettlingly in their sockets, as if her pupils were an etch-a-sketch trying to erase what they had seen.

Michael and Leslie adopted Rachel Fletcher's name for any pain that was too great to bear. When Leslie's father died of heart disease: *Rachel Fletcher*. When Michael was laid off: *Rachel Fletcher*. On that final day, when his car was packed, and he drove away, watching her disappear in the rearview mirror: *Rachel Fletcher, Rachel Fletcher, Rachel Fletcher*.

Rick stirs and rubs the sleep from his eyes. "This it?" he asks, taking in the abandoned house.

"No," Michael says, easing his foot down onto the pedal. "Next one."

He pulls into the drive. A single light glows firefly-yellow through the kitchen window. "Maybe you should stay here," he says.

Rick shrugs. "It's not like she doesn't know I'm coming."

"I know, but—"

Rick palms Michael's thigh. "Don't," he says, squeezing. "It'll be fine."

Michael stares into the nettled gulley behind the yard, waiting for his headlights to catch on a pair of gleaming eyes or the scales of a leaping fish. He is considering restarting the car and checking into a motel for the night when Leslie appears backlit in the doorway, a pilled cardigan sashed loosely around her middle.

"Hey, stranger," she calls, as Michael kills the engine and clambers out of the car.

The air is crisp. The breeze smells of rainwater on pine. Leslie waits on the landing, staring at Michael with what he imagines to be painkiller-induced joy. He walks to her and wraps her in a hug. She is all bone beneath his fingertips. With her mouth still nuzzled into his neck, he gently cups the back of her wigged head.

He hears Rick behind him and pulls away. "This is—"

"Rick." Leslie extends her hand. "So nice to meet you. Come on in. Ignore the mess. I'm still trying to get everything set for tomorrow."

She leads the way into the kitchen, where moonlight pools on the ground beneath the French patio doors. Michael's eyes flicker to the frames on the wall. Leslie riding the Raptor at Cedar Point, arms thrust into the air; Leslie at her nephew's wedding, face dewy and wide. He tries to reconcile the woman in the photographs with the one who stands before him now, her pallid skin impressed with a filigree of purple veins.

"Long drive?" she asks, collapsing into a cushioned chair. She rubs the back of her palm against her forehead, smudging one penciled-in eyebrow to a long, brown streak. "Can I get either of you a drink?"

"I'll take soda if you have," Rick says.

"Pop," Michael corrects. "I'll get it."

He pads to the pantry where they keep the drinks. The shelves are stocked for tomorrow's party with foods the Leslie of his memories would be loath to purchase: chips and candy, soda and beer. Michael fingers the plastic rigging between the soda cans. Leslie always used to complain that the rings were an environmental hazard, liable to pollute the oceans and strangle sea turtles. But what should she care for oceans now?

When Michael returns to the kitchen, he finds Rick standing in the planetary blue light of the refrigerator, wielding a bulbous head of ginger.

"It's for me," Leslie explains.

Michael cocks his head. His wife is gone, but here is this woman sitting in his wife's chair, wrapped in his wife's freckled skin, wearing her same kind and weary face.

"Soda?" Rick asks.

Michael tosses him the can, and listens to the snap of the tab, the hiss of the fizz. He has forgotten how eerie the woodlands' silence can be. Rick tips his head back and allows the brown liquid to stream into his gullet. Then, with alarming strength, he crushes the can in one fist and sets its flattened body down on the marble countertop.

Michael turns to Leslie, whose eyes are shut. "Do you need help setting anything up for tomorrow?" he asks.

"Mmm," she says, "I think I've got everything. My mom's been staying here, so she did most of the setup. I just need to finalize my outfit."

"Can we see it?" Rick asks.

Leslie pauses a moment, then blinks her eyes open and labors to her feet. "Sure," she says. "Just give me a minute. I'm slow going up."

Michael watches as she shuffles across the hardwood floor. He waits for the open mouth of the hallway to devour her frail body before shooting Rick a savage look.

"What?" Rick asks.

Michael shakes his head. "Let me show you the rest of the house," he says.

He leads the way from the kitchen, flicking on lights as he goes. In the dining room, he is overcome by the urge to yank open every drawer and catalogue all the objects she will leave behind. He reaches for the china cabinet, where he spots Leslie's favorite vase sitting on the topmost shelf. The vase is turnip-shaped, the white-waves color of the Atlantic on a drizzly day. Michael grips it by the neck and uses his shirtsleeve to swab dust from around the rim. Then he sets it in the center of the dining room table.

"Look at this," Rick calls.

Michael glances up and crosses the threshold to the living room, where Leslie's mother has arranged a semi-circle of folding chairs. Streamers festoon every surface. Rick stands at the foot of a bridge table set off to one side, studying the objects neatly arrayed on its surface. A sign above, scrawled in Leslie's trembling hand, reads "HELP YOURSELF."

Michael runs his fingers over the keepsakes: Leslie's porcelain hand-mirror; her camera; a set of scalloped, earthenware bowls; a watercolor of a lily. He is about to turn away when he catches sight of a familiar glass bottle, dangling from a silver chain. The bottle is the size of his thumb and filled with pink sand from the beach in Greece where he and Leslie honeymooned.

Michael pinches the chain and lifts it into the air, watching as the coral granules in the bottle tumble one on top of the other. He had given Leslie the necklace when they first married. He closes his fist around the glass and worms it into his back pocket. He can feel Rick's eyes on him and looks up, daring to be challenged. They stare at each other, soundless and unmoving.

Just then, the patter of Leslie's footfalls jolts them. "Where did you boys run away to?" she calls, and the kettle in the kitchen begins to sing.

*

Michael remembers little from the honeymoon. He remembers only the tract of sky at sunset: febrile, the color of a skinned tangerine; the sizzle of his feet over the hot cobblestones once walked by emperors; a donkey braying; the lassitude of the Mediterranean. He remembers the day he walked down to the beach alone. Leslie, sick with sun fatigue, had gone back to the whitewashed villa early.

Even now, Michael can picture the tanned face of the young man folding up umbrellas on the salmon-colored sand. The man, who couldn't have been more than a boy. The man, whom Michael slipped a Drachma banknote in exchange for a blowjob. The man, whose flushed cheeks and vacant brown eyes tormented Michael every day for the next twenty-two years of his life.

When all was said and done, Michael sat down in a webstrap beach chair and regarded the young man with the disdain he reserved for the people who reminded him of his most monstrous self. The man finished folding his umbrellas and strode back up the path, whistling.

*

When Michael and Rick reenter the kitchen, the room is dark. In the silvery moonlight, Leslie's edges are feathered and blurred, as though she has been done in crayon. She stands with her arms crossed, in a red silk gown that Michael recognizes. He and Leslie had squabbled about its exorbitant price two years ago; at the time, she had no occasion to wear it to. *I just want to feel beautiful*, she had said. Why was that not enough?

"Can one of you get my zipper?" she asks, walking toward them. She moves slowly, fisting her hair away from her neck. Rick steps forward and tugs the zipper up its track, his hand hovering at the clasp.

She spins around. "What do you think?"

Rick lets out a long, slow whistle of approval.

Leslie scans Michael's face. "It'll be better with makeup," she says.

Michael swallows down the lump in his throat. He levels his eyes on Leslie. She suddenly feels very large to him, and far away, like a city glimpsed through an airplane window. "You look…ravishing," he says.

He has the desire to say something more, but every word that comes to mind seems trite. They stand in silence until, at last, Rick clears his throat.

"It's late," he says. "I'm gonna turn in."

Leslie nods. "I've set you up in the guest room, just up the stairs, first door on the left."

"Great, thanks."

Rick swings his backpack over one shoulder and slinks toward the staircase. He has a dancer's physique, and his slim hips pendulum from side to side. After a few moments, Michael and Leslie tilt their heads up at the ceiling, where they hear Rick moving about in the room above.

"He seems nice," Leslie says. She crosses to the sink to put away the last of the dishes, humming to herself a tune that is more breath than music, and impossible for Michael to place.

"I'll get those," he says.

"They're already done."

She shuts the cupboard and wipes her hands on a blotted, balding rag. "So, what's he getting out of this?" she asks.

Michael opens his mouth, then closes it again. He thinks of Rick, of his youth, his boundless energy, of the rainbow-pride flag that hangs in place of a window curtain. He thinks of the night they first met. Michael had worn a too-tight paisley shirt, which pulled between his shoulder blades. Uncanny taxidermy fixtures jutted out from the wooden pillars overhead. Shot glasses sweated on the ebony bar.

Rick stood in the center of the room, pretending to rope the mechanical bull with an invisible lasso. At the sight, Michael felt a judder inside, and placed one hand over his heart; he had forgotten what this muscle could do. Later, the men kissed beneath the bristled snout of a boar, whose marble glare kept vigil over the crowd. Rick tasted of pizza. When he opened his mouth to speak, Michael was surprised by the faint Colombian accent that barbed his voice. *Top or bottom, Cowboy?*

Recalling the line, Michael feels the tips of his ears burn. At the start, he had liked how both he and Rick were, in some ways, beginners. He liked how Rick, at twenty-four, had never known a single person who had died, not even a grandparent. He liked how Rick called him *Mi corazón*— my heart.

Michael is about to ask Leslie what she knows about being someone's heart, when he notices that her hand has paled on the countertop. Her shoulders begin to tremble. The fabric of her dress dimples in the concave shadow of her stomach as she doubles over in pain.

"Hey," he says, stepping forward. He pries her fingers up one at a time.

She yields to his touch, as though she is boneless, made of water. "I've got you," he says, cinching an arm tightly around her waist.

*

For so long, the cheating had seemed almost too easy. Leslie never questioned why Michael decided to take up piano as an antidote to middle-age malaise, nor why he insisted on taking lessons twice a week with Jonathan Claffey, the neighbors' son. She never questioned the underwear with the stain in the crotch that she found nearby the gulley, which Michael said must have belonged to one of the hooligans who egged the Fletcher house. She never questioned why her husband was so frigid at night, rebuffing her every advance. Or, if she did, she never expressed these worries to him.

Perhaps Michael could have kept the charade up had he and Leslie not run into one of his ex-lovers—a striking, Irish-sort—at the Cinemark, whose eyes widened when Leslie introduced herself as Michael's wife. Leslie looked to Michael, her pupils dilating, jaw tensing, and in that instant, he knew that she knew.

In the car ride home, her hair smelled buttery, of popcorn. "I feel like my whole life—" she said. Michael waited, but she did not go on.

They pulled up to a stoplight, and Michael turned to face his wife, his throat gummed with excuses. Black trails of mascara coursed down her cheeks. Her expression was blank. She stared at him vacuously, as she would a stranger, and he wondered how she had so quickly secreted away whatever intimacy lay at her surface.

"What do you want me to tell people?" she said.
A car behind them honked, and Michael turned back to the road. "What?"

"I mean, do you want me to tell the truth?"

Michael sieved through the simple kindness of her question, hoping to catch something sharp lurking in its tenderness. "Tell them whatever you want," he said, too scornfully.

Tears pricked at his eyes. He told himself this was what he had wanted all along. Leslie reached over and laced her fingers with his over the gearshift. Her touch was warm, loving. Michael did not know how a person could be so good.

*

Upstairs, Michael sets Leslie down on the bed they once shared. The sheets smell of rotted flesh. On the bedroom carpet, he notices the oval impressions her slippers have left, like tracks in snow.

"Will you get the light?" she asks.

He does. In the darkness, he fumbles to the bed, sits at its edge with his head hung and his hands clasped in his lap. He hears Leslie's effortful breathing behind him. "Do you need me to get you anything?" he asks.

She runs her hand over the space beside her, smoothing the wrinkled sheets. "Lie down, will you?"

He climbs into bed, careful not to pull on the red silk of her dress. His body commas around hers. She is smaller than he remembers. The warmth that radiates through her back is shocking. He wonders for a moment if the doctors have it wrong, if she is not near to death at all.

"Wait," she says. "Shut your eyes."

"My eyes?"

"Are they closed?"

"Yes."

The mattress shifts as Leslie pitches forward. Michael hears a faint rustling and the clacking of bobby pins against the cherry-finished nightstand. He imagines her buzzed head, the down that frosts her skull.

She lies back down, closer to him, and he can feel her breath hot on his neck. "Hey, you have silver in your beard," she says. "You know that?"

Michael feels her fingers tracing over the basin-like curve of his chin. Her hands stall. Then, slowly, she leans in and kisses him. He can feel the ridges on her chapped lips, the places where her skin is flaking. She pulls away and nestles her head into his chest.

Just then, Michael hears the floorboards creak and glances up, startled. A shadowy figure stands in the half-lit doorway. Rick.

"I should go," Michael says, watching in his periphery as Rick turns around, making a hasty retreat.

"Wait." Leslie prayers her hands beneath her head and opens her eyes. "Stay."

Michael scratches at his beard. Groggy with exhaustion, he rolls from the bed. "Give me a minute," he says.

He plods his way from the room and down the hallway. The light is on in the guest room. Michael imagines entering, only to find Rick repacking his toothbrush into his toiletry bag, slipping his feet into his brown loafers, readying himself to leave. Michael will take Rick into his arms, explain the gossamer-thread sort of love that sprouts in the corners of a lifetime spent together, where neither party thinks to look. He will ask why it should not be possible for him to love them both. But Rick will merely snort, shove Michael away, say he is nothing but a foolish, dirty old man.

When Michael arrives at the room, he is surprised to find Rick standing by the window, hands balled into the pockets of his jeans. "What are you doing?" Michael asks, setting one hand to rest on the doorframe.

"Thinking," Rick says.

Michael strolls over to him, so that they are mere inches apart. Rick is a head taller, at least, and larger. Michael feels his heart quicken in his chest, the way it always does when he walks past someone on the street he knows could hurt him.

"How is she?" Rick asks. He is standing so close, Michael can make out the golden flecks in his brown, wrinkleless eyes, and the scar on his cheek where he scratched at a chicken pock when he was a boy.

Michael purses his lips. He waits, knowing that Rick will uncover the answer he cannot provide.

Rick nods and gestures to the window. "Look," he says.

Outside, the world is lacquered a chilled pink. Clouds scud across the lightening sky. Rime cloaks the winterweed. A slender-tailed bird alights in the tree just beyond the windowpane and begins to coo.

Rick reaches down and takes ahold of Michael's hand. Then, gently, he leads Michael back to the door. Michael suddenly feels very small. He remembers how, as a child, his father used to usher him to the bus stop at the end of the road each morning, where the other St. Jude's boys constellated in their woolen gray uniforms.

Rick crinkles his eyebrows. He gives Michael's hand a hard squeeze. "She needs you now," he says.

*

On the day Michael was set to leave Ohio, two years before, he paused in the kitchen before the French doors, wondering how he got here. Just yesterday, it seemed, he was a teenager whose pinky inched along the church pew toward the pinky of the boy who sat beside him. The next thing he knew, he was standing at the altar, staring into Leslie's eyes, and then, in a single blink, he found himself a middle-aged man, with back pains and a mortgage and a problematic hairline. The years were pancaked together, and he could not unflatten them.

The night before, Leslie had sunk down to the floor of their bedroom, wanting to know if it was her fault. He told her it wasn't and asked why it needed to be anyone's fault. But she was hurt, and he was hurt, and where there was hurt, there was blame. So he said, "No. I should have told you."

They did not kiss, but they apologized, each of them saying, *Sorry, I'm sorry*, over and over again, until the words had lost their meaning. She cried, and maybe he did, too, though in his memory he hadn't. In his memory, he held her, and she sobbed into his shirt, until two dark spots, the size of nickels, bloomed on his chest.

And now it was morning. In the daylight, Michael looked at his house, quiet and flooded with sun. He saw the kitchen as though for the first time, imagining what it would be like without him here. Leslie entered in her bathrobe, shaking him from his reverie. "Are you ready?" she asked.

Michael walked out to the car, lugging the last of his boxes. She watched him as he jammed the trunk shut. She said she wanted to watch his leaving for herself. Otherwise she would wake up in the middle of the night, expecting him to return.

"I'll see you," he said. He said it as if he were setting out for the supermarket. He turned the key; the engine sputtered to life. Michael waved, and then he drove away.

Exit signs studded the highway. At each one he thought maybe he would turn back. He drove and drove, until the world stopped looking like a place he knew. He drove until his body ached and he couldn't drive anymore. Then he parked the Camry on a seedy corner nearby the Holland Tunnel, where the whir of cars travelling in and out of the city lullabied him to sleep.

*

When Michael gets back to the bedroom, Leslie's eyes are closed. He crawls into the spot beside her and watches her lashes flutter as she drifts in and out of dream. Luminescence gathers in the folds of her red gown.

Beneath him on the sheets, a round object kneads into his back. He reaches down, and his fingertips land on a smooth, curved edge. Michael pulls it out and turns it over; the pink sand streams from one end to the other. He leans toward the nightstand and sets the bottle beside the wig.

Leslie stirs. "Everything alright?" she asks.

"Yes," he says, "go back to sleep."

She curls her legs up beneath her and reaches out, drawing Michael closer. Her eyes are wet and shining. Michael cups the soft of her shoulder.

"Are you in pain?' he asks.

"A little," she says. "The hospice nurse will be here in the morning."

Michael's stomach churns. "How bad is it?" he asks.

The room is quiet, save for Leslie's wheezing. Michael waits, wondering if she has fallen back asleep. But then, at last, the corners of her dry lips curl. She does not say it, but the words hang in the space between them: *Rachel Fletcher.*

Leslie yawns. "Will you wake me if I fall asleep? I want to see the sunrise."

"Sure."

Michael glances out the window. The first golden rays of morning have begun to dapple the sky, and pour into the room, swathing him and Leslie in ribbons of yellow.

"Thanks for coming," she whispers. She reaches over and clings to Michael's sleeve.

"Of course," he says, aware of her pulse beneath his fingertips, steady but faint. "I wouldn't miss it."

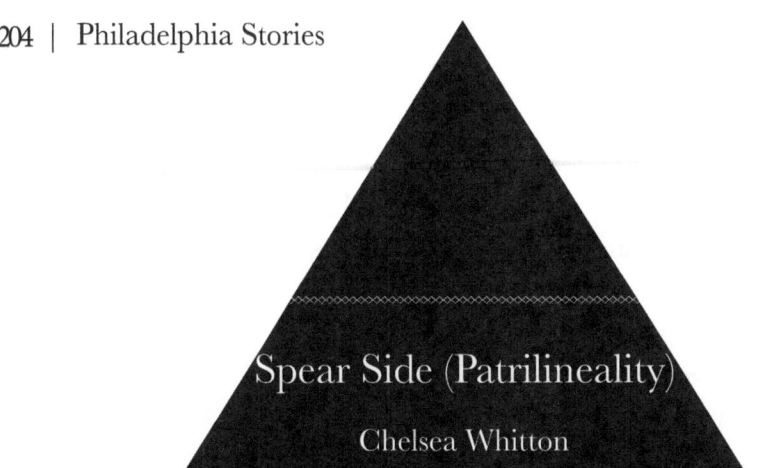

Spear Side (Patrilineality)

Chelsea Whitton

Your lopsided father stuck
the loose stars to your sky

one summer. Even now
they glow up there, as if,

like you, they are still dumbstruck
by the memory of his hulking grace.

With one foot on the bed, one on
the chest of drawers, his finger

pressed each phosphorescent
shard into eternity, too high

for anyone to tear them down.
It should have busted his ass

to do a thing like that. It did
—that kind of thing—eventually.

>>>

"That kind of thing, eventually,
will wear a man's skin thin," says mine.

His skin *is* thin, and mottled
from five decades in the sun,

on a vast green field that only winks
at abundance; does not, in fact,

yield anything up, save little flags
from holes, the occasional sky-borne

alien egg. True enough, he's burned
his skin to paper for this game.

But he does not, this time, for once,
mean golf. He means grief. *That* kind

of thing. He means leaving a child
in the ground, all fathers suffer.

>>>

In the ground, all fathers suffer
the fate of the warrior. In life,

it's a sky of tin gods. Each one's
a private lodestar, lost to all but us.

Whatever they did for a living,
our dads, however they hustled

and failed, they spun silvery roses
from gum foil, and blew Vaudeville

tunes through grass kazoos. And when
they told us how it was, we listened.

We believed their tales were true.
And so, however rent and upside-down

and patched, we flew their flags
until everything real blew away.

>>>

Until everything real blew away,
your father's father's father raised

a subsistence of cabbages above
the fruited plain. Nothing much

changed when the sky fell on us,
it is said he is said to have said. Only

the high folks got knocked down.
Haha. What *could* bring a poor man

low, apart from winter? Every soul
piled in one bed with the newspaper

stuffed to plug leaks in the windows.
Still, to be survived by all six children!

His salt-blind headstone seems to read:

God is fair to the faithful who toil!

>>>

God is fair to the faithful who toil.
Basically. Complicatedly. Squint

and try to see a version of events
in which good men are not heroic,

only good. Unmask that good
and you may find the face

of a previous father, not so
good. Meanwhile, and always,

and always without knowing why,
a procession of fathers stretches far

as infinity. Each one is in line to carve
his name over his father's name,

into the stone. It is only a stone,
but it shows them where to stand.

Trail of Ghosts

Devon James

When I was a junior in high school, I got a job at a flower shop. I worked there for almost five years, scraping money together for SATs and prom dresses. On the weekends I roamed South Jersey roadways and highways in the shop vans. Both vans, big or little, had filthy cupholders full of pennies, center consoles stuffed with fast food trash and business cards, broken starters, funky brakes, and were my chosen form of escaping home.

Being on the road was addictive. The vans were high above the pavement, where the echoes of my father's death, the debt he left my family, and its strain on my mother, couldn't reach me. I was secure in the way roller coasters feel secure when you're strapped in, just before the drop.

Big Bertha was my favorite van. From its height, I could see down into any car below. Maybe it was the feeling of control or maybe it was the feeling of breathlessness, that as high as I was, as far as I was from my problems below, I was still moving. As a restless teenager, this was a peaceful feeling.

The first time I drove Bertha was a few weeks after I got my license. I was 17. I grabbed the key from the shop and trekked across the street towards the parking lot. I didn't think I could handle a vehicle of her size, even if only to drive her across the street to the shop-front. I was used to smaller vehicles, and looking into other drivers' eyes, not the tops of their heads. Climbing upwards to reach the driver's seat was new territory for me. The seat was so far from the pedals I had to sit on the edge of the cushion to reach both gas and brakes. It would be months before I learned to move the seat forward.

The next time I drove her was also my first time delivering funeral flowers. I knew the location well. It was where my father's funeral was held ten or so years prior. My boss did the flowers for my father's service too, which meant they were delivered in the same van, Big Bertha.

I pulled into the driveway, set far back from the road by a hill jutting awkwardly above the street below. I braced myself for the flashbacks to come: four vases with a blue flower to represent my brothers, one vase with a pink flower for me. My mother crying. Sitting in the front row, the cremated remains of a former half of me resting in a box at the front of the room.

Before I entered the funeral home, I sat in the van, counting off arrangements, matching flowers to delivery slips, making sure none were forgotten.

I opened the side door, arms full with a funeral basket so large I couldn't see over it. I watched my feet, making sure to avoid tripping on any steps and destroying the flowers of mourning. After setting the arrangement down, I stood up to find myself facing the casket.

It was open and the corpse inside looked puffy and waxen. I averted my eyes though they kept gravitating towards his body. I couldn't look at him, yet I couldn't look away. His gray hair was slicked back perfectly atop his balding head. Years of living well had carved smile lines deep into his skin. His mouth had permanently set into a smirk.

I shifted my focus and found the carpet and wallpaper matched that of my memories. Dark floral patterns on the walls clashed, or perhaps meshed, with the deep green of the carpet. Behind me, the rows of chairs matched my memory too. I turned to see the chair I sat in the last time I was in the room, fifth from the left, front row.

My mother had been seated closest to the wall, first in line to receive guests, my brothers and I following her, positioned chronologically. Before us, instead of a coffin stood a table bearing the box of my father's ashes, and the five tiny vases.

Everyone had worn black as they huddled around pictures of a man no one would see again. I had smiled at them, awkwardly attempting to offer joy, failing entirely in that attempt.

That day ushered in an era of silence, of quiet tears spilt alone late at night. I don't remember much of what happened immediately afterwards. My mom finally finished the kitchen renovation they'd begun long ago. We went to Florida for our first vacation without our father. Eventually, money became tighter. My brothers and I became closer, conscious then of the ease at which a person goes from being there, to never being anywhere other than in the past tense. We were deeply connected to my mom too. As a unit, we spent no time looking back.

Maybe it had been too easy to walk out of that room. Maybe I had never really left it.

I left and came back with more flowers. Trip after trip, van to funeral home and back again, until finally it was over. I brought the final arrangement in and set it gently on the carpet in front of the casket. I looked at the silent and peaceful man and wondered how he would feel if he knew I was looking at him. I imagined his laughter and his hugs during the stories he would tell his grandchildren during the holidays.

I ran from the room without shutting the door. Bertha started on the first turn in the ignition, a rare feat, and I drove off so quickly I almost tipped her on her side.

Away from the room and the man and the memories, I wanted to go back to sit with him for a while but I had other deliveries to make. Birthday balloons, bridal flowers, "I'm Sorry" bouquets awaited.

Soon, I would learn how common it is to see corpses in the flower industry, how often it is not the flowers of the living, but rather casket decorations and peace lilies. How, more often than not, I would carry flowers whose recipients are in the process of being forgotten: silent arrangements, ones no one calls the sender about, as opposed to the flowers of the living.

In the hours before the services would begin, funeral home directors accepted the flower deliveries. After a while, these deliveries became quiet, peaceful places for me to be with the dead. Knowing I was one of the last people to share their private time with them, I began reading the obituaries, not just glancing at delivery dates and times, to glimpse who they were: veterans, nurses, teachers, students. I could learn how they died based on the wording, *Passed Suddenly* usually meant overdose or suicide, while *Is Now At Peace* usually translated into cancer or some other illness.

They were sometimes young, oftentimes old, and their loved ones were always listed at the end of the obituary. There, I learned how these people lived and who they left behind. People who were losing life partners, children, grandparents, mothers, and fathers. Then I would bring in the flowers ordered by those loved ones, and set them at the base of the caskets.

Quick and clean, in and out, bouncing around South Jersey, leaving a trail of ghosts behind, I'd strap myself into the safety of the van after each delivery. I'd blast NPR, or music, or both as I drove.

At the end of the night, I would park the van at the shop, hang the keys on the wall, then lock the door and leave, forgetting the names of the bodies I'd seen that day. I would trade their faces for those of the living and abandon the dead until my next shift.

I still notice when I'm near one of the funeral homes I used to deliver to. The familiarity of the routes have ingrained into my subconscious, next to the wallpaper patterns and obituaries, and ghosts of those whose funerals I'd crashed.

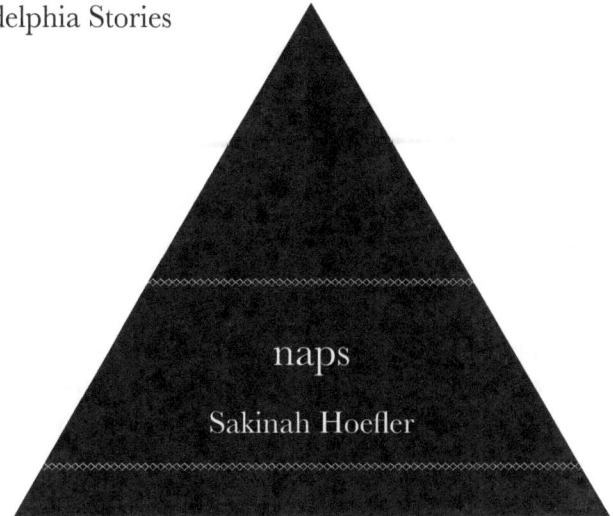

naps

Sakinah Hoefler

at pathmark, you would sneak bottles of pantene pro v shampoo and conditioner into your momma's shopping cart and each time, at the register, your momma would notice and tell the cashier you can take that one off, and each time you would scream, *I wanna have hair like those women in the commercials!* and each time she would just stare at you.

later your 4th grade teacher brought your momma in for a talk, not about your grades or your behavior, but your hair; your hair bothered her – one ponytail obeying gravity; the other, sticking skyward. her name was ms. alifoofoo and you stared at her jheri curl which were more poppin than your uncle's while she said, *your daughter needs to look decent for school. maybe you should get her a perm.* you don't remember what your momma said back but it happened on a thursday and by that following monday, you were starting your first day at a new school.

you learned religion at this new school and how to pray five times a day and you figured that you were now five times more likely to get the lighter skin, the long straight hair, and the brown eyes with flecks of green that you'd been asking for, and each morning you woke up, disappointed.

one day, your momma came home with two boxes of "just like me" and you and your sister held your noses while your momma spread the rotten egg white cream on both of y'alls hair, shampooed, then conditioned. after she blow dried, you couldn't wait for your hair to cascade in layers, you couldn't wait to flip your hair over your shoulders like the girls you read about in books. yes, your hair was softer. yes, your hair was a little straighter. but, your hair didn't look just like that girl on the box so you cried. your sister's hair fell out.

your momma took you to a salon and a professional added the extra step, the beveler, hair pulled and pressed between the heat of two ceramic plates. now, you could flip your shoulder-length hair as you pleased. now, you could almost be in a commercial. this became your habit for the next fifteen years.

you grew up.

your hair never grew past your shoulders but you found new ways to be grateful. your classmate in college told you your last name was german, making you pleased your family's slave owners were at least german, pleased because it sounded better to certain ears than johnson or williams. your surprised coworker met you for the first time and told you, you sounded white on the phone and you used that info and that voice to book a reservation at that restaurant you had been afraid to call before. you shy away from the ghetto, avoid the eyes of saggers, you get degree after degree trying to be equal. some days, you try to convince yourself to come out of hiding, that you'll beat anyone down who dare thinks they have something to say, in fact, there's a proud photo of you in the first incarnation of the "black girls rock" t-shirt with your hand around your guyanese neighbor and that photo gets more likes on instagram than any subsequent photo. some days, you're like, *hell yeah, bitches, my black is beautiful.* most days though, you pull out a scarf and cover your hair.

Elegy for Breath

Carlos Andrés Gómez

Picture the adolescent: mimicking
what makes him worthy. Pick his
most potent snapshot for click-
bait: fresh-faced but mean-
mugging; same mask I'd pull
clean across my jaw for any
Polaroid of me & my best friend
in eighth grade. Let's be clear: joke

stance—now used to justify
killing   make just   the just-
snuffed, just clumsy youth branded
bold-fonted & blood thirst. Peace
sign transmogrified to gang sign—
since the expert talking head
confirmed it. The expert talks &
confirms inside a rectangular frame
that renders most of him invisible.
Talks & confirms   two bullet-
points   from the bleached-
teeth interviewer. But nowhere
is the testimony of   breath
stifled, the practiced hands that
remained watched whenever they
ascended, whether in prayer or
surrender, holding a bag of groceries,
a cell phone, or a son. Nowhere
is that last sigh freed from his tired
lungs as the sixth shot   struck
the base of his skull   sprinting
with back turned. The neighbor describes
that final sound I did not hear   & yet
cannot   unhear. It is suddenly the last
sound I hear from too many people
I love: my brother-in-law, my four
nephews, my high school best friend,
my infant son. (Every police officer
is out in the world   defending
himself. Every one of them describes
the nightmares in which they see
a dark object against the darkness
that turns into fire & populates a rigid
void with lead. Every police officer

is a human being. He makes mistakes
sometimes. He got nervous. He thought
about his two kids & his pregnant wife,
it was fourteen days before retirement.
He's never missed a Sunday at church.
Believe me, it's true. I've seen him pass
the donation plate. Sometimes
he takes a naked, crumpled bill in his
calloused hands, wipes the sweat
& residue on his crotch.) I saw Jesus
on Easter Sunday   still resting
on the wall, a hooded sweatshirt
draped across his torso from the college
he was to attend just to make it all a bit
more decent. Everything you stare into
becomes a fist, a loaded weapon aimed
at your face. I wake up in a country
based on a single document made
to protect   every human being   equally
who is a wealthy, white man. The woman
I meet after my show in Myrtle Beach,
South Carolina has no response when
I ask her why the killing of three dogs
made her protest, made her write letters,
made her boycott, while the murder
of a defenseless Black child inspired
not a single word   from her lips?
Loud music; blocking the middle of an
empty
residential street; a wallet in a trembling,
outstretched palm; a back sprinting away
in fear; a woman after a car accident
knocking on a door for help; a toy
rifle in a Walmart in Ohio; a boy

in Money, Mississippi, walking, lost
in thought, a stutter from Polio, a whistle
he learned to cope with his stammer,
when the implication of   Blackness
is always absolution   from murder.
My son's first breath was with-
held: the cord that had nourished him
for nine months now choked   three
times   around his throat, as he fought
for life. Like his sister at birth. Like
the father on a sidewalk in Staten
selling cigarettes to support his six kids
to survive born fighting stayed fighting
to breathe. When my son   gasped
finally & then slumbered into dream,
his blooming tenderness unguarded as
a single orchid, I said a silent prayer
for the imagined crimes his world was busy
inventing, to condemn him for being born
Black   & having the courage   to breathe.

Lost Novella

Stephen St. Francis Decky

In 2004 I stopped reading books. I had just stopped smoking. I'd stopped smoking because I'd nearly completed writing a novella when my laptop sputtered and died. The data, despite some effort, was unrecoverable. I grieved like someone dear had died.

I'd been smoking since I was a Junior in high school. At that time, I was homeless; In a rare fit of mercy, my dad had kicked me out of his house that summer. Which left me free. But homeless. I spent the first night in a blur in the woods with a fire and some people I didn't know. I was free, and lost, and after a week, going through some sort of withdrawal from the anti-depression meds I'd left home without. That home had become a pressure-cooker of threats and hostility. There was no going back.

Instead, I stopped at a convenience store in Woodbury, New Jersey and for the first time in my life bought a pack of cigarettes. I lit one up outside. The jitters and withdrawal pangs softened in seconds; the relief was immediate and palpable. As the fog of anxiety faded, I sat down on the curb, opened a notebook, and began to write.

I smoked for 19 years. I'd been writing stories and painting and drawing since I was a child. But the smoking was to my fiction like canned spinach to Popeye: instant confidence and focus. I wrote obsessively, I made it a habit. I smoked upwards of 2 packs a day.

Later I published a couple short stories. They went nowhere but it didn't matter because I hadn't written my best piece yet. That one was still coming, and when it came, at the height of its formation - mid-delivery - it vanished.

Smoking did little to numb the despair. I'd begun seeing its effects in the mirror as well: I looked very *mid-30's, smoker*. This visual prompted me to take a day off from smoking. In the 19 years I'd been smoking I'd never gone an entire day without a cigarette. But I was going to take a day off. 24 hours. Instead of smoking I would eat cookies and ice cream and drink martinis and pretty much devour anything I craved except cigarettes.

That night I drank 4 and a half martinis. I woke up the next morning on the floor beside my bed. I felt bludgeoned but ecstatic: I'd just gone an entire day without a cigarette. I figured I'd wait a few hours and then have a smoke and a cup of coffee and resume my life. But mid-afternoon passed and evening arrived and I wondered what would happen if I somehow found the audacity to try the martini trick again.

It worked: I woke up the next day in my underwear on the porch, 48 hours smoke-free. It felt like the fabric of my life had been ripped; I had quit smoking.

8 months later, the pack I'd been working on when I quit was still in my backpack - a subconscious *Emergency Kit* - with 11 unsmoked cigarettes inside. I remembered this as I was leaving a convenience store on King Street in Northampton, Massachusetts. Embarrassed, I pulled the pack - Marlboro Reds, the ultimate sellout - out of my bag and tossed it into a trash can.

During the aforementioned 8-month contingency period, I climbed

Mt. Washington in less than 2 hours, did upwards of 300 push-ups daily, and started painting with renewed energy. I'd never painted with a purpose or audience but I could feel the possibility of one forming. Images began replacing text in my creative workflow. My written output dwindled until I was left with little more than Beckett-like, self-subsuming paragraphs of anti-fiction. The great novella was lost, and in its wake, my writing had become the literary equivalent of autolyzed yeast.

A side-effect of *not writing* was a burgeoning inability to read long-form works, i.e. *books*. The two processes had somehow been intertwined, and I was finding it impossible to focus on either. It was deeply worrisome, as I'd been a voracious reader for many years, and a battle at the intersection of inspiration and creativity seemed to be waging inside me.

At a bookstore in Philadelphia, I found and purchased a copy of Albert Camus' *L'Etranger* in the original French. I'd studied French in high school and retained some knowledge with occasional tutors, but reading literature *en français* was a new and suddenly necessary challenge: It forced me to concentrate at a level that had become second-nature in English, and the constant need to check my stack of French-English dictionaries satisfied - albeit faintly - the now-missing physical and gestural aspect of smoking.

I finished *l'Etranger*, some grossly pretentious Sartre plays, then *le Deuxieme Sexe*, all with a slowly increasing sense of ease. Later that year I travelled to France and found a copy of *Le Tour de la France par Deux Enfants* in Lyon, a Marivaux compendium in Chamonix, something by Nathalie Sarraute in Nice. I could understand Molière and Colette but couldn't keep up with anything modern: My comprehensive abilities were antiquated, and I developed a ready-made excuse in my perpetually-lagging conversational French:

> - *Je parle comme un enfant parce'que je pense comme un enfant en français*
> (I speak like a kid 'cuz I think like a kid in French)

Over the next 12 years, the only books I read in English were Houellebecq translations and systematically timed re-readings of Shirley Jackson's *We Have Always Lived in the Castle*. I read Marguerite Duras, Radiguet, La Fontaine and others in the original French, but with the sense I'd been trapped in a Robbe-Grillet loop of limited literary mobility.

....

Early in 2017, while recovering from surgery - and as if loosed from a longstanding fog - I began writing again: Mostly short and spastic stories and eruptions, but enough to open the door to reading in English again. It started with Marc Augé's *Everyone Dies Young*, then Ariel Goldberg's *The Estrangement Principle*. I re-discovered Nawel El-Sawaadi's *Woman at Point Zero*, then the suddenly/weirdly inspirational Cicero, then old favorites like Angela Carter, Mohammed Mrabet, Zora Neale Thurston, etc.

I started listening to audiobooks as well. While they were clunky and rare in 2004, they've become both accessibile and abundant in the interim, often reaching true eloquence. Listening to Ta-Nehisi Coates reading his own *Between the World and Me* after the chorus of voices reciting George Saunders' *Lincoln in the Bardo* was deeply revelatory.

Still, there's nothing like the presence of a book, and that physicality lingers *in perpetuity*: I can almost feel the de Beauvoir text I bought in Geneva early last summer and lost on the Broad Street Line in Philly; that copy of *Le Tour de la France* from Lyon still rests on my desk, ever-visible from the corner of my eye.

....

It's been nearly 15 years since I quit smoking. I stopped taking prescription anti-anxiety and depression medications soonafter. At that time, I felt - *fleetingly* - freed from the narcosis of short, long-term, and acceptable addictions. A slow-building ecstasy of heightened mental clarity whisked away many of the fears and worries that had been stifling my confidence since my earliest years. It was obvious, though, even as it was coursing through me, that the ecstasy wouldn't last; The feeling itself was strained by an array of side-effects, but like the addictions - and later, the literary anomalies - these eventually subsided, shifting from the harrowing insistence of the present to the fading but temporal archive of memory.

The novella is now but a blip in a long line of lost plans and ideas, but its influence on my story has been manifold. The future may have changed many times over, but I've learned that the potential for new creative prospects - even if temporarily obscured - is always there in some way, shape or form.

s.st.f.d. 07.18.

All Objects

Brittanie Sterner

Here are feet on the floor of a plane over Omaha:
Here are swatches of ground turning into ground
Here is voice mail from an unknown number
Here is every computer-generated test
Here is waiting with glass
Here is middle-night
Here are foreheads touching here are hands in space
Here is rope
Here is the braid that makes the rope
Here is a death one day
Here is another death
Here is another death
Here is perched investment
Here are plot equations from above
Here are characters for land and love
Here is unstoppable weather
Here is a bowl of ocean
Here is food digesting
Here is top of the bottom
Here is morning, again
Here is wake with a ship on the tongue
Here is a mouth of fog
Here are rotaries of birds
Here beads traffic in rosaries
Here graves imitate trees in rows
Here is orchard
Here is fruit clung and hatched
Here is a basket
Here are hands applied over Omaha, braiding highways
Here lawns cropped in rectangles
Here tillers in bunches transit
Here an accident that didn't make news
Here clipped migration
Here is lamp on a timer
Here letters spell electricity
Here is the room after leaving
Here is the light going off.

SITZ-i-zen

Bim Angst

The child was dead before Irina Putavich plunged her hands into the scalding water and lifted him startled-faced to the air. The baby was limp. As his round nose and the fat cheeks with which he so powerfully suckled rose above the shining scrim of clear water, he did not open his small heart-shaped mouth to suck in air. His head flopped back as Irina lifted him, the skin of her hands reddening around his waist as she drew him to her bony chest. *Misha Misha Misha* she whispered, as if she were trying to wake him.

It was the smell of Irina's hair smoldering that brought her mother, Vlada, trundling to the kitchen, where Irina knelt on the floor, the heat from the cast iron of the stove searing the loose ends of her hair. Vlada slid her felted feet across the new linoleum rug to peer over her 16-year-old daughter's shoulder. The beatific face of her grandson was losing its startling russet color. Crystalline droplets from the few golden curls at the back of his head broke ripples in the washtub from which still rose fingers of steam.

*

At the drowning of his son, Laszlo Putavich was not called from the mine. Instead, he returned home at the normal hour. The bricks of the alley walkway were wet, as he might have expected, but no trousers hung on the clothesline, and the washtub was tilted against the arbor as if it had been thrown. Laszlo entered the quiet kitchen to see his wife rocking in the big chair near the stove. Irina was wrapped in a sheet, her chin on her chest as if she were asleep, yet, softly, she moaned.

On the kitchen table sat the laundry basket, one wicker handle hanging loose. Laszlo did not detect the odor of the lye soap Irina used to scrub the miners' frayed clothes. Neither did the kitchen smell of lard or onions as it should have, but instead of hot metal and something that burned his nostrils and made his windpipe catch, something like the torching off of the last fur on a hide.

From deep within the house came the drone of prayer and a muffled half-sob. In the far room, Vlada was on her knees—how did she get down, he marveled, how would she haul her great bulk up? Vlada's oxen shoulders heaved. Beside her knelt Father Yspecky, the prayer for the departed on his lips in Russian.

It was then that Laszlo turned to the basket, where he saw the face of his swaddled son.

*

She had not been a beautiful bride, nor eager, but Irina had done her best to please Laszlo in the year and eleven months in which they had lain as husband and wife. It was not Irina's fault, Laszlo pondered, that Vlada was of the old country and treated Irina as if she were an ignorant serf. The new version of serfdom and soldiering as Franz Josef's conscript were exactly why Laszlo Putavich's parents had sent their sons from the vineyards of Uzhhorod Raion, why, in the company of his older brother, Laszlo had trudged across Europe to Hamburg wearing three layers of clothing, a pair of too-big shoes, and an uncle's overcoat.

Irina was, Laszlo knew, his best chance to avoid becoming the lost soul of a man without a country, a man without a family, a man who prayed but did not worship, who worked hard but lost his pay in the bottle. And so, when his friend Mykhail Kruchevich was crushed by a coal car that broke loose when the pillars were robbed in the Number 9 Clareville mine, Laszlo took old Misha's lunch pail to the home of his wife and daughter and sat with them through the wailing and banging of pots that followed. Two days later, in his embroidered shirt, Laszlo Putavich entered the blue-domed Russian Orthodox church for old Misha's funeral, not only to smooth the pall and bear Misha's poor coffin but to return from the graveyard with the dimpled hand of Misha's rotund widow tucked in his elbow and the offer of her remaining daughter in marriage pouring like oil into his ear. Before the month was out, Laszlo had an American-born wife and Vlada had a strong-bodied wage-earner under her roof.

At fourteen, Irina knew hard work and laundry. She rose to make her father breakfast, to pack his lunch into the metal pail while her mother slept, Vlada's rheumatism and bad heart swelling her limbs and giving her reason to lay abed. Irina's hands were raw and the texture of burlap. Yet Irina's narrow fingers worked nimbly, and she could starch and press flat the fine seams and lace edging of the table linens in the big houses of the English families to whom Vlada farmed her out. Irina was of America and knew both how to pinch the edges of pierogi and how to slice vegetables into the ridiculous shapes of budding flowers. Irina was of two worlds and knew both how to season halupki and how to braise a rack of lamb not big enough to simmer a broth. Before wax in a kistka hardened, Irina could draw a layer of design on an eggshell as had Christian women in the old country, and yet as a woman in this new place she could with a needle reattach a fancy mother-of-pearl button without a prick to the neck of the squirming boy still wearing the shirt. What Irina did not know of either world, Laszlo would gladly have taught her, if he had known any more than she.

All that Laszlo brought with him from the old country, beyond the poor clothes, were sunflower seeds and rootstock from the four varieties of grape his parents tended for the owner of the Slavic land on which the family had lived longer than anyone could recount. The night before her sons' leave-taking, Laszlo's mother pulled up a hot stone with a poker and withdrew a small jar of coins from the pit below. These few she had split into two pitiful stacks, sewing each coin and cuttings from the grapes into pockets she had fashioned in the hems of the threadbare overcoats she gave to Laszlo and his brother, Vasyli. Laszlo kissed his parents and sisters, and the next morning, he followed Vasyl's back, scraping seeds from the dead heads of his mother's sonyashnyki into his pocket as they passed. The boys settled into the feel of wearing shoes as they shuffled through the fields to a dirt road Laszlo had never seen before, the light of the known world burning up in the Carpathians behind them. One at a time, Laszlo ground the sunflower seeds of home in his teeth, flicking shell off his tongue to the dirt as Vasyli talked, talked, talked, and the two of them walked, walked, walked. Eventually, they met the ocean. Vasyli cut the coins from the hems of their coats and paid their steerage across.

The boys were like so many others on the far side. So many families. So many young men. Vasyli followed a braggart shipmate and his vodka bottle to a Hunkie settlement in Canada. Laszlo drew from his pocket a worn slip of finger-softened paper on which his mother had with the help of the priest carefully written in ink and capital English letters the name of the town to which his father's friend's cousin's eldest son had emigrated in the New World: CLAREVILLE. Beneath, in script, she or Father Grigori had penned *Pennsylvania*. Somehow, he did not remember how, Laszlo had arrived.

He had also been taken in, all three Orthodox churches welcoming him as yet another son of the motherland. After nights of sleeping on a storeroom floor, after days of eating red-beet eggs offered from a jar in the barroom he was allowed to sweep, Laszlo located countryman Stanis Shandrushavich and, for a time, shared a boarding house bed with this pal who could vouch for him when he made the rounds, using his most important new and difficult-to-pronounce word: *work*.

By the time he was invited to join the company of men smoking and sharing a bottle in the payday shade of Mykhail Kruchevich's back porch, Laszlo Putavich had through polite deference and the showing of adequate American cash secured his own bed and meals in the house of Baba Smolnyki, kitchen matron of Saint Michael the Archangel Russian Orthodox Church. Laszlo was not only well fed but adopted by the church's murder of crow-garbed babas, who were alarmed that he approached the age of 20 without a wife. This, along with the amount of coal he could shovel into a lokie car, assured that Laszlo's days as a man without family or roots would not last long. His name was mentioned more than once to Mykhail and Vlada Kruchevich.

Of Mykhail Kruchevich's five children—all daughters—only spindly Irina, age fourteen, remained at home. Irina caught no one's eye. Behind Irina, the babushka-ed Vlada loomed, casting a dark shadow on any thought a young man might entertain about the wraithlike girl. Even had Irina flesh and sway to spare, the men of Clareville who could speak English would have diverted their gaze to the sky or the frayed tips of their hand-me-down shoes had Irina drifted into view.

And drift Irina did. The child was, to all appearances, without a mind of her own. Some mistook this for stupidity, but Irina's quiet obedience to Vlada's barked commands shielded her not only from confrontation with the quick-to-slap matriarch but nurtured the fragile shoots of Irina's dreams. In her mind, Irina ranged widely. Sent beyond the confines of their yard to purchase butter or deliver laundry, Irina peered into yards and windows, walking fast enough to avoid Vlada's wrath. Irina saw that not all gardens grew cabbages. Beyond the patch, the windows were covered by lace—and in lamplight, the walls beyond the fine curtains were papered with colorful cloth and hung with gleaming mirrors. These led her to believe: She might, God willing, one day live a different life.

And then Laszlo happened onto the porch of the patch house Irina called home.

*

The morning before the afternoon Laszlo and Irina stood together hands on a Bible in the priest's wife's parlor, Vlada hauled herself up the sagging stairs to the second floor. She directed Irina to gather her church dress and bundle of nightgown, bloomers, and summer and winter stockings from the back bedroom she had shared with her sisters. Then, Vlada led Irina to the larger front bedroom dominated by the imposing headboard of what had been Vlada and Mykhail's marriage bed. On the coverlet, Vlada laid a gossamer white nightgown with smocked bodice. After the keg in the church hall smoker foamed its end, Laszlo appeared at the kitchen door with a paper sack of belongings. Vlada, who had been waiting in the rocker, led Laszlo on his first visit to the second floor, where the door to the front room was open, a lamp was lit, and Irina was curled under the quilt. Vlada laughed as she closed the door.

Laszlo set the sack on the floor and hung his jacket. He smiled shyly at Irina before he sat on the edge of the bed and removed his shoes. And then Laszlo Putavich, still wearing his new American-made shirt and trousers, stretched out on the felt mattress, nestled his beer-brained head into a pillow whose feathers still bore the scent of Mykhail Kruchevich's oiled hair, slung his arm over Irina, and fell drunk asleep.

The next morning, Laszlo Putavich presented Irina for the first time with the only fully mature and functioning male member she would ever encounter. The sound of a heavy stream in the night-pot woke Irina as dawn greyed at the windows. Irina had, of course, seen male privates in the snail- and grub-like forms they took on the small boys her duties required her to prepare for school or naps. But the member that her new husband Laszlo shook over the pot was as big as the spigot of a water pump. Laszlo had stepped out of his trousers and knee-length drawers, the hard globes of his tallow-white behind glowing. Still wearing his new shirt and white socks, Laszlo turned, his part in his palm. Seeing Irina awake, Laszlo grinned, and the thing in his hand stiffened.

Laszlo climbed back into the bed and lay gazing sweetly at Irina. Irina pulled the covers to her chin. Laszlo's thing stretched the sheet, pointing toward the ceiling with persistent rigidity. Once she had seen it, Irina could not take her wide eyes away from the spot where the dark tip pressed a bit of wetness onto the sheet. As the sun rose and Irina became more visible, Laszlo began to believe he was married and that there was now a woman next to him—and that she was his wife and would not refuse him.

Except refuse him she did. When Laszlo reached to embrace her, Irina slapped his face and bolted down the hall shrieking about Laszlo's deformity. His member not yet calmed, Lazlo was struggling into his pants when Irina reached the stairs, where Vlada blocked the retreat and commanded Irina to return to her marriage bed and attend to her wifely duty.

Laszlo let his trousers drop.

*

After a few weeks, female wailing and whimpering ceased to seep around the door and out the windows of the front bedroom of the house that had been Mykhail Kruchevich's. Irina's cheeks grew rosy. Laszlo whistled as he walked.

He brought her chocolates and cherries. She fried for him the biggest piece of meat and at the kitchen sink scrubbed his back with a brush. She burnished his getting-married shoes with melted candle wax and, when his barked knuckles split and festered, she salved his cuts with rendered chicken fat, wrapping his hands in clean strips of old sheets.

It was Vlada who pronounced the pregnancy. Watching her daughter throw laundry over the lines strung across the kitchen, Vlada gestured from the rocker for the girl to come close. Vlada's gnarled fingers cupped Irina's belly.

"Before the green leaves go red," she announced to Laszlo, who beamed.

Irina pondered how the baby had come to be in her belly, but Laszlo, his head on her shoulder as they lay in the big bed, thrust an index finger in and out of the circle he'd made with the other hand. Irina's eyebrows lifted in surprise, Laszlo imitated her, and they fell on each other laughing.

When baby Misha arrived, he brought with him the strings and clots of Irina's insides, washed from Vlada's slippery fingers after she pulled him from her screaming daughter the dark Sunday he was born. Misha's birth stained permanently the bed on which he had been conceived. Misha thrived, and Irina survived the fever, but the stitches with which the old doctor days later closed the bleeding chasm between Irina's legs healed into a scar half the size of a towrope and just as taut.

Relations for Laszlo and Irina changed.

*

In the weeks following little Misha's death, Irina Kruchevich Putavich returned to the back bedroom and curled like a potato bug to a ball. Morning and night, Laszlo touched her shoulder, which had no warmth. He bent to hear her breath and kissed her forehead when the brief breeze at her nostrils revealed her yet alive.

Grief, worry, and loneliness forced Laszlo Putavich to drink, and drink returned him to the company of Stanis Shandrushavich, his pal of boarding house days. Drink, however, especially whiskey, which they gulped with a slap of the thick-bottomed shot glass on the bar, led the normally sweet-tempered, happy-go-lucky Stanis to a state of mean-mouthed pushiness. But Stanis was known to produce, as if by magic, small goods and oddments—lengths of lokie rails his neighbors used to support their porches, metal piping and jointures used, alas, in their stills, along with lumber that mysteriously appeared beside their doors as they found need to repair the cladding of their outhouses. However, Stanis's material benefactions could not prevent those on the receiving end of his insults from sometimes punching his drunken, smirking maw.

Laszlo Putavich stood beside Stanis when Tador Milzewkevski missed his aim and stumbled, mashing his nose on the hard brass of the foot rail at Yushko's Bar. Tador's head slid off the rail in blood running as wide and thick as the stream at the butcher's drain. They let Tador lie.

Tador lay so long that Buzzy Lukavuch rolled him over with a foot, and the men at the bar, Stanis included, peered down at him, beer glasses in their hands. Someone threw water on Tador's face. He did not stir.

That night, it took five Cossacks of the Coal and Iron Police to pummel Stanis to the floor of his rented room while furniture broke and Baba Smolnyki, wailing in her nightgown, covered her eyes. Stanis was wearing only the union suit he slept in as he was dragged through the front door. The trial was swift, the verdict predictable. His name could not be found in the records, and illiterate Stanis could produce no document, consign no property, which would convince a lawyer to take his case. With sadness, Laszlo Putavich, himself possessing no document save the slip of paper on which his mother had written his American destination, held the roll of Stanis's clothes as Baba Smolnyki bound it with the knot-mended laces of his boots. Said bundle she pressed into the hands of Dorcas McElhenny, the Mick girl who peeled potatoes and onions for boarding house meals, with instruction to send it with her half-idiot brother William, whose lilting tenor could be heard blocks before he arrived to deliver ice at the county jail.

Stanis's name, like Laszlo's, was recorded nowhere but at the port of entry and in the Cyrillic script of St. Michael's church ledger, the pages of which Father Yspecky held in one hand as he gathered the hem of his cassock to mount the marble steps to the courthouse and plead for Stanis with Judge Hargrave Ellicot. Before he took the trolley back to Clareville, Father Yspecky knelt to say the benediction with the blubbering Stanis in his cell. Before the month was out, Stanis was on the train to Philadelphia under Coal and Iron guard, and no one in Clareville, not even Masha Trushkonic, who in shame bore his child seven months later, heard from or of Stanis Shandrushavich again.

*

Mykhail Putavich son of—Laszlo knew it proclaimed as his fingertips
traced the English letters of their names, carved in stone only in Amer-
EE-ka. Laszlo's grief burned into a desire for the recognition that would
establish him as head of his American family, more real to him than any
before. Laszlo prayed to become a SITZ-i-zen.

Irina had finished third grade. When she satisfied Vlada that she could
read and reckon well enough not to be cheated by butchers, farmers,
tinkers, sheenies, and the ragman, Irina was no longer sent to school. No
decent, hard-working man would marry a woman who might confuse
him with fancy words or waste time on reading. A good wife could cook,
sew, bear healthy babies, raise respectful children, run a clean and pious
household, and without a hitch wring the neck of any chicken she raised.
If she could grind and season kielbasa, so much the better. Fair looks were
not to be prized above these wifely skills. An educated girl was a ruined
woman. She guaranteed that even a good husband would, eventually,
be driven to drink, may the saints forgive him. Mykhail's hosting of the
Saturday bottle-passing and uneducated Vlada's wiles and sharp tongue
were never discussed—though what these might suggest was sometimes
pondered.

Laszlo himself read in Ukrainian and Russian and could reckon well
enough to track in his head and to the penny what his pay should be
for the lokie cars he'd loaded and the total he ran for shovelheads and
cowhide gloves, but he could neither write his name in English nor read
the documents which might secure him a place in this new country of
America.

On a little tablet, Irina penciled her few purchases—most recently
green thread matching the voluminous plaid skirt she had taken from the
rubbish at the home of her Tuesday-Friday English employer, cloth Irina
had carried home to make a winter jacket and two pairs of jumpers for
poor, then-growing Misha. They had lost the child, and although God
had secured their bond, Laszlo would see that American law kept him
with Irina. The salvaged length of plaid wool was spread across Irina's
knees, and she held the wooden spool of thread. Laszlo opened the fabric,
stacked Misha's garments and diapers, and rolled them into the wool along
with the spool. He kissed Irina's head and set the bundle in the empty

dresser drawer. Laszlo would take the test for citizenship in the United States of America. He would have his papers.

Before Laszlo returned to sit beside Irina, he took her tablet and pencil from the top of the dresser, along with the McGuffey's primer that she had slipped from a shelf and dropped in the deep pocket of her skirt while dusting the bedroom of sickly, sissy Luther Hathaway. Laszlo adjusted the pillows against the headboard and helped Irina slip off her shoes. He opened to a page marked with a prayer card, set Irina's finger on a line, and urged her to say the letters. Laszlo, looking first to the book, watched her mouth intently, pronouncing the sounds he thought she'd made. Each time Irina pointed to her mouth, signaling him to watch how the American sounds were shaped by lips and tongue, Laszlo wanted to kiss her but refrained.

Within a few weeks, Laszlo had filed his declaration of intent and could recognize the letters of the alphabet large and small, delighting Irina when he correctly identified all the capital letters of *self-rising flour,* and the small script o, c, l, and a in *Coca Cola.* Irina began to run her finger along a whole word, and Laszlo sought to move those words from his mouth, though they emerged sometimes as if they were shards of glass or tangled lengths of string. The J of June and July fell out of his lips as a halted breath, his Slavic tongue resting low in the channel of his mouth. The H in Heinz arrived accompanied by a back-of-the-throat growl Laszlo could not suppress, and inevitably, wherever the letter occurred, he rolled the R. The vowels were deep and released with the mouth open. *Work* was *wahrrk* and over was *ovair.* Some sounds were followed, inexplicably, by a sound similar to a soft, plosive E, not fully a sound of its own but more the halting of the tongue at the back of the teeth. And yet Laszlo caressed the words in his mouth and began to *rrEEdeh.* Each time he spoke a word in English, the words spelled *United States of America.*

Laszlo and Irina sat together on the overstuffed parlor sofa, the *McGuffey's Third Level Reader* across their adjacent knees. Laszlo followed Irina's finger and read word-by-word, his understanding keen, but the mechanisms of his tongue and teeth, his lips and breath, tumbling like stones at first but then dancing a heavy-footed mazurka that real Americans, if they listened carefully, might almost understand.

From the rocker, Vlada listened to the lessons in the parlor, her block-like feet pushing the old chair into the train-like rhythm with which she had for one year, two months, and fourteen days lulled and cooed Misha to sleep. Laszlo rested his hand on top of Irina's hand. Several evenings later, Laszlo's hand progressed to Irina's thigh. And then, one night, holding the primer, Irina settled not only onto the sofa but into the arm Laszlo slid around her shoulders. Vlada's fat fingers rolled the beads of her rosary and she prayed.

After the birth of Misha, Irina had lain with her back to Laszlo, who folded his muscled arms around the spikes of her ribs and shoulders, the back of her frail skull resting against his chest. She could hear his heart. He could smell the sweat and Ivory Soap in her hair. In the six months Misha had been with God, Irina had learned to force her body to rise, and she busied herself with chores and laundry. When Laszlo returned from the mine, the bricks in the alley had been swept and the air was heavy with the scent of frying onions. As Laszlo left his dirty boots at the door, Irina met him, and from the top step that made them even, she wiped the coal dirt from his face and kissed him. Though Vlada dozed in the rocker, Laszlo stripped to his drawers, washing not like a peasant from a bucket in the yard but like an American, at the kitchen sink.

The scar that roped the opening of Irina's private parts had diminished. Finding the scar no longer froze the air in Irina's lungs, and though she held her breath sitting down, all she felt there now was a numbness that grew in her groin and belly to a hard, Misha-sized heat. She missed the child, the loss a great gaping space inside her. She had, as all mothers must, she felt, come to think of the child not as the sun around which the earth moved but as sun and stars themselves, as heaven and earth combined. Misha had clung to her, crying to be lifted, his tears when finally she held him sparkling on his cheeks like drops of dew and summer rain on the petals of flowers. Misha had nuzzled in Irina's neck, played with her hair, and purred in her ear. Irina ached to feel that shape of love again.

And so, one evening Irina closed the book of American history passed down to her by Baba Smolnyki, whose current boarders were not fit for reading, and took Laszlo's hand. His head tilted, and in answer, Irina led Laszlo to the bedroom, where she unpinned her hair and set his hands to the button at her nape.

*

At noon, the 19th day of February, 1920, Laszlo Putavich, born most likely in 1894, a son of Zakarpattya Oblast in what was now

Czechoslovakia, stood with 20 others in the cavernous, oak-paneled courtroom of the Anthracite County Courthouse, kissed the last of the foreign coins his mother had sewn in his coat, and took the oath of American citizenship. Behind him as he signed each round letter of his name in English stood his wife, Irina, her cheeks filled out, her hair shining, her belly showing a definite roundness under the green plaid of the shawl draped over the shoulders of her winter coat.

"SITZ-i-zen" is from a manuscript of linked stories titled At the Surface of the Mine, set in the anthracite area. Bim Angst lives in Saint Clair, Schuylkill County.

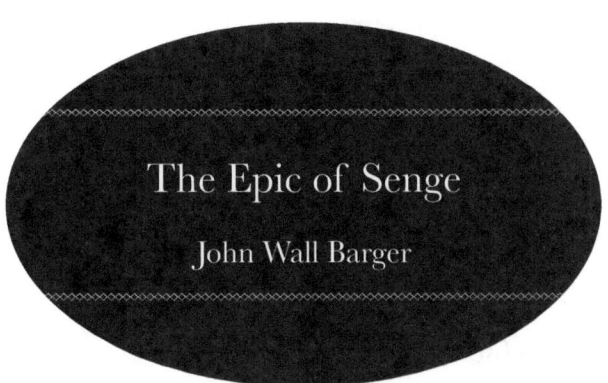

The Epic of Senge

John Wall Barger

We moved to Philadelphia from an Indian village
& shipped our big old tomcat, Senge.
We tried to keep him inside our row house,
tempting him with toys & snacks,
but he longed for village life:
fighting cats, hunting rats, walking the roofs
of the huts. He cried his lungs out:
"Freedom!" he cried. "Liberty!"
Sleepless, defeated, we opened the door:
Senge padded out in triumph.
He walked the sidewalks of West Philly,
manifesting all the lavish beauty

& violence of the village. Every day

he got lost. Today Tiina & I comb

the misty late-summer streets, searching.

Tiina—whose love for that cat

is fugitive & powerful—is so worried

she can't talk. As we step into Clark Park

I joke, "Maybe he caught a boat

back to India!" She emits a small,

dry laugh. We scan the park.

Dogs: fourteen. Cats: zero.

But it's nice. We sit in the damp grass.

Someone strums a woozy guitar.

Soft, distant singing. The sky, opening.

Under a maple tree: a pile, a form,

it is a body, an opossum. Twisted, seeping,

torn like a bag of rice. I say nothing.

Everything is wet. Record rain this year.

Even the kindness hovering in the high branches

is wet, glittering, pretty. Almost unbearable.

And *familiar*. The peaceful men

playing chess on fold-out tables.

The children blowing bubbles of light.

Like attending a warmhearted funeral,

which just happens to be your own.

Seaming

Kara Petrovic

My mother holds me down, her hands locked around my wrists as I am screaming, writhing in pain. It is midnight, or sometime after. The fluorescent lights of my room feel too bright, they burn against my skin, cursed with hypersensitivity. I can hear my mother cooing at me, gently whispering it is time to stop. Covered in cold sweat, my skin is slick, and my hair sticks to my forehead. This is a snapshot of my life at its lowest, which happens more often than I care to admit. It is a panic attack, or something similar, some days I cannot tell the difference. Yet, with unyielding patience, my mother hears my screams and we go into our usual song and dance: where my hands are scratching at my skin as if I were digging for gold, and her hands are petting my head, snaking their way around my body to make me still.

My mother never really understood mental illness, not when it first crept into my bed and made itself a home. She thought I was attention-seeking, the youngest child tired of raising their voice just to be heard, that this was the newest of my attempts to gain her affection. My mother thought she could shake it out of me, that if she grabbed me by my shoulders enough times or slapped me across the face hard enough I would snap out of it and be the child she had envisioned.

I am 22 years old now, and I have a cornucopia of diagnoses, all of which seem to be trying to outdo the other. In my youth, I was a lost soul — to put it kindly. A fire raged in my chest while a demon followed my every footstep: I was enamored with death.

If death was a man, with sickly grey skin and bones for fingers, he followed me throughout my adolescence, before I even knew how to correctly spell suicide. At 12 years old, I would write notes to my mother and leave them on the threshold of her bedroom, apologizing for being the way that I was, stating I knew she would be better off if I were dead.

I would watch her read these notes, hidden behind the pillars in the house. With the scoff of a laugh accompanied by a quick roll of her eyes, her staple response to my behavior, she would crumple the paper up. To her, this was a cry for attention, and I suppose in some way it was. It was also a cry for help, one she would make me wait several years to receive.

Meanwhile, I played surgeon with myself. I seemed to believe that if I cut deep enough I could find the source of my sickness and remove it from my skin. Since I had to eradicate this on my own, I had to navigate without a sense of direction. I would lock myself in my room and map out the corners of my brain, go hunting in the depths of my subconscious to try and locate the cause of my misery. At the dollar store, I would buy razors, take them home and break apart the safety barriers. I would mark up my arms, my legs, my stomach. I experimented at first, marking Xs all over my skin, but it quickly became methodical lines and, each new session, I challenged myself to dig even deeper.

A therapist once told me that the pain I carry is liquid gold, and it fills up the cracks inside of me and creates a new work of art each time— I stare at my pain and try to see the beauty in it, in its curves and twists, the knots in my forearms and the scars on my body. All I see are cracks. White lines that look nothing like gold. I trace my fingertips along the hypertrophic scars and, suddenly, I am engulfed in loneliness and vulnerability. Though I want nothing more than to hold on with an iron fist, I let go of the abyss and tell myself the wounds have healed. Yet they burn each time I see someone trying not to stare.

My mother believes pain can be expunged, as if my pain and I should separate. My mother says happiness is a choice. I promise I am trying to choose happiness every day, but maybe the words stick in my throat, maybe I'm so used to excelling as her disappointment that I can no longer tell the difference.

-

I am fifteen years old and I have been living with an unnamed illness for three years. It's November, 2011, and my sister and I are setting up the Christmas tree. My parents are still together, out for the evening at a concert, desperately hoping this date night will save their marriage. At some point in the evening, my lungs and heart plummet in my chest and my mind repeats one track. I sneak into my parents' bedroom and find my father's sleeping pills I had stumbled upon several weeks prior. I read the label with care, noting all the warnings. "Do not operate machinery. Take with food. Do not consume with alcohol."

Do not consume with alcohol.

Before I know it, I'm standing in front of the liquor cabinet, 26 pills in hand. I look through my options, and settle on the one with the highest alcohol content: tequila. I down the pills, chase them with the tequila, in seconds. The alcohol burns my throat, my body contorts in protest and I shiver as it enters my stomach. For a moment, nothing happens.

I walk upstairs into my bedroom. I pick out the outfit I would like to be found in: I change my shirt. I put one leg into my favorite pair of jeans.

When I wake up, I'm in the hospital. My mouth is black, covered in charcoal, and there are light burn marks on my chest. My mother sits across the room from me. Her thumbnail is in her mouth. She has been crying but when she realizes I am awake, her face hardens. I can hardly hear anything; the world is muted. She draws near and kneels by my bed. Her brown eyes I inherited are cold. "Listen," she says, "there will be a psychiatrist who comes to see you. You must listen to me. You must lie. You must not tell the truth. If you do, you will be hospitalized and this will ruin your life."

Ruin my life.

She coaches me, over and over, on the things I have to say. I stand up groggily and stumble towards the bathroom. She follows me, stands behind me, watching as I wash my face. She follows me back into the room, saying, "This was a mistake, an accident, you didn't know what you were doing."

"This wasn't an accident," I say, wincing as the words make their way from my throat.

"Don't be stupid. You must tell the psychiatrist, 'no, I don't have a history of this type of behavior.'"

When the psychiatrist visits me the following day, I say, "I made a mistake. It was an accident. I didn't know what I was doing."

I answer, "No, I don't have a history of this type of behavior."

When my 24 hours are up, I am released, and the next day I go to school as if I hadn't just died two days prior.

This becomes a standard play for us. The following year I make the same attempt. I steal painkillers, head to the liquor cabinet, swallow tequila. Again, I wake up in the hospital and follow the same script. When it happens again, and again, and again, we eventually manage to avoid going to the hospital, and it is my mother's turn to play doctor. As she wraps gauze around my wrists when I am 17 years old, her lips in a hard line though the rest of her face has softened over the years, I note her expertise: it had always been second-nature to her, healing my physical wounds in ways she could not mend the disorders in my mind.

Somewhere along the way, without much notice or declaration, everything changes. I have moved out and am living an hour's drive away. We see each other on weekends. Some weekends I skip. I ignore my mother's messages, her phone calls, and the more I do, the more they increase in frequency. No longer does she look at me with disdain. On this visit, I am 19 years old, sitting on the porch and smoking a cigarette with my mother. Even when we are the same, both smokers, we are different. She smokes thin sticks, I smoke 100s.

She asks, "How are you doing?"

I say, "Better than I have in years."

I look toward the setting sun as she flinches. I flick my cigarette away. The conversation is strained, painful, and I'm checking my phone at five-minute intervals; waiting for when I can take my train to a home that is no longer with her. She sends me care packages, tells me not to worry so much, kisses my forehead, and I realize this is the most attention I have gotten from her in years. Except now, I think, I no longer need it. I am independent, grown, away from her. I am eating healthy, sleeping well, saving money. For all intents and purposes, I am well and stable.
But I am not cured.

The illness returns.

I find myself coming home more and more. My mother welcomes this. We have a family dinner every Sunday, just the two of us, and I can see the happiness etched into her face. I feel her warmth for the first time in years, and I suddenly begin to loathe when it is time for me to return to my house.

At the end of the year, I move back home and nestle myself into her. She calls me baby, and reminds me that the world is not my enemy, and neither is my mind. I realize, then, that finally: neither is she.

-

My mother never understood mental illness, no, but she grew to accept me. We had lived in parallel, traveling in the same direction, never once touching. In the years that followed my first splitting of skin, I learned to come to terms with my mind. My darker inclinations left shadowy traces on me that I have filled with gold. My body is a work of art I cherish, each mark a reminder not of my lowest, but of what I have survived. I fell out of love with my own melancholy. In ways unclear to me, my mother did the same.

-

My mother holds me down. After a few minutes, my breathing evens out and my tears dry themselves on my face.

That night, we sleep together, cocooned around each other and still.

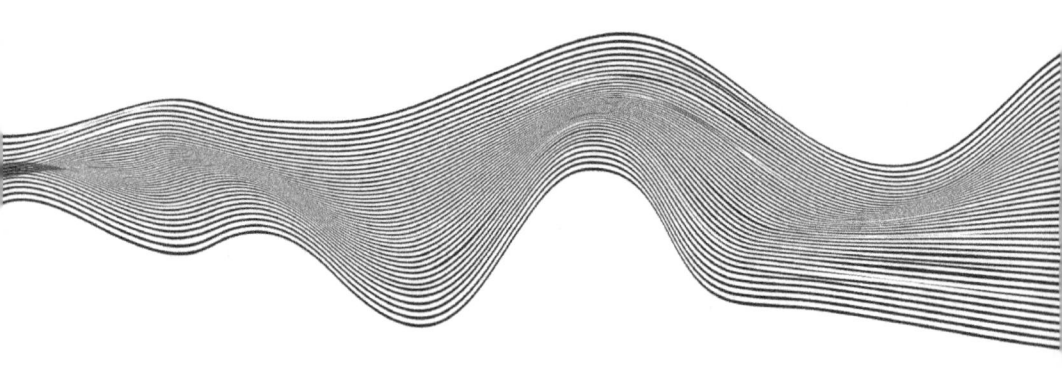

Nine-Year-Old Suicide in Reverse

Chad Frame

for Jamel Myles

A candle unsnuffs, its smoke drawn back in,
its guttering, finger width flame relit.
The bright blue JanSport rises from the floor
and hooks its straps around your slight shoulders.

You dart backwards down the carpeted stairs.
The door unslams. The yellow bus backs up
around the cul-de-sac. Your eyes unclench.
The children suck words back away from you.

High-fletched F, its bulbless semiquaver.
Lofty A, its slopes unassailable.
Selfsame, cliquish GG, backs turned to shun.
Surprised O, rolling, caught up in all this.
And T, the final, burning cross of it.

That morning, unknowing, your mother smiles,
untousles your hair like wind smoothing grass,
and sits. Inky clouds of coffee billow
past her pursed lips like possessing spirits.

Mysteries of the Universe

Roger Hart

The premonition hits as I walk down Park Street to the university. One foot up in the air and bamm! Knocks me back like a punch in the gut or a mysterious pain in the chest. A premo that sends a chill down my spine despite the warm spring morning. I try to shake it off. I have things to do.

Crows squawk in the maples and oaks, a holy racket. In the

distance the university band rehearses for the halftime show of the first home football game four months away, another holy racket. The smell of fresh baked bread and donuts drifts from Sweet Melissa's Bakery on Lake Avenue.

I try to wash the ugly inkling, the déjà before the vu, out of my mind by concentrating on the cottonwood fluff floating in the air, the noisy crows scolding me, the fat dandelion blossoms blanketing the lawn. A large limb from a sycamore tree has fallen across the sidewalk in front of the physics lab. The dew-covered grass in the shade of the red bricks and ivy of Rodman Hall needs mowed. Cleaning up downed limbs, mowing, trimming, mulching flowerbeds, seeding the muddy areas around the greenhouse. Maintenance stuff. My job. Need to get everything looking tiptop for graduation.

The premonition gnaws at the sunny day. It's a dark thundercloud threat just over the horizon, lightning flashing, thunder booming. I hope it's a false warning, a fake forecast.

I've had a few, both good and bad, fake and not. Take the one when Sloane and I were camping in the Boundary Waters, our first date, although we didn't think of it as a date. We'd known each other three weeks. Morning fog blanketed the campsite so thick we couldn't see the water a few feet beyond our beached canoe. Dew dripped from the needles of the pine trees, landed on the rocks with little plops. I closed up the camp stove, and we took our cups of coffee inside the tent, sat on our sleeping bags with Yogi hunkered down bear-like between us. "A moose," I mumbled a few minutes later, just as the coffee was beginning to cool.

"What?" Sloane asked.

"Outside the tent," I said. I hadn't heard a thing, no hooves crunching on pinecones or sloshing through water, no chomping of aspen, no snorting. Pure premonition.

Sloane gave me her Ph.D. in theoretical physics look. I couldn't even recite the title of her doctoral thesis, which had something to do, she explained, with cosmic rays called Oh-My-God particles. I had no clue what Oh-My-God particles were despite her attempts to explain, but I took comfort in her admitting no one else knew much about them either. Sloane says space-time is curved by gravity and that virtual particles pop in and out of existence, but she doesn't buy into premonitions, prophesies, omens, or signs.

Holding onto my cup, I crawled to the tent flap and flipped it aside. Ten feet away and staring at our red canoe was a giant moose although, I guess, all adult moose are giants. I touched my finger to my lips and pointed. Yogi, curious but cautious, watched, sniffed the air. No growl or bark. The moose grazed around our campsite then stepped into the lake and urinated, which sounded like a bucket of water being dumped or a waterfall dropping from a respectable height. "Premonition," I said a bit smugly.

Sloane shook her head.

I tried throwing a little of her theoretical physics stuff at her. "Didn't you tell me yesterday as we were paddling across the inlet that quantum things in the future can influence the present? Maybe the future moose in front of our tent signaled it would be there."

Sloane smirked. "Future events influencing the present is only true in the quantum world," she said.

Sloane is driven in an indoors/office/journal reading sort of way. Although she had traveled to conferences in several countries and a dozen major cities, this was her first camping trip. I wanted to ask how one thing could be true in her quantum world and not ours, but the moose had moved on, and she was packing up, preparing to move out.

Later that day, the moose day, two young women wearing nothing but hats paddled by us, which has nothing to do with this story.

"Morning," I said, doing my best not to focus on their as yet un-tanned breasts.

"Morning," they answered.

After they'd rounded a bend behind us, Sloane, sitting in the bow, turned, cocked her eyebrow. "Well? No comment?" She spoke softly as sounds carry over water, and she didn't want the topless paddlers to hear.

"I'd worry about mosquitoes and sunburn," I said, "but it's a free world."

Sloane puzzled over my answer for a second. "In the spirit of sisterhood," she said, and then facing forward, pulled off her sweatshirt and bra.

I stared at her back, the way it narrowed near her waist, the smooth skin, the soft bumps of her spine. "Oh, look," I said, pointing at an island behind us, tricking her into turning around. "Thought I saw a bear."

She squinted at the island, and then at me. "Yeah, right," she said, daring me to stare.

A bare-breasted theoretical physicist sitting in the bow of my canoe. Who could have imagined?

Sloane says we met by mistake, but I say we have a cosmic connection. When the science department has a lecture I attend. I like seeing slides of galaxies, nebulas, the colorful clouds of Jupiter. When I was in high school we had careers day, and I signed up for cosmetology, which I had mistakenly assumed was cosmology. The instructor, a woman with fluorescent blond hair and bright red lipstick, asked each of us to describe our interest in cosmetology. "Wrong class," I muttered.

Sloane, applying for a position in the physics department, gave a lecture on dark energy and mistook me for another prof. Instead of wearing my maintenance clothes, boots and a blue shirt with *Russ*, my name, stitched in red above the pocket, I wore a sport coat and tie, having come from my niece's recital. (Lucy's only ten and plays the violin.) After the lecture I complimented her, and she asked about my research focus. "Oh, I go in circles," I said, referring to mowing the lawn, but she thought I was talking code for work with the Hadron Collider. We went to dinner where her mistake became obvious as I had no clue what she was talking about: Hilbert space, vacuum energy, the fine tuning problem. She laughed when she discovered I mowed the lawn, and when we returned from our

Boundary Waters canoe trip she moved in with me, saying I was a mystery and she liked mysteries. We've been together nine months, something my mother calls a pregnant amount of time.

Her look: white blouses and not a wrinkle in them. Black skirts that show off her long legs. She's thin and has reddish-blond hair, which she wears in a no-nonsense, professional above-the-collar cut, a style the instructor in the cosmetology class might have liked. Her lips stretch across perfect teeth and her hazel eyes sparkle when she smiles. She doesn't wear glasses, which is surprising her being a theoretical physicist who is always buried in a book.

Anyway, all this has little, maybe nothing, to do with my premonition, but, as Sloane says when describing her quantum particles, we really have no idea what is real and what isn't, so I've included it here in an effort to be as honest as possible even though honesty is a seldom admired characteristic today despite lip service by politicians, religious folk, the FBI, and the Boy Scouts.

The spring semester is almost over, and dandelions cover the campus commons. Arnold Dickey, the head of maintenance, ordered ten gallons of Roundup and told me to spray last spring and fall. I don't trust Roundup despite assertions by DuPont that it's safe. I got rid of it, burned it in the incinerator, then sprayed the lawn with water. I don't understand Arnold's love of Roundup. He was in Vietnam, got sprayed with Agent Orange, which has been linked to his Non-Hodgkin's Lymphoma and was made by Dow Chemical, which is now part of DuPont, so you'd think he'd be suspicious of chemical sprays and chemical company claims.

Arnold catches me as I approach the maintenance shed. Before he went through chemo Arnold looked like Willie Nelson what with his beard, western hat, and long, white pigtails, but his hair and beard are gone, replaced by bald, although he still wears the black western hat. I think he's going to warn me about the dandelions, which isn't really a premonition as much as a hunch. There's a difference.

Arnold owns a hangdog expression and gets right to the point. "Sloane," he says. "How do you feel about her getting the trip?"

Trip? I squint. "What trip?"

He waves his hand in the air, trying to remember the name. "The Antarctica thing."

I don't know about any Antarctica thing. Sloane going to the South Pole is something I can't imagine. Our canoe trip to the Boundary Waters was her equivalent of going to the moon.

"Maybe I shouldn't have said anything. Maybe she's going to surprise you."

"When?" I ask.

"Maybe over dinner. I don't know."

This is the way Arnold talks, expecting you to fill in between the lines. Arnold also has spells, gets confused, maybe the chemo, maybe something else. Arnold calls me Wes sometimes when I'm Russ, maybe a beginning dementia thing, maybe exposure to Roundup. "No," I say, "I mean when is the South Pole thing?"

He looks up in the trees, maybe trying to remember, maybe watching a squirrel. With Arnold, everything is maybe. "This summer, I think. Going to be there six months." He pauses, points at the dandelions and shakes his head. "That Roundup ain't doing shit," he says. And then remembering, "Maybe she said something and you forgot."

Sloane works late, sleeps late. Much of her work is done at her office desk. Most of it is math without numbers, just letters and squiggly lines, sometimes a graph. I've seen it. Why would she want to do that in Antarctica? "Must be a mistake," I say. "She's a theoretical physicist. They go to conferences in big cities, sit indoors. They don't go to the South Pole. We're going camping this summer."

"Can't be in two places at once," he says.

But you can, or at least those quantum things Sloane talks about can. Here and there at the same time. Unbelievable. It's like a habit with them.

I haven't talked with Sloane since lunch yesterday. She nudged me with an elbow to the ribs when the alarm went off this morning, but she went back to sleep before I rolled out of bed, so we haven't had time to talk about the South Pole or her being in two places at once.

Arnold, like me, has not had much luck in his love life, and he tends to be cynical about relationships. That's why he worries about Sloane. He thinks she's stringing me along, which has nothing to do with the string theory of the universe she often mentions.

I dismiss Arnold's off-hand warning the way I dismissed ten gallons of Roundup and this morning's premonition. I toss Antarctica in my mental incinerator. Melted. Gone.

I'll stop by Sloane's office later, after I take care of the sycamore limb blocking the sidewalk next to the physics building, after I pretend to kill the dandelions. We'll have lunch together, and she can tell me something new, maybe explain how gravity curves space or how those quantum things can be in two places at once. I'll ask about the Antarctica thing, which goes to show my mental incinerator is not working.

When Sloane goes for a walk to ponder, she takes Yogi. What a sight! Yogi weighs 140, twenty pounds more than Sloane. When we went to the Boundary Waters, Yogi and I swam despite the water being so cold my fingers, toes, and personal body parts went numb. He stayed by my side, kept an eye on me. That's the Newfoundland way. His chin is white and his eyes are milky. He is slow to get up, and he sits gingerly, but he loves to swim.

Students greet me as they head to their classes. "Hi, Russ, "Morning, Russ," they say. My name is stitched in red letters above the pocket of my blue shirt, which I have already mentioned, so they know me and that I can unlock their dorm room doors when they forget their keys. They watch, a few do, as I cut up the sycamore limb and haul it away. Sycamores love water and the physics building is on high dry ground, so I have no idea what the tree is doing here. I sometimes wonder what I'm doing here, too.

Anyway, by the time I finish taking care of the limb and pretend to Roundup the dandelions, it's lunchtime, and I enter Rodman Hall, the physics building. Sloane's office is on the third floor, the floor with the view of the football stadium and the river. I knock on her door and it swings open. "Oh," she says. "Is it that time?"

In the beginning we ate lunch together a couple times a week at one of the tables in the faculty lounge off the cafeteria, days when she didn't have meetings or a class, but we stopped doing that for reasons I don't know. It happened. A mystery. When the weather warmed up and everything began to green, we sometimes walked home and had lunch there, sat on the back steps and watched Yogi sniff around the yard, cock his arthritic hip on the bushes.

Today, however, the day of the bad premonition, I order delivery from Busy Day Café before heading to Sloane's office. I don't have to specify what we want. It's always the same. "Lunch for Russ and Sloane," I say. I'm in Sloane's office five minutes when Jerry whose-last name-I-don't-know shows up with the white bag holding our sandwiches, a vegetarian wrap for Sloane, a steak sandwich for me. Sloane drinks Coke despite my warnings about it being a lot like Roundup. I drink water.

We make small talk. She's amused by my granting amnesty to the dandelions but otherwise she's preoccupied. Sloane is desperate to understand the universe. "Is it those Oh-My-God particles?" I ask, nodding at the papers on her desk.

She goes, "What? No. Just thinking. We need to talk." She looks at the office door the same way Arnold went blank staring off at the squirrels and for a second I think something is going around, a distraction bug or virus.

I wait for the talk we need to have but none comes. I avoid the Antarctica thing because I don't believe it's true and because I'm afraid if I ask it will be, sort of like those quantum things that come into existence when you observe them. There's a connection here I can't explain. "Hey," I say, trying to drum up a little enthusiasm. "I'm looking forward to the lecture tonight."

She sips the Coke, leaving a smudge of lipstick on the straw. "Oh,

Russ, are you sure you want to go?"

I take a bite of my steak sandwich. It's huge. Her veggie wrap is green and small. Maybe that's how Sloane stays so thin. I'm confused as to why she thinks I might not want to go. I go to all the physics lectures. I like hearing about the unknown, and I've not made a fool of myself by asking a question, stupid or otherwise. I just listen. "Sure," I say. "I'm going."
"Going where?" a voice behind me asks.

Rocky, the grad student she's supervising. I want to say, Oh my god, it's Rocky, but what I actually say is, "Hey, Rock. The lecture tonight."

Rocky's eyes never look straight at you but off to the side, like you're really six inches to your left. He's thin and pale and cultivating the Einstein look with his wild hair. He wears dark-rimmed glasses and needs to change his name or switch his major to geology.

"Excuse me," he says to Sloane, stepping behind me and my steak sandwich. "Do you have time this afternoon to look at my calculations . . ." and then his voice trails off as he mumbles things like Planck's constant, dimensions, and vacuum energy.

Sloane gives me a look that says she needs to take care of this and it would be a good time for me to run home and let Yogi out for a few minutes. She can say all that with one look, a twitch of an eyebrow, pursed lips.

I grab my sandwich and thermos of water—no plastic bottles for me—and nod to Rocky, who flinches despite my not touching him. I save the last two bites of the steak sandwich for Yogi, who will give me a look that says thanks.

Later, after sitting on the back deck with Yogi and him giving me the look that says thanks, I walk back to the university where right off I'm confronted by two students, a young man wearing flip-flops and a tie-dyed shirt and a tiny, wide-eyed, granola-type girl, who may or may not be his girlfriend. Both are holding cell phones, like this might be the way they talk to each other. "Russ," she says. The tone of her voice suggests she's locked herself out of her room. Again, this is not a premonition but a hunch based on voice, body language, and her blocking my path.

"What can I do for you?" I ask, and she points at the grass, at the tiny pink flags warning that the dandelions have been sprayed with an herbicide and they should stay off the lawn for twenty-four hours.

"You're poisoning the environment," she says. Her tie-dyed friend nods.

"It's not poison," I whisper. "I put flags there so everyone would think I sprayed the dandelions." I hope this doesn't get back to Arnold who would be sorely disappointed in me.

The girl, wearing a Greenpeace badge on her jean blouse and half a dozen silver rings dangling from her ears, takes a defiant stance. "Herbicides are poisonous," she says. She snaps a picture of the pink flags with her cell phone. "You're killing microorganisms in the soil. Animals will track this back to their homes. Birds will eat poisoned worms."

I bend down and snap off a dandelion. She jumps back like I'm going to attack her with it. I bite the dandelion. She gasps. The guy stares at me. "Cool," he says.

For a second I think the dandelion has a sickening sweet smell, a bitter taste. I worry that Arnold came out with more Roundup, real Roundup and not water, and dowsed the dandelions. I pick another, a fat, bright yellow one with moisture still clinging to the bloom. I sniff. There's no sweet smell and the blossom tastes like salad without the dressing.

The girl is confused. Maybe I'll die in front of her and maybe I'm telling the truth. She tugs at the sleeve of her boyfriend's tie-dyed shirt, and they slip away, careful to not step on the grass.

Another thing I learned from Sloane was that things, quantum things, exist only when they interact with other things. If they don't interact, they don't exist. I asked Sloane to explain. She started, took a deep breath, stopped. "Electrons, photons, all the tiny bundles of energy that make up atoms, don't exist unless they interact with something."

"Yeah," I said. "But how is that possible?"

"It's hard to explain," she said.

Although she assured me I had nothing to worry about, I welcome these interactions with students. We exist!

A lot of the things I learned from Sloane came during our canoe trip to the Boundary Waters. "What came before the Big Bang?" I asked as we paddled across a smooth stretch of water. Yogi's ears perked up like he wanted to hear the answer too.

"There was no before," she said. And then she asked, "What's wrong with those trees?"

"They're aspen. Probably the Aspen Blotch Miner. It's an insect."

"Will it kill them?"

"Probably not. And how can there be no before?"

"There was no time."

We paddled close to shore. The wind had shifted and we were alert for any sudden change in the weather while I tried to grasp how there could be no time. A few seconds later—see, there's time—I touched my finger to my lips and pointed at the bird swimming ahead of us.

"What is it?" she whispered.

"A loon."

We went back and forth all afternoon, me asking questions about the universe, how an electron could be in two different places at the same time, what is dark matter, and Sloane asking questions about the Boundary Waters, what were the smooth rocks where we beached the canoe, why was the area so rich in iron ore, what was the story of the Native Americans who had lived here, and where had they gone.

I've heard dozens of science lectures, and I've read a few books, but I'd never had a chance to ask questions of an expert. My job during those science lectures is to be quiet. Talking with Sloane I felt the way a music lover taking a canoe trip with Adele or Prince might feel, like a football fan talking with Jimmy Brown, the greatest running back of all time.

We fell into something special on that trip, if not love, something moving in that direction. Sloane had a wicked sense of humor and several times we laughed so hard we almost tipped the canoe. At night, after the mosquitoes quieted down, we'd stretch out on the smooth slab of rock along the shore, hold hands and stare at the stars while Yogi snored beside me. I tried to imagine a universe that went forever and then tried to imagine one that didn't. Was there intelligent life somewhere out there staring back at us? How did this universe get started and why were we here? Sloane was looking for the answers. Loons called back and forth, their songs both beautiful and haunting.

Sloane talked all winter about the two of us going on a return trip to the Boundary Waters. "I want to see a bear," she'd say. I have the permit and a couple weeks off in August. That's why I don't think Antarctica is a real thing.

I get ready to mow despite the mower's roar annoying the professors who are trying to teach electricity and magnetism, particles and waves. A few professors have become so outraged by the mower's roar that they fight back. We have battles. The physics professors have threatened to shoot me with lasers and turn on powerful magnets that would suck the fillings out of my teeth. I let the tractor backfire and make an extra sweep past their windows when these things happen. I hate cutting the dandelions, but a job is a job, so I make sure the mower deck is secure, fire up the tractor, and begin making loops around the green. Mowing is a good time to think.

Do premonitions have an expiration date? How can you tell the fake from the real? These are things Rozzi and I argued about when we were on patrol outside Kandahar. Rozzi claimed if you never told anyone your premonition it wouldn't come true. He hoped it might keep at bay the nightmare scenarios we all foresaw. He also said premonitions had no expiration date. I argued everything died sooner or later, even premonitions.

I can't shake this morning's premonition, which is like a bad dream, a disturbing movie playing on a screen behind my eyes. Made me feel hollow. If this premonition were a movie there'd be sad music playing, maybe a cello or bagpipes, maybe the theme from the movie *Starman* at the moment Jeff Bridges is about to leave and never come back. I would describe it except for hoping Rozzi was right. If I keep it under wraps it won't happen.

I go around and around, the circle of mowed grass growing smaller with each loop. I take comfort in knowing the dandelions will be back. The sun is fat and bright, the first really hot day this spring, and my neck is burning.

After work I walk home, I call Sloane's office as I put a pizza in the oven.

"Russ," she says. "Sorry. I'm going to dinner with Dr. Franz and Dr. Ahman before their presentation tonight. We're on our way now."

I hear other voices and laughter in the background. "Okay," I say. "I love you."

"Okay," she says. "Got to go."

I eat half the pizza. Yogi's bones are tired, and he ignores my offerings of the crust.

As I walk toward the lecture hall the whistling of the spring peepers and the smell of fresh cut grass cheer me although they do not wipe out the ghost of this morning's premonition. When I arrive the room is half full of grad students and their friends. I don't spot Rocky's wild hair. The two giving the lecture and the physics faculty have not yet shown up, still hobnobbing, I suppose, at the Other World Tavern across town.

I take a seat near the front and save the seat next to me for Sloane although she will probably sit in the first row with the other physics professors. This does not bother me. I understand how she might want to lean over and whisper a quantum question or comment to one of her peers who will whisper theoretical things to her.

Five minutes before seven they show up and take their seats in the first row. Sloane turns in her seat, spots me and nods. I wink back and let out my breath, which I didn't realize I'd been holding. After long introductions the lecture begins.

The first speaker, a physicist responsible for experiments with photons, explains that when two quantum particles are close to each other they become entangled. They can then be sent their separate ways and still, somehow, maintain a mysterious connection when thousands, even millions, of miles apart.

I like the idea two particles can remain connected when far apart. I think Yogi and I have that. I hope Sloane and I do, too.

Next up, is an older woman who repeatedly swings her head to the side to get her long, going-to-gray hair out of her eyes. Her theory is that the universe is a hologram, nothing more than a projection stored in a two dimensional membrane surrounding the universe. "Which is real?" she asks. "The three dimensions we think we know or are we and our world like the images in a mirror, mere projections?"

I can't sit still any longer. Maybe it's the weight of the bad premonition. The thought that we are nothing more that images is too much. I raise my hand.

The woman smiles, leans forward and nods.

"But we're more than images," I say, hoping I haven't missed the entire point, hoping, too, I'm not embarrassing Sloane. I tap my chest, the spot over my heart. "I'm solid."

The woman nods a few more times to acknowledge my question. "But you aren't solid. You are mostly empty space. And that very tiny bit of you made up of protons and neutrons and electrons? Well, they're not solid either. They're bundles of energy that pop in and out of existence. It's a great mystery, isn't it?" And then there are more questions, eager grad students wanting to impress their professors and each other. I stop listening. When the lecture is over, when the speakers have been thanked and everyone heads for the door, there's a tap on my elbow.

"Russ?" she says. "You okay?" She sits, one vacant chair between us.

"Are we entangled?" I ask.

"That happens only in the quantum world," she says.

"Are you going to the South Pole?"

She doesn't appear surprised by my question. "Yes. I don't like the cold and it's outside my realm of experience. But I'm looking forward to it." She glances at her group as they wait for her by the door. "We can talk later."

I say I understand although I don't. I want to ask about our trip to the Boundary Waters and if she plans on living with me when she comes back from the South Pole, but I already know the answers. Sloane pats my knee and says she has to run.

The auditorium is mostly empty when I leave. On my way out the door I bump my elbow. Solid.

As I walk across campus my mind races from one thought to another. Yogi is having trouble getting up and down and this may be his last trip to the Boundary Waters. A couple sitting by the lake laugh and lean into each other. The spring peepers sing. Usually I take comfort in seeing the night sky full of stars, but tonight is an exception. I feel alone. Temporary. My premonition haunts me. I feel like I'm no more than a character in someone's story, and I might, my entire world might, at any moment, blink out of existence.

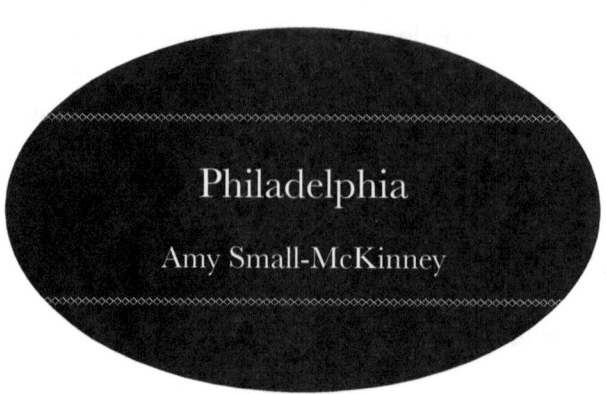

Philadelphia

Amy Small-McKinney

Beauty was hard for me to find on a spare cot or in the back
of a truck, when I had no home. & then I did,

when beauty had bars on its windows & a Coleus sat on my sill
with its purple hearts & old Tony sold me necessities
& came to know my name & the butcher without a thumb brought a
    Thanksgiving turkey
to my front door & young Tony upstairs lost a finger in some war, or so
    he said.
I was happy to hike the flight of stairs to sit with him and talk.
He borrowed a glass vase, nothing more, &

at the nearby market, startled pigs & cheeses hung on racks,
women peddled chestnuts & nutmeg, their voices ancient pigeons
    promising no hunger.

A Vietnamese restaurant, the place for cheap soup with long noodles &
    airy leaves floating.
A boat, I could sit for hours & row away from loneliness.

No one knew what they meant to me then.
The green leafy soup stars or the nine-fingered butcher,
his attentiveness filled me like a luxurious meal.

To tell you I was hungry is beside the point, very young,
left home, no choice, love rationed like air.

Now I think I know beauty,
look up at stars, some have names,
are gifts for birthdays.
What I want to say: how little I know of anyone's life.

We are a country, a world, a universe of division.

We imagine this must be beauty:

Doesn't everyone love Evie's homemade *Nduja*, her hair pulled back in
    a chignon?
Or this: A woman drinks morning coffee, mistrusts newly leveled fields,
worries for her seed beds.
Or: Summer & a man sits beside the stoop of his sweltering house
    playing checkers, waits
at least five minutes to move his piece.
& I have found it, at times, when the train rumbles under my window,
its constancy a parliament of beautiful owls, returning.

In the Woods

Curtis Smith

The cut ran fifty yards, a scar halfway up the hillside. The cut scoured by glaciers, or so the boy had been told. He climbed atop a boulder larger than a car, and he imagined the hill and all he knew entombed in ice. The boy's steps careful as he descended into the cut, the bothering of roots and rocks. The boy tacked an envelope to a fallen oak. The wood riddled with bugs, and the boy ran a finger over the bullet holes and thought about the days his father had brought him here to shoot. The boy retreated, and at thirty yards, he unshouldered his father's deer rifle. He loaded a single cartridge and secured the bolt. The rifle was heavier than the .22 he'd learned with, but the boy was older and stronger now. He steadied the rifle and placed the scope's crosshairs on the paper. He didn't love shooting, but he liked this—the sense of a world stilled, the woods breathing with him, the rocks aware of his beating heart. He rooted himself, an anchoring in his boots, his spine straight, and squeezed the trigger. The kick knocked his shoulder, and he lurched back but he kept his feet. His ears rang, and the echo pulsed between the trees before the quiet rushed back.

Their house stood in a clearing at the hill's base. The house built by his grandfather, white clapboard, moss on the roof. Generations of settling had robbed the structure of its straight lines. Pictures hung crooked, or appeared to. A dropped ball would roll until it reached a baseboard. A gravel drive slanted down to the two-lane road, and beyond that, a longer slope that ran to the river's edge. The boy had seen the river cover the road, and although the water had yet to reach their home, the boy knew this was inevitable. The back door slammed, and the old lab that had been his father's hunting dog followed the boy to the yard's burn barrel. The boy covered the barrel's ash with a layer of cardboard and cartons. Junk mail. The bills they'd ignore until the envelopes stamped with red warnings arrived. The grass around the boy and dog silver with frost, and when the dog peed, steam rose.

The boy considered the hillside, his gaze lost amid the naked trees. The hill blocked the morning sun and shielded them from a nor'easter's winds, but when the storms pushed from the west, the drifts grew deep. On the nights the wind whistled across the frozen river, their crooked house shook, and the boy listened to the roof's groan and slept little, fearing collapse, a burial beneath wood and snow. He squirted fluid into the barrel then struck a match. He paused, waiting to feel the heat on his fingers before dropping the match. The flames caught, a gasp of oxygen, a pull the boy felt in his lungs. He watched the flames, his hands buried in his pockets. The dog, which had lurched back with the flames, now came sniffing to the boy's side.

On the road, a black pickup slowed. The truck lost from sight, but the boy heard it pull onto the riverside's shoulder. The engine killed, the doors and gate slammed. The leafless forest offered little cover to the men who set upon the hillside's rocky path. The men stocky, black skullcaps and thick beards. They didn't carry rifles, but they soon would. The boy wondered if they noticed him or the smoke from the barrel or the dog that offered a brief, feeble bark. The boy had seen their truck from the school bus window, its oversized tires, its decals and gun rack. Common courtesy should have directed the men to knock at their door. An asking of permission. A thanks for sharing the land. Perhaps they believed the land beyond the clearing was open despite the weathered No Trespassing signs the boy's father had posted. Perhaps the men knew the boy's father was gone, and they believed there was no need to seek consent from a woman and her boy. The men walked on then vanished into the woods. The boy turned to the dog. "Come on, girl."

The boy and his mother ate long after dark. Thanksgiving leftovers and tomorrow she'd teach him to make soup from the carcass. Her late shifts at the warehouse, the ride that took over an hour on snowy days. She often returned from work dazed. The pace. The warehouse's acoustics. The hours on her feet. The boy had always loved her, but he'd grown to appreciate her. Her devotion. Her strength and sacrifices. He fed the woodstove, and the dog curled close to the warmth. The boy hoped to shoot a deer in the coming week. They'd stock the freezer. He'd help provide. He was down to ten bullets, but he reasoned if he was patient, if he heard his father's voice—his urgings to be certain, to breathe deep and melt into the woods' stillness—he'd be OK. He washed the dishes, the water cold after his mother's shower. He returned to the living room to find her asleep on the couch. He turned off the TV and covered her with a blanket. Outside, headlights, the cars and trucks navigating the dark and the twists of the river road.

The next morning, the boy woke before dawn. They used to go to church on Sundays, but that was another life. His mother gone, as she would be every weekend for the next month. The chance for overtime, and perhaps they'd even have enough for Christmas presents, although the boy assured her he didn't need anything. The boy made coffee, savoring its warmth more than its flavor, but firing up the woodstove could wait until he came back. He bundled up. In the mudroom, he grabbed his father's crowbar. The dog followed, its movements slow in the cold, its black eyes upon him. The boy stood in the open doorway, letting the dog have its choice. Outside, the dark of starlight, the river's churn.

The boy crossed the clearing and entered the woods. He aimed his flashlight on the path, and the rocks and leaves passed like a stream. The cold in his lungs, and balancing it, the kindling of muscle. He thought of all the times he'd followed his father up this trail. When he dreamed of him, they were often in the woods, his father's back to him, the boy struggling to keep pace.

The boy waited for the dog to catch up before turning off the path. He petted her, a habit he engaged in more and more, the understanding of her age and a future in which he'd miss her. He looked up. A thousand branches fragmented a sky just beginning to lighten. He'd have the dark for a while, the hill's western shadows, a sensation that had always made him think of the river's fish, a submersion, yet in a world so often turned upside down, who was to say whether the river was the darkness or the light above?

The flashlight's beam passed across the branches' tangle until it settled on the tree stand. "Stay," he told the dog. He heard his father, his talks of doing the right thing, and the boy apologized as he grasped the first rung nailed into the wide trunk. In the boy, a balance of footing and grip. Then a deeper balance, the equaling of what was right and what was just.

He grasped the next-to-last rung. The sky above lighter, and he became the fish rising to the bait. He looked down. His dog lost in the darkness. He thought of falling, the breaking of bones. Of dying alone. He wedged the crowbar under the rung below the stand. He jerked, and from the wood, a groan. The rung pulled away in fits. He caught his breath. The sky lighter, the gray of ash. He swung the crowbar, striking the plank's back. The thuds echoed until the plank dislodged. The dog barked. The boy stepped down a rung and went back to work.

He rose early again the next morning. He sat perched in the tree stand, and in his father's orange vest, he felt like an exotic bird waiting on the sun. The vest smelled like his father, gun oil and grease. The perch a half-mile from the other tree stand, and the boy imagined the trespassers, their anger, their thwarted schemes. The boy lifted his chin, and his exhaled breath rose. He found peace in accepting the truth that the world owed him nothing. Below, a rustling, and the boy waited, knowing the darkness would fade.

Contributors

CNF

Kara Daddario Bown is a Philadelphia-based freelance writer. Her writing examines the diverse ways in which illness and loss can affect the human experience. She has performed at The Moth StorySLAM and GrandSLAM. Her work has been published in *The Belladonna, The Pennsylvania Gazette, Philadelphia Stories*, and *The Penn Review*. She holds a Bachelors in English and Creative Writing from the University of Pennsylvania.

Stephen St. Francis Decky is a multimedia artist and writer whose work has appeared in festivals, collections, and museums both nationally and internationally, including The New Britain Museum of American Art and The Museum of Fine Arts, Nagoya, Japan. His films have screened at the Camden International Film Festival, the Philadelphia Unnamed Film Festival, and the VOID International Animation Film Festival in Copenhagen, Denmark, among many others. He has taught Animation and Digital Media classes at several schools, including Tufts University and Lycoming College, and his fiction has appeared in *Berkeley Fiction Review* and *Luna Negra*, as well as being nominated for a Pushcart Prize. He currently lives and works in Philadelphia.

Nancy Farrell is a lifelong writer of autobiographical essays and poetry. She is inspired by old family stories and photographs, and with personal memories that continue to stir emotion. She suspects her love of nostalgia comes from her late father, who delighted in talk of long-lost friends and their antics on the streets of South Philadelphia. Nancy and her husband, Jack, share three grown daughters with whom they happily spend most of their spare time. Nancy works as a legal assistant in Media, PA.

Rachel Garman is a storyteller residing in State College, Pennsylvania. She graduated from Penn State in 2015 with a degree in print journalism and currently works for the university's central marketing department. A proud native Philadelphian, she enjoys spending time outdoors with her husband and dog, pronouncing water as "wooder," and following the exploits of the Flyers' mascot, Gritty.

Devon James is a recent graduate from Rowan University's Master of

Arts in Writing program where she received the Toni Libro Medallion Award upon graduating. She was a featured reader for Moonstone Poetry's New Voices series, and won second place in SCCC's undergraduate writing festival. She currently teaches writing as an adjunct at several local colleges.

Patrick McNeil works at the Homeless Advocacy Project. His fiction and nonfiction have appeared in places like *Cleaver Magazine* and *The Head and the Hand*'s Chapbook Series. He is the organizer of Philadelphia's own Backyard Writers Workshop, and founder of the Writers Retreat in Tufo, Italy. Community is important to him.

Kara Petrovic is 23 years old and is living in Toronto, Ontario. They are a survivor of trauma four times over and are living with a variety of mental health disorders. They have self published a collection of poetry, *beyond rock bottom* in 2017 and have been published in *CONKER* magazine in 2018 and 2019. Their poetry has also been published by *Train Journal*. Also in 2019, they self-published another collection titled *forget-me-not*. They have also been selected for Toronto's Emerging Writers Reading Series. They are currently working on a book of fiction with a co-writer in New Jersey. Philadelphia holds a special place in their heart, as their father and younger sister currently reside there. They identify as genderfluid and pansexual.

Jennifer Rieger is the English Department Chair at Upper Merion Area High School and an English professor at Cabrini University. An advocate for her students, she devotes her time to empowering young people through reading, writing, and acts of love. Jen holds a BA in English, an MA in English Literature, an MFA in Creative Writing and has been published in *Chautauqua Literary Journal, Wisconsin Review, BUST Magazine, The Sigh Press, Philadelphia Stories*, among others. Jen's book, *Burning Sage*, a collection of personal essays reflecting on unconventional motherhood, unconventional teacherhood, and her accidental, and quite flawed, role-model existence, will be published this spring.

* Please note: When "The Fix" was first published in *Philadelphia Stories*, my name was spelled incorrectly.

Ona Russell is the author of three award-winning historical mysteries and has been published in a variety of other venues. She holds a PhD in literature from UC San Diego where she also taught for many years. Although she lives in California, she considers herself a Philadelphian once removed—her mother was born there, her brother lives in Narberth, and her great uncle was the late architect, Louis I. Kahn. Her new novel *Son of Nothingness*, will be published in 2020. For more, please visit: onarussell.com.

FICTION

Bim Angst "Sitz-i-zen" writes from the small town of Saint Clair, Schuylkill County, in Pennsylvania's anthracite coal region. Angst writes across genres and has been the recipient of fellowships to Yaddo and from the National Endowment for the Arts, among others. She's working now on a novel based on Pottsville's Nicholas Biddle, the African American man among the first whose blood was shed in hostilities of the American Civil War.

Kate Blakinger "Hothouse Lounge" has published fiction in the *Gettysburg Review, Harpur Palate, Iowa Review*, and *New Stories from the Midwest*. She holds an MFA from the Helen Zell Writers' Program at the University of Michigan, where she was awarded the Meijer Postgraduate Fellowship. She has also received fellowships from the Elizabeth George Foundation, Jentel, the MacDowell Colony, and the Kimmel Harding Nelson Center for the Arts. In 2018, Blakinger was elected to local office as a Democratic committee person. She lives in Philadelphia with her family.

Dana De Greff "How to Make a Baseball Player Cry" holds an MFA in fiction from the University of Miami. She is the author of *Alterations* (winner of the 2018 Rane Arroyo Chapbook Series), and recipient of the 2018 Lillian E. Smith Writer-in-Service Award. She has been accepted or awarded scholarships from TENT, the Tin House Summer Writers' Workshop, The Key West Literary Seminar, and the Lemon Tree House Residency in Tuscany. Her work appears in *PANK, Origins Journal, Philadelphia Stories*, and more. She is currently at work on two novels and is a Visiting Professor of English at St. Thomas University.

Jenna Geisinger "How to Get Lost" is a fiction writer from South Jersey. She recently moved north to pursue her MFA at William Paterson University, where she is expected to graduate in May. Her short story,

"Face to Face" will be published in the *Masters Review: Volume VIII* anthology in October. Jenna is currently writing a manuscript of historical fiction set in Prohibition-era New York City. When not writing, Jenna and her fiancé explore their new home one bakery at a time.

Sara Graybeal "Coal" is a writer, teacher, and spoken word artist living in Greensboro, NC. She is the former artistic director of the Poeticians, a performance collective based out of Point Breeze, Philadelphia. Sara's work has been published in *Moon City Review, Floating Bridge Review, Sixfold, the Asteroid Belt Alamanac*, and elsewhere. She is an MFA candidate at the University of North Carolina at Greensboro.

Lauren A. Green's "Leslie" work has appeared in Glimmer Train, Conjunctions, American Short Fiction, and elsewhere. She lives in Austin, where she is a Michener Fellow at the University of Texas.

Roger Hart "Mysteries of the Universe" has had published stories and essays in *Natural Bridge, The Tampa Review, Passages North, Runner's World*, and other magazines and journals. His short story collection, *Erratics*, won the George Garrett Contest and was published by the Texas Review Press. He holds an MFA from Minnesota State. As a former science teacher he's still fascinated by the mysteries of the universe and the human heart. He lives in Iowa and is working on a novel under the supervision of his wife and two giant dogs.

Rachel Howe "Like Nothing Happened When the Leaf Bug Bites I'll Be Looking Out the Window at You Smoking in the Rain" runs a volunteer program that brings Temple University students to volunteer in North Philadelphia high schools. She has taught writing at Rowan and Temple Universities as well as the Community College of Philadelphia. She also runs creative writing workshops for kids at local recreation centers and libraries. Her work has been published in *Philadelphia Stories, Dark Matters, The Philadelphia City Paper, The Philadelphia Inquirer*, and a variety of radio programs. Ms. Howe holds an M.A. in Creative Writing from Temple University. She lives in South Philadelphia with her partner and four children

Robert Johnson "Bird Fever" lives and writes in South Bend, Indiana. He holds an MFA from the Iowa Writers Workshop. He taught writing in high school and college and worked many years in commercial television. Robert's story "Bird Fever" won the Marguerite McGlinn Award in Fiction in *Philadelphia Stories* magazine in 2015 and was nominated for a Pushcart Prize. His story "The Continental Divide" won the *Hudson Review*'s 2019 Short Fiction Contest. Other stories have appeared in *Barcelona Review, American Fiction, Midwest Review* and elsewhere and have been finalists in Glimmer Train, Narrative, Pinch Literary Journal and other journals.

Dennis Lawson "Like Nothing Happened" is a fiction writer and writing instructor based in Newark, Delaware, where he lives with his wife and daughter. He writes both literary and crime short stories. Dennis received an MFA in Creative Writing from Rutgers-Camden in 2012. He was awarded an Individual Artist Fellowship from the Delaware Division of the Arts as the 2014 Emerging Artist in Fiction.

Oindrila Mukherjee, "Cul de Sac," teaches creative writing at Grand Valley State University. She has a Ph.D. in literature and creative writing from the University of Houston. Her work has appeared in *The Kenyon Review Online, Salon, Crab Orchard Review, The Colorado Review, The Greensboro Review, Los Angeles Review of Books, the Oxford Anthology of Bengali Literature* and elsewhere. She has written extensively for the Indian magazine *Scroll* and is a contributing editor for the journal *Aster(ix)*. She is currently working on a novel and a collection of stories.

Curtis Smith, "In the Woods," has published over one hundred stories and essays. He's worked with independent presses to put out four novels, five story collections, two essay collections, and a book of creative nonfiction. His next novel, *The Magpie's Return*, will be released in 2020.

Sharon White, "Minato Sketches," won the AWP award in creative nonfiction for her book *Vanished Gardens: Finding Nature in Philadelphia. Boiling Lake (On Voyage)*, a collection of short fiction, is her most recent work. She is also the author of two collections of poetry, *Eve & Her Apple and Bone House* and a memoir, *Field Notes, A Geography of Mourning*. Some of her other awards include the Marguerite McGlinn Prize for Fiction, the Neil Shepard Prize, the Italo Calvino Prize in Fabulist Fiction, the Leeway Foundation Award for Achievement, and a National Endowment for the Arts Fellowship.

POETRY

Joe Cilluffo's first book of poetry, *Always in the Wrong Season*, was recently published by Kelsay Books and is available on amazon.com. In addition to *Philadelphia Stories*, Joe's poems have appeared in journals such as *Philadelphia Poets*, *Apiary*, and the *Schuylkill Valley Journal*. He was the Featured Poet for the Fall 2014 Edition of the *Schuylkill Valley Journal*, which nominated Joe's poem, "Light," for the Pushcart Prize. Joe recently had a (third!) surgery on his left foot, and hopes this time it works!

Autumn Konopka is a poet, activist, runner, and coffee lover. She teaches, parents, and tries to make the world a better place in and around Philadelphia. Her poems have appeared or are forthcoming in *Coal Hill Review*, *Main Street Rag*, *Apiary*, *Literary Mama*, *and Crab Orchard Review*, among others. Her chapbook, a chain of paper dolls, was published by the Head & the Hand Press (2014, Philadelphia). In 2016, she was poet laureate of Montgomery County, Pa., selected by Pulitzer-prize winning poet Carl Dennis. Autumn has a BA in English from the University of Pittsburgh and an MFA in poetry from Antioch University. Currently, Autumn teaches writing courses in and around Philadelphia, curates a bi-monthly poetry series in the Philly suburbs, and serves as President of the Board of Directors for the Philadelphia Writers' Conference. Find her online:autumnkonopka.com.

Emily Rose Cole is the author of a chapbook, *Love & a Loaded Gun*, from Minerva Rising Press. She is the 2015 winner of Philadelphia Stories' Sandy Crimmins award and has also received awards from *Jabberwock Review*, *Winning Writers*, and the Academy of American Poets. Her poetry has appeared or is forthcoming in *Best New Poets 2018*, *Spoon River Poetry Review*, *The Pinch*, and *Southern Indiana Review*, among others. She holds an MFA in Poetry from Southern Illinois University Carbondale and is a PhD candidate in Poetry and Disability Studies at the University of Cincinnati.

Kelly McQuain is the author of *Velvet Rodeo*, which won the Bloom poetry prize. His poetry and painting has appeared in *Philadelphia Stories*. Other publications include: *The Pinch*, *Painted Bride Quarterly*, *The Philadelphia Inquirer*, *Spunk*, and *Cleaver*, as well as such anthologies as *Men on Men*, *Drawn to Marvel*, *LGBTQ Fiction and Poetry from Appalachia*, *Eyes Glowing at the Edge of* the Woods: Fiction and Poetry from West Virginia; Best American Erotica, and Rabbit Ears: TV Poems. He has been a Sewanee Scholar and a Lambda Literary Fellow, and he has received two fellowships from the Pennsylvania Council on the Arts. www.KellyMcQuain.wordpress.com.

Warren Longmire is a black man, a writer, a software engineer, and an educator from North Philadelphia. He is the co-founder of the Excelano Project Spoken Word Collective and the Director of Poetry Events for Blue Stoop. You can find his writing the journals including *American Poetry Review, Painted Bride Quarterly, Eleven Eleven* and *The New Purlieu Review* and on his instagram @alongmirewriter.

Robin Kozak was born in Chicago, Illinois and grew up in Wyomissing, a bedroom community outside Reading, Pennsylvania. She received degrees from Ohio University and the University of Houston, and her writing has appeared or is upcoming in *Antioch Review, Arkansas Review, Crazyhorse, Field, The Gettysburg Review, Hotel Amerika, Philadelphia Stories, Sequestrum, Witness,* and other publications. Among her awards are two Creative Artist Program grants from the city of Houston and the 2016 Sandy Crimmins Prize for Poetry. An authority on antique and estate jewelry, she currently is finishing *Berkowitz,* a collection of short fiction.

Shevaun Brannigan's work has appeared in such journals as *Best New Poets, AGNI,* and *Slice.* She is a recipient of a Barbara J. Deming Fund grant, and holds an MFA from Bennington College.

Alejandro Escudé's first book of poems, *My Earthbound Eye,* was published in September 2013 upon winning the 2012 Sacramento Poetry Center Award. He received a master's degree in creative writing from UC Davis. Alejandro works as an English teacher, having taught at the secondary level for many years. Originally from Argentina, he immigrated to California at an early age. A new collection, *The Book of the Unclaimed Dead,* published by Main Street Rag Press, is now available on the MSR website. Alejandro lives in Los Angeles with his dog, a feisty terrier named Jake.

Kayla Coolican is a freelance writer and poet based in Somerville, MA. Born and raised in Northern New Jersey, Kayla is a graduate of Lesley University and a student of the Cantab Lounge. Drawing inspiration from

Ariana Reines, Kaveh Akbar, and Anis Mojgani, Kayla enjoys pairing her written work with quirky illustrations and blind contours. She looks forward to completing her first chapbook soon.

Nancy L. Davis publishes poetry and fiction. Her work has appeared in *Philadelphia Stories, Primavera, The Ledge, Cooweescoowee*, and *Cutthroat*, to name a few. Recent awards include a Pushcart Prize nomination in Poetry, First Prize in the Sandy Crimmins National Prize in Poetry, Honorable Mention in the Lorian Hemingway Short Fiction contest, and Finalist in the Joy Harjo Poetry Prize. Her poetry chapbook, *Ghosts*, was published by Finishing Line Press in July 2019. Davis earned her MFA at the University of Massachusetts in Amherst and was an Associate Professor of English for 25 years at Harper College in the Chicago area.

Barbara Daniels' book of poetry, *Talk to the Lioness*, will be published this year by Casa de Cinco Hermanas Press, which also published three of her chapbooks, *Black Sails, Quinn & Marie*, and *Moon Kitchen*. Barbara's poetry has appeared in *Prairie Schooner, Mid-American Review*, and other journals. She received three fellowships from the New Jersey State Council on the Arts.

Ken Fifer has published four collections of poetry, the most recent being *After Fire* (March Street Press). He was a finalist in the 2019 Gunpowder Press poetry book contest. His poems and translations have appeared in *Barrow Street, New Letters, Ploughshares, The Literary Review*, and other fine journals. He has a Ph.D. in English Language and Literature from The University of Michigan. He was a 2019 finalist for the Gunpowder Press Book Contest.

Sakinah Hofler's work has appeared or is forthcoming in *Hayden's Ferry Review, Mid-American Review, Bettering American Poetry*, and elsewhere. She has won the Manchester Fiction Prize and the Sherwood Anderson Fiction Award. Previously, she was shortlisted for the Manchester Poetry Prize. A former quality and chemical engineer for the United States Department of Defense, she's currently a PhD student and an Alfred C. Yates Fellow at the University of Cincinnati.

Chelsea Whitton is an internationally published poet and essayist. She is the author of *Bear Trap* (Dancing Girl Press, 2018) and is a PhD candidate at the University of Cincinnati. Her poems appear or are forthcoming in issues of *Copper Nickel, Cream City Review, Poetry Ireland, The Atlanta Review*, and *Forklift-Ohio*, among others. She is the recipient of the 2018 Sandy Crimmins National Poetry Prize, and will join the staff of The Sewanee Writers' Conference next summer. Raised in North Carolina, she spent her twenties in New York, and now lives in Cincinnati with her husband, Matthew, and their cats, Puck and Merle.

Charles Carr is a native Philadelphian Educated at LaSalle and Bryn Mawr College, holds a Masters in American History. In 2007 Charles was *The Mad Poets Review* First Prize Winner for his poem "Waiting To Come North." Charles has two published books of poems; *paradise, pennsylvania* and *Haitian Mud Pies And Other Poems*. Charles' poems have been published in various print and on-line local and national poetry journals. He is host of Philly Loves Poetry a live monthly broadcast on PhillyCAM. Charles has also hosted a Moonstone Poetry series at Fergie's Pub. In 2013 Charles read poems as part of the international 100,000 Poets For Peace at The Garden of Remembrance in Dublin, Ireland.

Carlos Andrés Gómez "Elegy for Breath" is a Colombian American poet and the author of *Hijito* (Platypus Press, 2019), selected by Eduardo C. Corral as the winner of the 2018 Broken River Prize. Winner of the Atlanta Review International Poetry Prize, Lucille Clifton Poetry Prize, and the Sandy Crimmins National Prize for Poetry, Gómez's writing has been published in the *New England Review, Beloit Poetry Journal, BuzzFeed Reader, CHORUS: A Literary Mixtape* (Simon & Schuster, 2012), and elsewhere. Carlos is a graduate of the MFA Program for Writers at Warren Wilson College. For more, please visit: www.CarlosLive.com.

Chad Frame's work has appeared in *decomP, Barrelhouse, Rust+Moth, Menacing Hedge, Philadelphia Stories*, and elsewhere. He was the 2017 Poet Laureate of Montgomery County, Pennsylvania, serves as the Poetry Editor of *Ovunque Siamo: New Italian-American Writing*, is a founding member of No River Twice, a poetry improv performance troupe, and the founder of the Caesura Poetry Festival and Retreat. He was interviewed and featured on the radio program "The Poet and the Poem" by Grace Cavalieri from the Library of Congress.

Brittanie Sterner currently directs the Free Library's One Book, One Philadelphia project. She holds a BFA in poetry from Emerson College and an MS in Arts Administration from Drexel's Westphal College.

Amy Small-McKinney's poems have been published in numerous journals, for example, *The Cortland Review, Construction, American Poetry Review, The Indianapolis Review, Connotation Press, Tiferet, Philadelphia Stories, Anomaly,* and elsewhere. Her poem "Birthplace" received Special Merits recognition for the 2019 Muriel Craft Bailey Poetry Contest and will appear in *The Comstock Review.* Her second full-length book of poems, *Walking Toward Cranes,* won the Kithara Book Prize 2016 (Glass Lyre Press). Her poems have also been translated into Romanian and Korean. Small-McKinney teaches community poetry workshops in Philadelphia. She has an MFA in Poetry from Drew University.

John Wall Barger's poems have appeared in *American Poetry Review, Alaska Poetry Review, Rattle, The Awl, The Cincinnati Review, Poetry Ireland Review,* and *Best of the Best Canadian Poetry.* His poem, "Smog Mother," was co-winner of *The Malahat Review*'s 2017 Long Poem Prize. His fourth book, *The Mean Game,* came out with Palimpsest Press in spring 2019. He lives in West Philadelphia and is an editor for *Painted Bride Quarterly.* johnwallbarger.com

Cover Art

Row 1 (top) L-R
Maggie Hobson-Baker *Fire,* Maryanne Buschini *Drillers 1910,* Catherine Kuzma *Crossing Over,* Nancy Kress *Towards the Light*

Row 2 L-R
Anne Leith *Valley Forge 1,* Linda Dubin Garfield *Light of Morning,* Pamela Lee *Celestial Bodies I,* Christina Tarkoff *Jamal-Music in Rittenhouse Square*

Row 3 L-R
Jeff Thomsen *Valley Forge with Fall Sunshine,* Tilda Mann *Point of No Return*

Row 4 L-R
Lois Schlachter *Spring Fling,* Laura Rutherford Renner *A Snow Day*

Row 5 L-R
J. Rossi *Trees in Orange*, Alice Dustin *Still Life Abstracted*, Dae Rebeck Sanchez *The Pool Series: Ophelia*, Kathleen Spicer *Stella*

Row 6 (bottom) L-R
José Ortiz-Pagán *Mandragora 2*, Catherine Quillman *Academy Artists*, Christine Walinski *Lift Every Rock*, Heather Devlin Knopf *Frida*

Artists

Maggie Hobson-Baker *Fire*
Maggie Hobson-Baker, an artist, designer and Associate Professor of Studio Art and Design lives and works in the Philadelphia Area. Interested in the dialogue between traditional and digital platforms in the creation of art and visual images, Hobson-Baker works with her iPad and Bamboo Tablet as well as traditional materials. Her work reflects her love of shape, color, nature and design. A breast cancer survivor, *Fire* is a self-portrait of her journey through treatment.

Maryanne Buschini *Drillers 1910*
Maryanne Buschini is from Valhalla NY and lives in Malvern PA. She graduated from Kansas State University with a BFA, holds a master's degree from University of the Arts and studies at the Pennsylvania Academy of the Fine Arts and the Barnes Foundation. Her narrative figure painting has earned awards in juried shows. Buschini's solo exhibition at the Fireside Gallery at Main Line Unitarian Church in Devon PA remains on view from October 27 - December 1, 2019. www.maryannebuschini.com/solo.

Catherine Kuzma *Crossing Over*
Born in Philadelphia and residing in New Jersey, Catherine Kuzma earned her Bachelor of Arts degree from Rutgers University. Kuzma's award-winning oil paintings have been shown nationally and locally in Philadelphia, New Jersey and NYC in solo, group, and juried exhibitions. Publication of her work includes the cover of the July 2018 Tishman Review. Sparking the rich, meditative process of painting, nature and landscape serve as the initial inspiration for Kuzma's paintings. More can

be viewed at www.catherineluzma.com.

Nancy Kress *Towards the Light*
For many years, Nancy Kress studied landscape painting, working realistically, en plein air. Today, her figurative work and landscapes combine realism with abstraction. Kress is a member of Philadelphia/Tri-State Artists Equity and InLiquid. Her work has been included in exhibits throughout the Philadelphia area including the Delaware Center for the Contemporary Arts, Art in City Hall, Goggle Works Center for the Arts, 3rd Street Gallery and Pleiades Gallery in NYC.

Anne Leith *Valley Forge 1*
Anne Leith spends her time painting nature and places, both in the plein air tradition and in the studio. With an MFA from the University of Pennsylvania and an MA in Contemporary Art History, she credits other artists as her teachers and inspiration. She also works like a fiend to achieve the same top-level results in her own paintings. Leith is a professor of art in several colleges and art centers in the Philadelphia area and creates video documentaries and oral histories.

Linda Dubin Garfield *Light of Morning*
Linda Dubin Garfield, an award-winning printmaker and mixed media artist, creates visual memoirs exploring the mystery of memory and the magic of place, using hand-pulled printmaking techniques, photography, collage and digital imaging. Garfield is founder of ARTsisters, a professional artists' group which empowers artists and their community. She also founded smART business consulting which aids emerging artists. Garfield serves on several non-profit boards, including The Da Vinci Art Alliance for whom she served as president.

Pamela Lee *Celestial Bodies I*
Pamela Lee is a project-based artist, yoga instructor and writer living and working just outside Philadelphia since 2004. She earned a BFA in Fine Art from The School of The Art Institute of Chicago in 2001 and an MFA in Jewelry/Metals/CAD/CAM from Tyler School of Art in 2006.

Christina Tarkoff *Jamal - Music in Rittenhouse Square*
Christina Tarkoff is a representational oil painter who loves to paint people. Her paintings tell stories that cross traditional barriers such as

gender, age, and race to help us understand the most important art of all — "The art of being human." Tarkoff has been honored with numerous awards from local Philadelphia organizations, including the 2019 Manayunk Arts Festival's "Best Emerging Artist" award. In 2018 she was awarded a Knight Foundation cash honorarium for her painting "Dancing in Rittenhouse Square."

Jeff Thomsen *Valley Forge with Fall Sunshine*
Jeff Thomsen grew up in Glenside, PA, and attended Abington High School, the College of William and Mary, and Temple University Law School. In 1991, Thomsen enrolled in the certificate program at the Pennsylvania Academy of Fine Arts. Thomsen lives in Havertown, PA, where he maintains his studio when not painting and drawing out of doors.

Tilda Mann *Point of No Return*
Tilda Mann is a painter primarily working in oil. Mann's narrative work derives from her everyday life and memories. On a formal level Mann is interested in color, shape and texture. She trained at the Pennsylvania Academy of Fine Art and lives in Wynnewood, PA. Mann grew up in Los Angeles, and is still influenced by the vivid colors that surrounded her childhood days there.

Lois Schlachter *Spring Fling*
As a graduate of Pennsylvania Academy of Fine Arts, Lois Schlachter was formally educated. In the graduate program of life, she paints whatever comes into her head, working directly from her hand to the canvas with little to no planning. With her love of line, handsome and vibrant color, Schlachter leads the viewer into her world of rhythm and comfortable composition.

Laura Rutherford Renner *A Snow Day*
Laura Rutherford Renner is an artist whose paintings on wood depict contemporary life in New Jersey and Pennsylvania. Her work has been included in various juried exhibitions and shows, recently as a juried member of Artists Gallery in Lambertville, NJ, and at the iconic Philadelphia Sketch Club. In addition to her painting career, Renner is a practicing Occupational Therapist and the published author of several biographical articles for OT journals. She lives in Collingswood, NJ.

J. Rossi *Trees in Orange*
J. Rossi is a colorist. The way she looks at life comes across in the vibrant colors and the expressive way she paints. For the last seven years Rossi has indulged her passion for painting; taking studio art classes, workshops and master classes with many distinguished mentors and teachers. She also paints in the Abstract Studio at Community Arts Center in Wallingford. Her work appears on exhibit in the Philadelphia area and has been awarded prizes.

Alice Dustin *Still Life Abstracted*
Alice Dustin, long time resident of Ardmore, Pennsylvania, has been drawing since early childhood. She began painting in oils more recently (1997) and in 1999 began showing her work in galleries. Awards for her paintings include those from the PAFA fellowship, the Woodmere Art Museum, Wayne Art Center's National Juried Show, Fleisher Art Memorial, and Artists Equity. She teaches oil painting at Main Line School Night.

Dae Rebeck Sanchez *The Pool Series: Ophelia*
Dae Rebeck Sanchez in a fine artist who has shown in galleries and art centers regionally and abroad. Rebeck Sanchez works primarily with acrylic paints, photo-based transfers and collage on wood. Her narrative, sometimes surreal layered paintings focus on women, the circus, and urban/suburban decay. She studied at the Institute of American Indian Arts in Santa Fe, New Mexico and Moore College of Art in Philadelphia.

Kathleen Spicer *Stella*
Kathleen Spicer creates painted wood sculptures and reliefs such as "Stella" (currently in the Brantley/Webster collection) and has shown extensively across the country since 1983. She has been awarded seven public art commissions with one underway at New Market West in Philadelphia. Her work has most recently been acquired by Temple University and Penn State. Her awards include recognition from the New York Foundation for the Arts. Upcoming shows include a two-person exhibition at The 431 Art Gallery titled "Shiny Objects" opening in March 2020.

José Ortiz-Pagán *Mandragora 2*

José Ortiz-Pagán is a visual artist and a cultural administrator. His Philadelphia community-based art projects focus on conversations around inclusion within local communities as well as achieving diverse cultural manifestations. He is a key developer of the PEW Center for the Arts' funded initiative "Bring Your Own Project (BYOP.) Ortiz-Pagán exhibits his award-winning work internationally and has developed projects with several organizations including Second State Press, Taller Puertorriqueño, Chemical Heritage Museum and the Art Anthropology Museum at the University of Puerto Rico.

Catherine Quillman *Academy Artists*

Catherine Quillman became a mixed-media artist and illustrator after leaving a 20-plus year career as a suburban staff writer for *The Philadelphia Inquirer*. She was the paper's only reporter to be granted personal interviews with the late Andrew Wyeth. She has also written about other members of the Wyeth family and is the author of five regional books including *100 Artists of the Brandywine Valley*. She can be reached at www.catherinequillman.com.

Christine Walinski *Lift Every Rock*

Christine Walinski studied Fine Arts at Keystone College and received her BFA and Art Education Certification from Tyler School of Art. She finds inspiration in nature, color, shapes and lines. Her work often reflects on memories of growing up in nature, nostalgia and past experiences. She is both a city mouse and a country mouse. Walinski lives with her super creative family in Manayunk and teaches art classes in the area. View work at www.christinewalinski.com.

Heather Devlin Knopf *Frida*

Heather Devlin Knopf is a Philadelphia-based artist/illustrator, writer, and educator. She teaches at Moore College of Art and Design and at Arcadia University. A graduate of Carnegie Mellon University, she earned a BS in Graphic Communications Management and later earned an MFA in Illustration. Knopf illustrated the picture book *The Cow in Patrick O'Shanahan's Kitchen*, published by Little Pickle Press, and is currently working on her next picture book project.

15ᵗʰ anniversary acknowledgments

It would be impossible to thank everyone who helped *Philadelphia Stories* reach its 15ᵗʰ anniversary on just one page.

Publishing 5,000 copies of *Philadelphia Stories* each quarter, and 2,000 copies of *PS Junior* and *PS Teen* bi-annually, without ever missing an issue can only be done with the dedication of our volunteers, who donate hundreds of hours each year because they believe in our mission to cultivate a community of writers, artists, and readers across the Delaware Valley.

We also would not be able to keep the magazine in print and free without the support of our donors. Unlike other literary magazines, *Philadelphia Stories* isn't financially supported by universities or large foundations. We are fortunate to the have the generous support of the McGlinn, Hansma, and Sullivan families for our contests, and a grant from the Philadelphia Cultural Fund to support part of our operating expenses, but the bulk of our support comes from individual donors.

When I think about who to thank for helping *Philadelphia Stories* reach this important milestone, one word comes to mind: *community*. Thank you for being a part of this community, for helping us connect 360,000 writers and artists to readers since we launched in 2004, and for helping us grow this community with others who are passionate about supporting the local arts.

Christine Weiser, Co-Founder and Executive Director

PhiladelphiaStories

Cultivating a community of writers, artists, and readers across the Delaware Valley

A MAGAZINE THAT CREATES COMMUNITY

I would like to support local art & literature by making a contribution today.

MONTHLY PLEDGE:

O $5/Month   O $10/Month   O $20/Month   O Other _____

ONE-TIME MEMBER PLEDGE:

O Michener ($30-$49)   O Potok ($500-$999)   O Buck ($50-$99)

O W. C. Williams ($1,000+)   O Whitman ($100-$499)   O Other _____

NAME _____   ADDRESS _____

CITY _____   STATE _____   ZIP _____

EMAIL _____   PHONE _____

CARD NUMBER (MC, V, DISCOVER) _____   SECURITY CODE _____   EXPIRATION _____

Thank you for your generous support of Philadelphia Stories

To donate online please visit **www.philadelphiastories.org/donate/**, or mail to: Philadelphia Stories, 93 Old York Road, Ste 1/#1-753, Jenkintown PA 19046

CALL FOR SUBMISSIONS

Philadelphia Stories is a free print magazine that publishes fiction, poetry, essays, and artwork from writers and artists from PA, NJ, and DE and makes it available to 5,000 readers every quarter.
We'd love to see your work!

Find submission guidelines at
www.philadelphiastories.org
Free to submit year-round!

PS Teen is an annual magazine published each
Fall featuring local writers and artists aged 13-18.

PS Junior is by local writers and artists aged 12 and younger,
which will be published each Spring.

Submissions open year-round:
www.philadelphiastories.org/junior